A MACRO THEORY WITH MICRO FOUNDATIONS

RICHARD J. SWEENEY

Assistant Director
Office of Policy Research
U. S. Treasury Department

Published by

H78 **SOUTH-WESTERN PUBLISHING CO.**

CINCINNATI   WEST CHICAGO, ILL.   DALLAS   PELHAM MANOR, N.Y.
PALO ALTO, CALIF.   BRIGHTON, ENGLAND

ISBN: 0-538-08780-3
Library of Congress Catalog Card Number: 73-90122

1 2 3 4 5 D 8 7 6 5 4

Printed in the United States of America

PREFACE

This book tries to help reconcile micro and macroeconomics. The more or less strict separation of micro and macro analysis at the undergraduate level, and frequently the graduate level, often seems to irritate students and undermine their economic education. They resent having one theory for single firms, households, or markets, and another, very different, for the macroeconomy. Often they come to regard both as sterile games, or to value one and dismiss the other. ("I like macro but hate micro" is a frequent remark, and the reverse is sometimes heard.) Hard-won theorems in one course are reversed—or ridiculed—in another. The schism continues to the professional level, though recent years have brought some integration, and many economists seem to want more such progress. It is really not a sign of virtuosity in the professional economist to move from micro theory to a separate, conflicting macro theory with the schizophrenic ease demanded of students.

This book applies the standard model of a monopolist-monopsonist —familiar from the principles course—to the macroeconomy by aggregating individual firms responses. Microeconomics courses sometimes present the firm as being continuously at its profit maximum, though this is in no way essential to micro theory. Many problems can be analyzed by showing the attempts of firms to maximize wealth and their failures because of imperfect information. Thus, the newer micro emphasis on problems of information is also rich in implications for macro theory—and the result is a better job than the standard macroeconomic Keynesian system.

Much of micro theory is the *equilibrium* theory of *perfect competition*. Both equilibrium and perfect competition are powerful tools, but students too often gain the impression that they are the sum of micro theory. Macro theory commonly takes a particular aggregated, perfectly competitive, general equilibrium system—the Keynesian system—and modifies it with an ad hoc limitation on its equilibrating tendencies, to induce phenomena that simulate the disequilibrium of the real world. Thus, in a macro system that would otherwise show a perfectly competitive general equilibrium, unemployment results from a liquidity trap, or rigid money wages, or money illusion, or rigid real wages, or rigid prices (take your choice). Meanwhile, all markets except the labor market are in perfectly competitive equilibrium—the system is on the *IS* and *LM* curves. Neither micro nor macro theory gain students' respect by the spurious claims of either equilibrium or pervasive perfect competition. This book analyzes macro disequilibrium with the simplest micro theory of price- and wage-setting power.

The theory of decision making over time, subject to disequilibrium and error, can rapidly become so complex as to yield no results at all. Consequently, this book makes explicit simplifying assumptions, always for the ultimate purpose of giving clear-cut macro results. Students respect the effort to make these assumptions explicit, and usually find them acceptable means to the goal of results.

This book makes greater use of the micro theory of the firm than of the household. Chapters 1-6 are a coherent whole, starting with foundations and going through short-run policy. They rely on the simple model of the monopolist-monopsonist, make the simplest possible assumptions about the household sector—for example, a consumption function linear in disposable income—and use *IS* and *LM* curves. Thus, they can appropriately be used at any level beyond the first part of the intermediate macro or money course.

Chapter 7 uses the micro theory of the household to discuss the influence of *wealth* on the macro system. The analysis is more difficult than before, fewer results are unambiguous, but policy recommendations are not much changed. Chapter 7 also introduces a business demand for money, with no effect on the macro results derived earlier in the chapter. Chapter 8 briefly discusses some questions that arise for the model when the economy has two produced goods instead of only one as usually assumed, for example in the Keynesian system.

I wish to thank Professor Axel Leijonhufvud of the University of California, Los Angeles; Professors William H. Branson and George de Menil of Princeton University; and the many hundreds of students who learned various parts of this book and showed some heartening enthusiasm for its effort.

CONTENTS

1 INTRODUCTION

This book develops a new, general, short-run, one-sector macro model of a closed economy, based on the microeconomic theory of price-and-wage-setting firms, and derives policy implications from it. This introductory chapter explains the value and usefulness of such a model, sketches its rationale, and outlines the following chapters.

1.1. Criticisms of Current Macro Theory

A general macro model of a closed economy analyzes the product, money, bond, and labor markets.[1] Any new general macro model competes with those previously built. If the new model is worthwhile, either it must yield results different from other models', or it must yield the same results from logically more acceptable premises. This model does yield many results different from the usual ones, and it does so with assumptions more reasonable than those used in other models.

The largest class of general short-run, one-sector macro models is the Keynesian system.[2] This system uses the IS and LM curves as building blocks. It is the standard theory taught in intermediate macro courses, and there are many expositions.[3] Many seemingly different

1 This is in contrast to the multiplier-accelerator model, for example, which ignores everything save the demand for output.

2 See Axel Leijonhufvud, *On Keynesian Economics and the Economics of Keynes: A Study in Monetary Theory* (London: Oxford University Press, 1968), for a brilliant discussion of the great differences between Keynes and the Keynesians.

3 See, for example, Chapters 2 and 3 of Martin J. Bailey, *National Income and the Price Level; A Study in Macroeconomic Theory* (2d ed.; New York: McGraw-Hill Book Co., 1971); J. R. Hicks, "Mr. Keynes and the 'Classics': A Suggested Interpretation," *Econometrica*, Vol. V (April, 1937), pp. 147–59, where the curves were introduced; Warren Smith, "A Graphical Exposition of the Complete Keynesian System," *Southern Economic Journal*, Vol. XXIII (October, 1956), pp. 115–25; Franco Modigliani, "Liquidity Preference and the Theory of Interest and Money," *Econometrica*, Vol. XXII (January, 1944), pp. 45–88; Robert Mundell, "An Exposition of Some Subtleties in the Keynesian System," *Weltwirtschaftliches Archiv*, Vol. XCIII (December, 1964), pp. 301–12; and many intermediate textbooks, such as Thomas Dernburg and Duncan McDougall, *Macroeconomics* (4th ed.; New York: McGraw-Hill Book Co., 1972); and Gardner Ackley, *Macroeconomic Theory* (New York: Macmillan Co., 1961). Recent attempts by monetarists to portray monetarism as the Keynesian system but with assumptions different from the Keynesians' about elasticities (for example, of the demand for money) seem to obscure the issues: see Milton Friedman, "A Theoretical Framework for Monetary Analysis," *Journal of Political Economy*, Vol. LXXVIII (March, 1970), pp. 193–238, for such an attempt.

models are merely the same model exposited differently and can easily be put in standard Keynesian terms.[4]

These Keynesian models come in two versions, the full employment, general equilibrium version and the unemployment version. The latter is more interesting, for unemployment is a significant problem demanding an explanation. Fixing one and only one price variable above its general equilibrium value introduces unemployment into the full employment, general equilibrium Keynesian system. Movements of prices coordinate the system, and imposing a given value on some price variable breaks down the coordination of the system. Among the prices authors have chosen to fix are the nominal wage rate, the price level, the rate of interest—through the liquidity trap—and the real wage rate.

Dissatisfaction with this model is widespread. Many criticisms, both explicit and implicit, have been offered. No model can hope to meet all objections,[5] but this book discusses one which meets some of the major specifications laid down by critics.

The more recent theoretical literature lists some of the major desiderata of a satisfactory macro model. First, the model must have an explicit microfoundation for the behavior of macroeconomic variables. Changes in macro variables must be the aggregate result of the behavior of individual decision makers. The model must rigorously analyze the behavior of firms and determine macroeconomic results on the basis of consistent aggregation.[6]

Second, the model must describe and analyze behavior when there is disequilibrium as well as when there is equilibrium. In particular, it must describe behavior when business finds itself off its demand and supply curves and when households and firms cannot buy and sell as much as they like at going prices.[7]

Third, the macroeconomic state of the world must influence micro decisions, and micro decisions must determine aggregate variables;

4 Thus, Patinkin's static theorem on the neutrality of money in Don Patinkin, *Money, Interest, and Prices* (2d ed.; New York: Harper & Row, Publishers, 1965), can easily be incorporated in Keynesian analysis. (Bailey, *op. cit.*, includes real balances in the consumption function at one point, making his model formally identical to Patinkin's.) The argument in George Horwich, "Tight Money, Monetary Restraint, and the Price Level," *Journal of Finance*, Vol. XXI (March, 1966), pp. 15–33, can be put exactly in Keynesian terms.

5 Nor should a model meet all objections, since some are ill-conceived.

6 See Edmund Phelps, "Money Wage Dynamics and Labor Market Equilibrium"; Edmund Phelps and Sidney Winters, "Optimal Price Policy under Atomistic Competition"; and Armen Alchian, "Information Costs, Pricing, and Resource Unemployment," *Microeconomic Foundations of Employment and Inflation Theory*, edited by Edmund Phelps et al. (New York: W. W. Norton & Co., 1970).

7 See Robert Clower, "The Keynesian Counterrevolution: A Theoretical Appraisal," *The Theory of Interest Rates*, edited by F. H. Hahn and F. P. R. Brechling (New York: Macmillan Co., 1965); Leijonhufvud, *op. cit.*; and Alchian, Phelps, and Winters, *op. cit.*

but macro variables must influence micro decisions even when no micro decision maker knows the values of the macro variables. Thus, aggregate unemployment should affect actors in the labor market, but without the stipulation that decision makers must know or care about aggregate unemployment. For example, Australia compiles figures on vacancy rates, while the United States for a long time did not. But the same theory should be able to explain each country's labor markets.[8]

Fourth, the model must abandon the logically unsatisfactory device of the Walrasian auctioneer to describe disequilibrium processes. Not everyone can be a price taker when there are disequilibrium prices which must be altered.[9]

Fifth, producers should react to disequilibrium first with quantity adjustments and then with price adjustments. In the shortest run, the system displays quantity adjustments rather than price adjustments.[10]

Sixth, there must be explicit micro underpinnings of the macro investment-demand function.[11]

Seventh, the treatment of time should be sophisticated enough at least to allow for the possibility of extending the analysis to describe the behavior of the system over time.[12] To understand how the system's foundations change over time requires investigation of its microfoundations. If the complexity of the system forbids analytical derivation of the time path, analysis must at least arrive at the point where the model can be simulated or estimated.[13]

1.2. Sketch of the Remaining Chapters

Chapter 2 develops a model of the representative firm, providing explicit micro foundations for the behavior of the business sector.

8 See Phelps, "Money Wage Dynamics and Labor Market Equilibrium," *op. cit.*; and Dale Mortenson, "A Theory of Wage and Employment Dynamics," in Phelps *et al., op. cit.* Each assumes that firms have beliefs about the numerical value of unemployment in their market.

9 See Kenneth Arrow, "Toward A Theory of Price Adjustment," in Moses Abramovitz *et al., The Allocation of Economic Resources* (Stanford: Stanford University Press, 1959); D. Cogerty and G. Winston, "Patinkin, Perfect Competition and Unemployment Disequilibria," *Review of Economic Studies,* Vol. XXXI (April, 1964), pp. 121–26; Clower, *op. cit.*; Leijonhufvud, *op. cit.*; Phelps and Winters, *op. cit.*; and T. Koopmans, *Three Essays on the State of Economic Science* (New York: McGraw-Hill Book Co., 1957).

10 See Leijonhufvud, *op. cit.*; and Alchian, *op. cit.*

11 See James Witte, "The Microfoundations of the Social Investment Function," *Journal of Political Economy,* Vol. LXXI (October, 1963), pp. 441–56, where the existence of any investment demand function and its micro underpinnings is denied. Dale Jorgenson, "The Theory of Investment Behavior," *Determinants of Investment Behavior*, edited by Robert Ferber (New York: Columbia University Press, 1967) also denies this; and Haavelmo seems to in T. Haavelmo, *A Study in the Theory of Investment* (Chicago: University of Chicago Press, 1960).

12 See Phelps, *op. cit.*

13 In conventional analysis, there is no concern for how the *IS* curve, for example, changes over time.

It analyzes a "typical" firm's reactions to changes and aggregates such behavior in a consistent way (first point in the list of desiderata). The firm has monopoly and monopsony powers—it decides on prices and wages (fourth point). The model analyzes firm behavior in and out of equilibrium (second point). When the firm is not in equilibrium, it adjusts its output and sales in the shortest run, changing prices only periodically (fifth point). Firms are affected by macroeconomic variables, but neither know nor care about the numerical values of these variables (third point). The individual firm has an investment function which it derives by maximizing the value of its operations. Aggregation of these micro functions yields an aggregate investment demand function (sixth point). Finally, basing the firm's behavior only on the goal of profit maximization, subject to the demand and supply curves it expects to face, provides the foundations on which to build a sequence of decisions through time. Such a sequence requires only a specific hypothesis about the formation of expectations, for such a hypothesis generates demand and supply curves which the firm expects to face, and profit maximization on the basis of these curves explains firms' behavior (seventh point in the list of desiderata).

The model allows a decision maker to set prices and to maintain these prices for a certain length of time. During the period in which price setters maintain prices, whenever decision makers settle on a price vector different from the equilibrium vector there is a general disequilibrium. Unemployment, excess capacity, and excess demand for output are all symptoms of general disequilibrium and are explicable in terms of firms' choosing a disequilibrium price vector. Firms choose such a vector because they lack the knowledge which would lead them to choose the equilibrium vector.

The macro theory rests on the microeconomic theory of the price-and-wage-setting firm. To derive operational results, assume the typical firm is a wealth-maximizing monopolist-monopsonist and acts as though perfectly certain of the consequences of its behavior. The firm's problem is to decide on the wealth-maximizing price to charge and wage rate to offer. Now, whatever price and wage it decides on, it expects to be on its demand and supply curves, for it reduces wealth to offer a given number of workers a wage larger than necessary or to sell a quantity of output for a price lower than could be had. When the firm sets a price and wage that put it off its demand and supply curves, it is contributing to the general disequilibrium. But it is off its demand and supply curves only by mistake, for the wealth-maximizing firm wants to be on its demand and supply curves at all times.

General disequilibrium means that firms are off their demand and supply curves, due simply to mistakes. How do such mistakes come about and persist? The firm acts on its "best guess" about demand and supply. Unfortunately, best guesses are easily wrong. As soon as the firm recognizes that it was wrong (and this may take a good deal of time), and as soon as the firm has formulated a new best guess (and this also may take a good deal of time), it tries to correct its error by acting on its new best guesses about demand and supply. However, these new best guesses may themselves be incorrect. If they are, disequilibrium persists.

Chapter 2 builds a model of the representative firm's decision making. The firm is currently selling its output at a certain price and hiring labor at a certain wage. It is discovering how much it can sell and buy with these policies. On the basis of this new information, it must decide how to change its price and wage. Chapter 2 derives the magnitudes of the changes in the firm's selling price and wage offer. It also derives the quantity of output the firm expects to sell at the new price, the quantity of labor services it plans to use to produce this output, and the quantity of capital it wants to add to its stock to produce this output. It shows how current macroeconomic variables affect these microeconomic decisions. It aggregates functions showing these relationships so they then apply for the entire business sector of a one-output economy.

Chapters 3 and 4 use these functions with IS and LM curves to build a simple general macro model. The model neglects wealth effects on the household sector and neglects businesses' demand for money. (Both of these are introduced in Chapter 7). Chapter 3 discusses the system when there is excess capacity; and Chapter 4, when there is positive, excess, aggregate demand for output.

Chapter 5 studies the determination of the actual level of employment, as distinguished from the level firms desire, which Chapters 2, 3, and 4 investigate.

Chapter 6 derives some policy implications from the model. (1) Policies often have effects exactly opposite those predicted by other models. For example, restricting the supply of money may spur inflation. (2) Design of fiscal and monetary policy requires detailed knowledge of functions which are currently ignored. For example, much work has been done on the sensitivity of the demand for money to changes in income and the interest rate, but the sensitivity of the labor demand function to changes in income and the interest rate has never been compared with the sensitivity of the demand for money to these changes. Such a comparison is necessary to determine whether expansionary fiscal policy leads to an increase or decrease in the demand for labor. (3) High interest rates, other things being equal, contribute to inflation and in no way dampen it. (4) Measures designed to fight inflation by reduction of aggregate demand often will not work and currently are being used in-efficiently. (5) A mixture of monetary and fiscal policies is virtually certain to be superior to either used alone.

Chapter 7 remedies omissions of Chapters 3 and 4 by introducing wealth effects on the household sector and a business demand for money. The results derived are not too different from the earlier chapters', and this justifies their omissions. Policy conclusions are virtually unaltered.

Chapter 8 extends the analysis to a two-sector model with different consumption and capital goods. Though the analysis is richer, policy implications are relatively unaffected.

The next chapter turns to the micro-theoretic foundations of the model.

2 THE MICROECONOMIC MODEL OF FIRM BEHAVIOR

This chapter constructs a model showing how a typical monopolist-monopsonist reacts to changes in such macroeconomic variables as aggregate demand, the expected rate of inflation, and unemployment. The results are aggregated, giving behavior functions for the business sector.

2.1. The Assumptions of the Microeconomic Model of the Firm

This chapter develops a model of how the firm decides on its pricing and wage policies and its desired (planned) output, investment, and hiring.

The central assumptions of the argument are: (1) the wealth-maximizing firm has monopoly power in the output market and monopsony power in the labor market, but does not engage in rivalrous competition with other firms; (2) the firm acts under conditions of perfect certainty, though it can be wrong in the beliefs on which it bases its policies; (3) the firm changes its policies only periodically; and (4) the firm holds no inventories. Any unsold output wastes away before the start of the next period.

The period structure of the model is important. The firm announces to the market at large at time t the price and wage policy it will follow during period t, from time t to time $t + 1$. By hypothesis, the firm does not change this policy during the period.[1] It bases its decisions on information about its product demand curve and capital and labor supply curves for period t. But it must decide on its policies for that period before time t; for it prepares for them before time t, making the necessary investment to have the desired stock of capital by time t.

The firm plans to be on its output demand and labor supply curves, so the stock of capital, K_t, and number of workers, N_t, the firm wishes to employ completely specify its decisions, given the relevant demand and supply functions. For example, N_t and the labor supply curve give the wage rate, w_t.

The problem, then, is to choose K_t and N_t. But ΔK_{t-1}, which is $K_t - K_{t-1}$, is ordered and delivered before time t. Thus, $K_t = (\Delta K_{t-1} + K_{t-1})$ is selected before time t.

---

1 The firm determines the length of the period. Chapter 5, section 3 discusses why the firm changes prices and wages only periodically.

The representative firm makes its decisions to maximize the present value of its operations from the present, $t = 1$, to the end of its horizon, $t = h$. Assume, solely for convenience, that it finances all investment with retained earnings. Then, the amount which it turns over to owners in any period t is the value of its sales, $P_t Q_t$, less its wage bill, $w_t N_t$, less its gross investment spending, $P_{K,t} I_t$ (where P, Q, I, and P_K are the price the firm charges, its output, its investment, and the price of capital goods, respectively); or, it pays dividends of:

$$P_t Q_t - w_t N_t - P_{K,t} I_t \qquad\qquad \textbf{2.1.1}$$

Assume there are perfect capital markets in which any firm may buy and sell at the going price (no monopsony here), and all capital is eternal and nonwasting.[2] Thus, any capital in existence can be bought and sold as are new additions to the stock. Since there is no depreciation, the firm's gross investment, I_t, is equal to net investment, $(K_{t+1} - K_t)$. Dividends at time t are then:

$$P_t Q_t - w_t N_t - P_{K,t} (K_{t+1} - K_t) \qquad (t = 1, h - 1) \qquad \textbf{2.1.2}$$

The firm's horizon is h, at which it plans to go out of business. The firm plans to disinvest its entire capital stock in period h, i.e., sell it off, or:

$$\Delta K_h = -K_h \qquad\qquad \textbf{2.1.3}$$

The present value of the firm, PV, or the present value of its operations, is precisely the present value of the dividends the firm pays between now, $t = 1$, and the end of the firm's horizon, $t = h$, which includes the scrap value from equation 2.1.3; or if i_{j-1} is the one-period interest rate in period j,[3]

---

2 That is, there is no depreciation of any sort. Appendix 1, section 4, introduces a fairly general scheme of depreciation which leaves the text's results virtually unchanged.

3 Interpret $P_{K,h} K_h$ as the scrap value of K_h. Since capital is eternal and nonwasting, K_h can be sold for the same value as an equal number of units manufactured in period h. It will become clear within a few pages that the firm's horizon does not influence its current behavior (unless $h = 1$). Current decisions about the more distant future will be revised in light of new information, and are, in any case, not binding; for the firm does not make contracts for more than one period at a time.

$$PV = P_1 Q_1 - w_1 N_1 - P_{K,1}(K_2 - K_1)$$

$$+ \sum_{t=2}^{h-1} \frac{1}{\prod_{j=2}^{t} (1 + i_{j-1})} \cdot [P_t Q_t - w_t N_t - P_{K,t}(K_{t+1} - K_t)]$$

$$+ \frac{P_h Q_h - w_h N_h + P_{K,h} K_h}{\prod_{j=2}^{h} (1 + i_{j-1})}$$

2.1.4

The necessary conditions for the firm to be at an interior maximum are:

$$\frac{1}{\prod_{j=2}^{t} (1 + i_{j-1})} \{MRP_{K,t} + P_{K,t}\} - \frac{1}{\prod_{j=2}^{t-1} (1 + i_{j-1})} P_{K,t-1} = 0$$

$$(t = 2, h) \quad 2.1.5$$

$$\frac{1}{\prod_{j=2}^{t} (1 + i_{j-1})} \{MRP_{N,t} - MFC_{N,t}\} = 0$$

where $MRP_{K,t}$ and $MRP_{N,t}$ are the marginal revenue products of capital and labor respectively, and $MFC_{N,t}$ is the marginal factor cost of labor.[4] Notice there are no conditions for $t = 1$. The firm is already in period 1, at or beyond time 1, and is already using K_1 and N_1, having decided on them before $t = 1$. In light of current experience, the decisions may be inoptimal; but the relevant decision now is for period 2.

There are two equations for every pair of variables (N_t, K_t), containing these variables and no others. The system of equation 2.1.5 is *decomposable*, allowing solution for (N_t, K_t) without simultaneously determining any other variables. Setting $t = 2$ in system 2.1.5,[5]

4 These conditions are discussed in Appendix 1.

5 Consider the timing of payments. In fact, payments are spread throughout the period; but they are treated as if they all occurred at the start of the period, payments during period 1 from $t = 1$ to $t = 2$ all taking place at $t = 1$. i_1 is the rate that rules between $t = 1$ and $t = 2$. Thus $P_1 Q_1$ is received at $t = 1$, while $P_{K,1} \Delta K_1$ is disbursed at $t = 1$. Next period's revenue is received at $t = 2$, so its discounted value is $P_2 Q_2/(1 + i_1)$. The alternative is to have the payments take place at the end of the period. It might appear that this would make the interest rate in the marginal conditions be i_2. That is, it might seem that the current interest rate has no effect on decisions. Such a conclusion seems strange and is, in fact, incorrect. Moving all payments from the very start of the period to the very end makes i_2 the only relevant rate for this period. Bonds earning i_1 were bought before $t = 1$ and of course i_1 has no effect on current decisions. Moving the payment date makes i_2

$$MRP_{K,2} - P_{K,1}\left(i_1 - \frac{\Delta P_{K,1}}{P_{K,1}}\right) = 0$$

2.1.6

$$MRP_{N,2} - MFC_{N,2} = 0$$

Interpreting $P_{K,1}(i_1 - \Delta P_{K,1}/P_{K,1})$ as the implicit rental rate on capital,[6] these very neoclassical conditions require that the marginal revenue product of capital equal its rental rate and the marginal revenue product of labor equal its marginal factor cost.

Before section 4 imposes a shock on system 2.1.6 to derive compara-tive statics results, sections 2 and 3 consider the individual terms af-fecting the marginal conditions for $t = 2$.

2.2. Two Interpretations of the Discount Rate

Consider interpreting the discount rate in the present value ex-pression as either: (1) the interest rate of neoclassical theory, or (2) the cost of capital in finance theory.

First, in neoclassical capital and interest theory with perfect cer-tainty, all that concerns the firm's owners is the present value of the dividends paid them, that is, the present value of the firm. Each period has a single interest rate at which any economic unit may borrow and lend as much as it likes. The neoclassical model demands that all current and future markets clear, and all prices be known with certainty. In the present model, current markets do not necessarily clear and future ones need not. However, the firm sets prices and wages in an attempt to make its markets clear. Neglecting that the firm "ought" to act under a regime of uncertainty about the future, maximizing the present value of operations is rational; and given a single borrowing and lending rate, expected future, short-term interest rates and the cur-rent market rate are the appropriate discount rates.[7]

The discount rate may also be interpreted as the "cost of capital", which is a kind of weighted average of market rates which themselves reflect risk. The extensive literature on the cost of capital has developed this notion in theoretical finance, and macroeconomic model builders

---

the relevant rate for this period, the rate earned on bonds bought this period. Whether i_2 is known during the entire period or only just before $t = 2$ makes no difference to the firm considered. But the capital goods industry must have its orders at $t = 1$ in a Wal-rasian (though not in a Hicksian) context, and this requires that i_2 be known at $t = 1$. Thus, in this case, i_2 serves the very role of i_1; and it seems more straightforward to date payments at the start of the relevant period.

6 Section 4 of this chapter justifies this interpretation.

7 Since the model does not commit the firm for any period beyond the next, the ques-tion of whether the firm is wrong in its expectations of future interest rates does not seriously arise.

have also discussed it.[8] The logic of the second interpretation of the discount rate as the cost of capital is that the rate can be applied to decisions just as in the first case.[9] Thus, in both cases, the firm wants to maximize its present value.

In the first interpretation of the discount rate, with perfect capital markets, whether the firm finances investment with retained earnings or bond sales does not matter. In the second interpretation, assume either: (1) the firm always finances with the leverage which induces the lowest discount rate and then uses this discount rate in equation 2.1.4, or (2) the firm is in a range subject to the Miller-Modigliani propositions on the invariance of the value of the firm with respect to leverage, so the question of leverage does not arise.[10]

2.3. Influences on the Output Demand and Labor Supply Conditions Facing the Monopolistic-Monopsonistic Firm

The firm influences output price and the wage it pays labor, but it buys and sells capital at a given price. Assume the firm has competitors and realizes that the terms on which it can sell output and hire labor in period t depend on the prices and wages of its competitors. But assume the firm believes its policies do not influence competitors. Let some index of competitors' prices in period 2, P_2^e, affect the price the firm can charge in that period, and some index of competitors' wage offers in period 2, w_2^e, affect the wage the firm pays workers.

Indices represent the effect of competitors' prices and wages on the firm's demand and supply curves for two reasons. First, if every price has so different an effect from every other that aggregation is impossible, then the assumption of no rivalrous competition becomes more tenuous, for some firms would be more important then and would watch each other. If a firm does not believe its actions can slip unnoticed through some index, it must ponder competitors' reactions.

8 See Ezra Solomon, *The Theory of Financial Management* (New York: Columbia University Press, 1963), especially Chapters 3, 8, and 10. See also James Duesenberry, *Business Cycles and Economic Growth* (New York: McGraw-Hill Book Co., 1958), especially Chapter 5, which develops the notion of the marginal cost of funds.

9 In the second interpretation, the discount rate is the cutoff rate. The firm should use capital up to the point where the percentage rate of return on capital equals the discount rate. The percentage rate of return on capital in the model when capital is nonwasting is the future, marginal revenue product of capital, divided by the current price of capital, plus the percentage rate of price appreciation of capital which the firm expects. Thus, the last unit of capital yields the marginal revenue product of capital plus the price appreciation on the unit of capital; and, dividing these two terms by the current price of capital, the result should equal the cutoff rate. This marginal condition can, in fact, be obtained by rearranging the first of equations 2.1.6.

10 See Franco Modigliani and Merton Miller, "The Cost of Capital, Corporation Finance, and the Theory of Investment," *American Economic Review*, Vol. XLVIII (June, 1958), pp. 261–97.

Second, these indices are later aggregated (in section 5 of this chapter) to represent the business sector's general beliefs about prices and wages. While it is conceptually possible to have many different prices or price indices influence the firm, the interpretation of several different aggregate indices in a one-sector macro model would be strained.

Assume that the higher is P_2^e, the higher is the price the firm can charge for any given quantity in period 2; and the higher is w_2^e, the higher is the wage rate the firm must offer to attract a given number of workers in period 2. Let any experiment that varies the prices and wages of individual competitors but leaves the indices P_2^e and w_2^e unchanged have no effect on the terms on which the firm sells output or hires labor in period 2. Assume that the higher is output, the lower the price the firm can charge; and the more workers it wants, the higher the wage it must pay.

These assumptions may be formalized as:

$$P_2 = \overline{P_2}(Q_2;\ P_2^e,\ u_{P,2})$$

$$\frac{\partial P_2}{\partial Q_2} < 0,\ \frac{\partial P_2}{\partial P_2^e} > 0,\ \frac{\partial P_2}{\partial u_{P,2}} > 0 \qquad \textbf{2.3.1}$$

and

$$w_2 = \overline{w_2}(N_2;\ w_2^e,\ u_{w,2})$$

$$\frac{\partial w_2}{\partial N_2} > 0,\ \frac{\partial w_2}{\partial w_2^e} > 0,\ \frac{\partial w_2}{\partial u_{w,2}} < 0 \qquad \textbf{2.3.2}$$

The variable $u_{P,2}$ is parametric to the firm and represents "general conditions" expected in the product market in period 2 and their influence on the expected demand curve of that period. Assume $u_{P,2}$ varies directly with changes in current real aggregate demand, Y_1^d, thus relating the macroeconomic state of aggregate demand to effects on microeconomic decisions made now for period 2. This is reasonable, for increases in Y_1^d increase the typical firm's current demand, presumably increasing the demand it expects next period. The variable $u_{w,2}$ is parametric to the firm and represents "general conditions" expected in the labor market in period 2 and their influence on the labor supply curve expected in that period. Assume $u_{w,2}$ varies directly with changes in the current aggregate percentage rate of unemployment, Nu, thus giving another macro determinant of micro decisions.[11] The higher is Nu, the more workers currently apply for jobs and the more workers the firm expects to attract next period for any given wage rate.

11 Chapter 5, section 2, provides a detailed rationale for this relationship.

As long as $u_{P,2}$ varies with Y_1^d, and $u_{w,2}$ varies with Nu, the firm need not know the statistical value of aggregate demand and unemployment in any period. The firm need notice only the effect of these macro variables on the individual firm's situation, not the cause of the effect.

The firm's expectations of next period's average price level, P_2^e, and wage rate, w_2^e, are:

$$P_2^e = \widetilde{P}_1 + \widetilde{P}_1 \left(\frac{\Delta P}{P}\right)_1^e \qquad \textbf{2.3.3}$$

and

$$w_2^e = \widetilde{w}_1 + \widetilde{w}_1 \left(\frac{\Delta w}{w}\right)_1^e \qquad \textbf{2.3.4}$$

where $\widetilde{P}_1$ and $\widetilde{w}_1$ are what the firm believes are the current average values of, and $(\Delta P/P)^e$ and $(\Delta w/w)^e$ are the expected percentage rates of change in, the prices and wages in which it is interested. The expected rates of change are conceptually free to vary independently of $\widetilde{P}_1$ and $\widetilde{w}_1$, and the firm need not always be right about the actual values P_1 and w_1.

The firm's production function is:

$$Q_t = Q(K_t, N_t);$$

$$\frac{\partial Q_t}{\partial K_t} \geq 0, \frac{\partial Q_t}{\partial N_t} \geq 0, \frac{\partial^2 Q_t}{\partial K_t^2} < 0, \frac{\partial^2 Q_t}{\partial N_t^2} < 0, \frac{\partial^2 Q_t}{\partial K_t \partial N_t} > 0$$

$$\textbf{2.3.5}$$

which, for simplicity, does not change over time. Both factors display nonnegative but diminishing marginal productivity. The factors are complements, or an increase in one raises the marginal productivity of the other. Depreciation can easily be introduced by modifying equation 2.3.5 to treat it as a factor of production.[12]

Four further assumptions are crucial to the comparative statics results. First, an increase in employment increases the marginal revenue product of capital,

$$\frac{\partial MRP_{K,t}}{\partial N_t} > 0 \qquad \textbf{2.3.6}$$

and since the order of differentiation in a mixed partial is irrelevant,

$$\frac{\partial MRP_{N,t}}{\partial K_t} > 0 \qquad \textbf{2.3.7}$$

---

12 Appendix 1, section 4, takes this approach and shows that the comparative statics results are virtually identical to those of the following section.

This implies the two factors are complements, but places only very minor restrictions on the curvature of the demand curve.[13]

Second, when the firm can buy all the capital it wants, the marginal cost curve is linear and horizontal.[14] (Virtually all studies show that United States firms with market power operate in a range of constant or even decreasing per unit costs.[15]) When the firm cannot buy all the capital goods it wants, this assumption implies its marginal cost curve has a positive slope; for the firm produces with increasingly suboptimal factor combinations as output expands.[16]

Third, let variations in current, real aggregate demand change $u_{P,2}$ proportionately; and let changes in $u_{P,2}$ shift expected demand proportionately and isoelastically relative to the *price* axis.[17]

Fourth, let variations in P_2^e shift demand proportionately and isoelastically relative to the *quantity* axis.[18]

The second and third assumptions together can be shown to imply: (1) when there is excess capacity and the firm can buy as many capital goods as it demands, increases in Y_1^d do not affect inflation; and (2) when there is positive excess aggregate demand, increases in Y_1^d increase inflation—two intuitively and empirically plausible properties of a model.[19] Given the second assumption, the third is the only one consistent with noninflationary, steady-state growth, with all firms growing at the same rate as the economy. Since it is desirable that the typical firm be able to display this behavior pattern, the assumption of a horizontal marginal cost curve partly justifies the third assumption.[20] Note that proportionate and isoelastic (relative to the quantity axis) demand shifts with changes in P_2^e are necessary and sufficient to allow an inflationary, stationary state—and it is desirable that the firm be capable of displaying this behavior pattern.[21] Further, such a reaction is useful in deriving the effect of inflationary expectations.[22]

13 Hence the earlier assumption that $\partial^2 Q / \partial K \partial N > 0$.

14 From the point of view of period 1, period 2's marginal cost is *long run* marginal cost, since both capital and labor are freely variable between the two periods.

15 Declining marginal cost strengthens the policy recommendations of this book, so couching the analysis in terms of constant marginal cost understates the argument.

16 See Chapter 4, section 6, and Appendix 1, section 3. Note that when capital is not freely variable, period 2's marginal cost is a short run marginal cost.

17 See Appendix 1, section 5.

18 See Appendix 1, section 5.

19 Chapters 2 and 3 consider case (1), and Chapter 4 discusses case (2). M. Kalecki, *Theory of Economic Dynamics* (rev. 2d ed.; New York: Monthly Review Press, 1968), assumes the typical manufacturing firm is a monopolist with a horizontal, marginal prime cost curve up to capacity; and increases in demand raise output but not price until capacity is approached—but Kalecki provides virtually no analysis.

20 For a further discussion, see Appendix 1, section 5, and also section 4 of this chapter for graphical isoelastic demand shifts.

21 What of the real balance effect? It presumably operates through aggregate demand and hence u_P. Continuing increases in prices, with unchanged real aggregate demand and no change in i imply steady expansion of the money supply at the same percentage rate as inflation—the stationary state case of steady state growth.

22 See footnote 20.

Five interesting parametric changes affect the system of equations 2.1.6: variations in current, real aggregate demand, Y_1^d, and hence in $u_{P,2}$; in the percentage rate of unemployment, Nu, and hence in $u_{w,2}$; in competitors' expected prices and wages, P_2^e and w_2^e; and in the rate of interest, i_1.

The micro results of changes in macro variables can be aggregated to give macro results.

2.4. The Comparative Statics Results

Shocking the system of equations 2.1.6 produces the comparative statics results in Table 2–1.[23]

TABLE 2–1

SUMMARY OF COMPARATIVE
STATICS RESULTS FOR THE FIRM*

Parameters	\multicolumn{6}{c}{Variables}					
	K_2	I_1^d	N_2	Q_2	P_2	w_2
Y_1^d	+	+	+	+	0	+
i_1	−	−	−	−	+	−
Nu	+	+	+	+	−	−
$\widetilde{P}_1$	+	+	+	+	+	+
$\dfrac{\Delta P}{P}e$	+	+	+	+	+	+
$\widetilde{w}_1$	−	−	−	−	+	+
$\dfrac{\Delta w}{w}e$	−	−	−	−	+	−
$P_{K,1}$	−	−	−	−	+	−
$\dfrac{\Delta P_{K,1}^e}{P_{K,1}}$	+	+	+	+	−	+

*Interpret all tables as follows: The first row says that an increase in Y_1^d causes an increase in K_2, I_1^d, N_2, Q_2, and w_2, and no change in P_2. The second row says an increase in i_1 causes a decrease in K_2, I_1^d, N_2, Q_2, and w_2, and an increase in P_2. Interpret the other rows similarly.

Recall that an increase in the stock of capital raises the marginal revenue product of labor—shifts the MRP_N curve up—and an increase

---

23 Appendix 1, section 2, discusses the relatively weak conditions, in addition to those already specified, under which increases in $\widetilde{w}_1$ or $(\Delta w/w)^e$, or decreases in Nu, will increase w_2; and increases in $\widetilde{P}_1$ or $(\Delta P/P)^e$ will increase P_2.

in employment raises the marginal revenue product of capital—shifts the MRP_K curve up. This assumption is crucial.[24]

The parametric variations are a change in: (1) the demand function; (2) the labor supply function; and (3) $P_{K,1}(i_1 - \Delta P^e_{K,1}/P_{K,1})$, the implicit marginal factor cost of capital services.

Figure 2-1 illustrates an increase in $\widetilde{P}_1$ or $(\Delta P/P)^e$. The preceding section assumes that an increase in the average price the firm expects its rivals to charge next period raises the demand curve the firm expects to face proportionately and isoelastically at the initial equilibrium quantity. Since the marginal cost curve is horizontal, output increases. Capital and labor are complements, so the quantity demanded of each rises. The price the firm sets for next period rises. Desired investment, equal to the desired minus the actual capital stock, rises.

Figure 2-2 illustrates an increase in current aggregate demand. A rise in this period's real aggregate demand increases the firm's current demand; and the firm interprets this as indicating that next period's demand is higher than otherwise. The firm views the increase in demand as isoelastic at the initial equilibrium price. Then, the firm does not change price, but expands output by increasing its use of both labor and capital.

Figure 2-3 illustrates an increase in the average wage the firm expects its rivals to offer, or a decrease in current unemployment. The higher the firm expects its rivals' wage offers to be next period—the higher is $\widetilde{w}_1$ or $(\Delta w/w)^e$, or both—the higher it thinks its labor supply curve will be, inducing a decrease in desired employment. Since labor is complementary to capital, the decrease in labor lowers the MRP_K curve and hence reduces the quantity demanded of capital. The upward shift in the labor supply curve raises the marginal cost curve, inducing a rise in price and fall in output.[25]

The higher is current unemployment, the lower the firm expects its labor supply curve to be next period, inducing a higher labor demand than otherwise for next period.[26] The increase in labor raises the MRP_K curve, so the firm plans to have a larger stock of capital. The lowered labor supply curve lowers next period's marginal cost curve, inducing an increase in output and fall in price.

Finally, $P_{K,1}(i_1 - \Delta P^e_{K,1}/P_{K,1})$ is the implicit rental rate of capital, equal to the implicit marginal factor cost of next period's capital services. If a firm buys a unit of capital now, paying $P_{K,1}$, and expects

24 This assumption is the basis of the effects on one factor of changes in the other factor's market. However, the assumption is not crucial to policy recommendations, though rejecting it requires reworking of many of the details of the essay.

25 The assumption that factors are complements implies this.

26 Figure 2-3 shows the vertical shifts appropriate for changes in w^e_2. Changes in Nu also change the supply curve's slope. See Appendix 1, section 2.

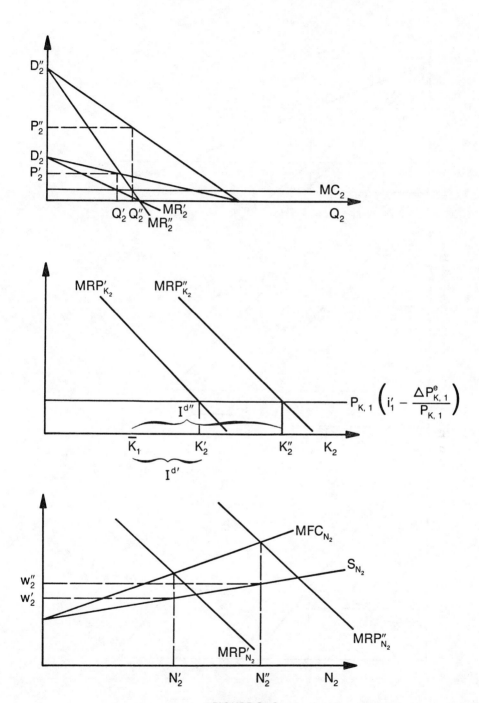

FIGURE 2-1

AN INCREASE IN RIVALS' PRICES

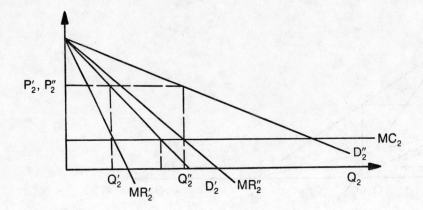

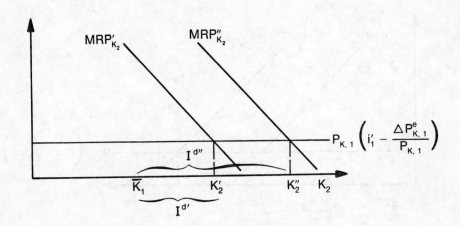

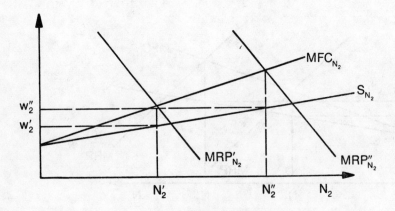

FIGURE 2-2

AN INCREASE IN AGGREGATE DEMAND

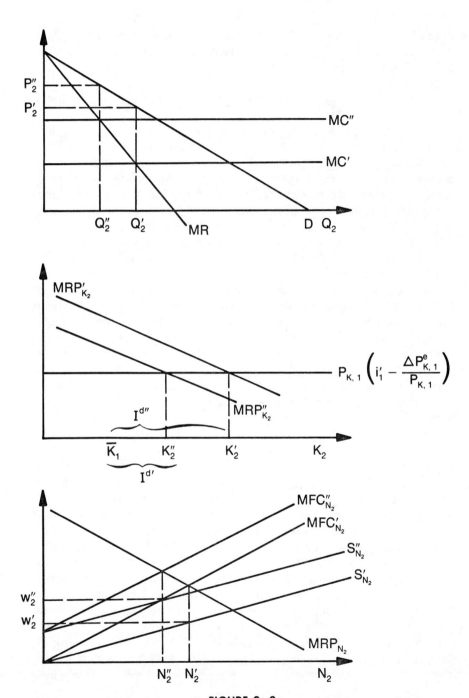

FIGURE 2-3

AN INCREASE IN LABOR COSTS

to resell it next period for the same price, it expects to lose only $i_1 P_{K,1}$, the interest on $P_{K,1}$. Suppose, however, that it expects price to rise by $\Delta P_{K,1}^e$. Then, it expects to lose:[27]

$$i_1 P_{K,1} - \Delta P_{K,1}^e = P_{K,1}\left(i_1 - \frac{\Delta P_{K,1}^e}{P_{K,1}}\right) \qquad 2.4.1$$

An increase in i_1 or in $P_{K,1}$ raises the marginal factor cost of capital services, while an increase in $(\Delta P_{K,1}^e/P_{K,1})$ lowers it. Figure 2–4 illustrates the effect of an increase in i_1. This raises the marginal factor cost of capital services, thus decreasing the quantity of capital the firm wants to use. This decrease in capital lowers the MRP_N curve, reducing the quantity of labor the firm demands and lowering the wage offer in period 2. The increase in the marginal factor cost of capital services raises the marginal cost curve for next period, inducing a fall in quantity and rise in price.[28] The effects of changes in $P_{K,1}$ and $(P_{K,1}^e/P_{K,1})$ are completely analogous.

The experiment in Figure 2–4 is to raise the rate of interest and find the comparative statics results, with all other parameters facing the firm unchanged. The demand curve each firm expects to face remains unchanged. On the macro level, government increases the interest rate while holding constant real aggregate demand. The government can do this by lowering the money supply while raising real government demand for output. With aggregate demand constant, there may be shifts in demand at the firm level, some firms finding current demand higher than otherwise, others finding it lower. These shifts in current demand cause shifts in expected future demands.

One shift in expected demands is between the consumer and capital goods sectors. Increasing the interest rate initially decreases current private investment demand, hence lowering the demand capital goods producers expect to face next period. The increase in the interest rate seems to affect capital goods firms both as an increase in costs and as a decrease in demand. But with a fall in private investment demand, government must raise some other component to keep aggregate demand constant. One possibility is to increase its demand for the output of each capital good by exactly the amount that the increase in interest has lowered private demand. This holds constant aggregate demand and current—and hence expected—demand for every firm. Here, there are no problems of sectoral shifts.

Government might instead provide the needed stimulus to aggregate demand by cutting personal taxes. The household sector might

---

27 All this depends on the continuing assumption that there is no depreciation. Appendix 1, section 4, relaxes this assumption.
28 See footnote 25.

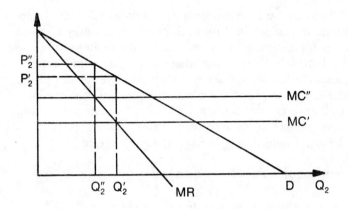

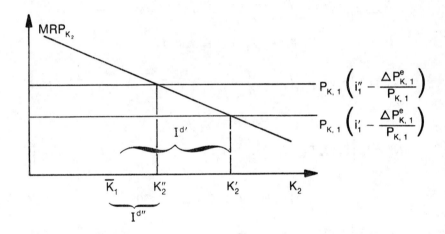

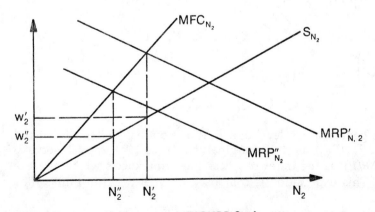

FIGURE 2-4

AN INCREASE IN CAPITAL COSTS

react to this tax decrease by increasing its demands to offset the interest-induced change in the demand for each good (trucks may be used for hauling hay or for camping). However, it is unrealistic to suppose that the shifts in demand will not be against capital goods and in favor of consumer goods (10-ton lorries are not very suitable for camping). In a macro model with one produced good, this sectoral shift can logically have no influence at all. Chapter 8 shows it is quite interesting when the macro model has separate consumer and capital goods sectors —though single period behavior is not significantly affected.

2.5. The Micro Results Are Aggregated

The micro results are summarized in functional form as:[29]

$$P_2 = F\left[P_1 Y_1^d, P_{K,1}\left(i_1 - \frac{\Delta P_{K,1}^e}{P_{K,1}}\right), \widetilde{P}_1 + \widetilde{P}_1 \frac{\Delta P^e}{P}, \widetilde{w}_1 + \widetilde{w}_1 \frac{\Delta w^e}{w}, Nu\right]$$

$$F_2, F_3, F_4 > 0; F_5 < 0; F_1 = 0$$

$$w_2 = G\left[P_1 Y_1^d, P_{K,1}\left(i_1 - \frac{\Delta P_{K,1}^e}{P_{K,1}}\right), \widetilde{P}_1 + \widetilde{P}_1 \frac{\Delta P^e}{P}, \widetilde{w}_1 + \widetilde{w}_1 \frac{\Delta w^e}{w}, Nu\right]$$

$$G_1, G_3, G_4 > 0; G_2, G_5 < 0$$

$$N_2^d = H^*\left[P_1 Y_1^d, P_{K,1}\left(i_1 - \frac{\Delta P_{K,1}^e}{P_{K,1}}\right), \widetilde{P}_1 + \widetilde{P}_1 \frac{\Delta P^e}{P}, \widetilde{w}_1 + \widetilde{w}_1 \frac{\Delta w^e}{w}, Nu\right]$$

$$H_1^*, H_3^*, H_5^* > 0; H_2^*, H_4^* < 0 \qquad\qquad \textbf{2.5.1}$$

$$K_2^d = K\left[P_1 Y_1^d, P_{K,1}\left(i_1 - \frac{\Delta P_{K,1}^e}{P_{K,1}}\right), \widetilde{P}_1 + \widetilde{P}_1 \frac{\Delta P^e}{P}, \widetilde{w}_1 + \widetilde{w}_1 \frac{\Delta w^e}{w}, Nu\right]$$

$$K_1, K_3, K_5 > 0; K_2, K_4 < 0$$

$$Q_2^s = Q^*\left[P_1 Y_1^d, P_{K,1}\left(i_1 - \frac{\Delta P_{K,1}^e}{P_{K,1}}\right), \widetilde{P}_1 + \widetilde{P}_1 \frac{\Delta P^e}{P}, \widetilde{w}_1 + \widetilde{w}_1 \frac{\Delta w^e}{w}, Nu\right]$$

$$Q_1^*, Q_3^*, Q_5^* > 0; Q_2^*, Q_4^* < 0$$

P_1 is the general price level and $P_1 Y_1^d$ is nominal aggregate demand. $P_{K,1}(i_1 - \Delta P_{K,1}^e/P_{K,1})$ is the marginal factor cost of capital services. $\widetilde{P}_1 + \widetilde{P}_1(\Delta P/P)^e$ is the index of prices the firm expects which affect its demand. This expectation is composed of what the firm thinks these

---

29 F_1 equals zero on the assumption the firm can buy all the capital goods it wants. Chapter 4 develops the argument that F_1 is positive when the firm can buy only fewer capital goods than it desires.

prices are currently and the rate of increase it expects. A similar inter-
pretation is put on $\widetilde{w}_1 + \widetilde{w}_1(\Delta w/w)^e$. Nu is the aggregate unemployment
rate.

The functions in equations 2.5.1 may be treated as aggregated merely
by putting a different interpretation on the arguments. Assume that
the aggregate of decisions taken by the business sector behaves as do
the decisions of the representative firm. This is plausible. For example,
if there is an increase in aggregate demand, some firms must enjoy
an increase in current demand. If every firm in the economy reacts
according to the model, and if every firm has some weight in whatever
index is used, then the indices behave as predicted.

But there are problems of consistency. The hypothetical increase in
aggregate demand just mentioned might have fallen on a different set
of firms. While one set would behave qualitatively like any other, the
quantitative results might be quite different. Some industries may be
more subject to random disturbances which are not serially correlated,
and hence these industries will be less influenced by increased demand
today when estimating future demand. Further, the two sorts of industries may have very different production functions; where one
industry responds to increased demand by hiring many workers and
buying a few units of capital, the other reverses this pattern.

Aggregation changes the interpretation of the variables $(\Delta P/P)^e$
and $(\Delta w/w)^e$. Previously these were a kind of weighted average of how
an individual firm expected relevant prices and wages to change. Now
interpret these as an average of individual firms' indices of expected
rates of inflation. The macro variable $(\Delta P/P)^e$ is then the rate of inflation the business sector expects. Though based on a shaky aggregation
as are all macro variables, it allows discussion of inflationary expectations, as in Chapters 3 and 4 and particularly in Chapter 7, sections
4 and 5.

Treating equations 2.5.1 as aggregate functions, assume that $F(\cdot)$
and $G(\cdot)$ are homogeneous of degree one in the first, second, third, and
fourth arguments; and K, H^* and Q^* are homogeneous of degree zero
in the same arguments.[30] The function $F(\cdot)$ in equations 2.5.1 may be
rewritten as:

$$\frac{\Delta P}{P} = f\left[Y_1, \frac{P_{K,1}}{P_1}\left(i_1 - \frac{\Delta P^e_{K,1}}{P_{K,1}}\right), \frac{\widetilde{P}_1}{P_1}\left(1 + \frac{\Delta P^e}{P}\right), \frac{\widetilde{w}_1}{P_1}\left(1 + \frac{\Delta w^e}{w}\right), Nu \right] \quad \textbf{2.5.2}$$

Consider the interpretation of $P_{K,1}/P_1$, $\widetilde{P}_1/P_1$, and $\widetilde{w}_1/P_1$. As in all models
with one produced good, $P_{K,1}$ necessarily equals P_1 on the aggregate
level, so $P_{K,1}/P_1$ equals unity. On the macro level in models with one

---

30 When mentioning a function but not listing its arguments, it is conventional to
replace the arguments with a dot, as in $F(\cdot)$ or $G(\cdot)$.

produced good, variations in relative prices are nonexistent. But the short run in the present model is easily adapted to two sectors, particularly since all firms have already set their prices in the short run and the price level is thus unambiguously defined. Chapter 8 pursues this further.

With the other two ratios, there are two problems. The first problem is consistency. Some index P_1 can always be found just by arbitrarily selecting weights. Now, there is some index $\widetilde{P}_1$ on the micro level that is an average of what the firm believes are the relevant current prices. Treating equations 2.5.1 as a system of macro functions, P_1 is an average of these averages and represents the general price level the business sector believes to hold currently. Suppose firms know the prices they use to construct $\widetilde{P}_1$. Does the general price level P_1 equal $\widetilde{P}_1$? Secondly, firms may be wrong in their beliefs about the wage and price policies of their competitors.

Assume there does exist an index P_1 such that P_1 equals $\widetilde{P}_1$. The second problem is not very interesting per se, and since mistaken beliefs do not change qualitative results, they are ignored. Assume then $w_1 = \widetilde{w}_1$ and $P_1 = \widetilde{P}_1$.

Similar to equation 2.5.2,[31]

$$\Delta P/P = f[Y, i - \Delta P^e/P, \Delta P^e/P, w/P(1 + \Delta w^e/w), Nu]$$

$$f_i, f_{w/P}, f_{\Delta w^e/w}, f_3 > 0; f_{Nu} < 0; f_y = 0; \frac{\partial \Delta P/P}{\partial (\Delta P/P)^e} = f_3 - f_i \gtreqless 0$$

$$\Delta w/w = g(Y, i - \Delta P^e/P, \Delta P^e/P, w/P, \Delta w^e/w, Nu)$$

$$g_y, g_{\Delta P^e/P}, g_{\Delta w^e/w} > 0; g_i, g_{w/P}, g_{Nu} < 0$$

$$\Delta N^d = H[Y, i - \Delta P^e/P, \Delta P^e/P, w/P(1 + \Delta w^e/w), Nu, N]$$

2.5.3

$$H_y, H_{\Delta P^e/P}, H_{Nu} > 0; H_i, H_{w/P}, H_{\Delta w^e/w} < 0; H_N = -1$$

$$I^d = I[Y, i - \Delta P^e/P, \Delta P^e/P, w/P(1 + \Delta w^e/w), Nu, K]$$

$$I_y, I_{\Delta P^e/P}, I_{Nu} > 0; I_i, I_{w/P}, I_{\Delta w^e/w} < 0; I_K = -1$$

$$AQ = AQ[Y, i - \Delta P^e/P, \Delta P^e/P, w/P(1 + \Delta w^e/w), Nu]$$

$$AQ_y, AQ_{\Delta P^e/P}, AQ_{Nu} > 0; AQ_i, AQ_{w/P}, AQ_{\Delta w^e/w} < 0$$

---

31 The partial derivative f_y equals zero here because F_1 equals zero in equations 2.5.1. See footnote 29, p. 22 and Chapter 4, section 6, where f_y is positive when the firm cannot buy as many units of capital as it desires. Appendix 1, section 2, shows that under mild conditions $f_3 - f_1 > 0$.

Examining equation 2.5.3 on the micro level, Q_2^s represents the quantity the firm plans to produce and sell in period 2. On the macro level, AQ represents aggregate, planned output of the business sector for period 2. Output may fall short of this if business attracts fewer workers than planned. Next period's aggregate demand may exceed AQ, implying positive excess aggregate demand as in Chapter 4, or fall short of AQ, implying excess capacity as in Chapter 3. AQ sets an upper bound to next period's real income, and hence an upper bound to real growth.[32] In equilibrium growth, there is zero excess demand for output; and the economy grows at the same rate as AQ.

Notice that $G(\cdot)$ is the only function in equations 2.5.3 that has w/P and $\Delta w^e/w$ as separate arguments rather than the single argument $w/P(1 + \Delta w^e/w)$, and that the partial $g_{w/P}$ has a different sign from $g_{\Delta w^e/w}$. To understand this, rearrange $G(\cdot)$ in equations 2.5.1 to:

$$\frac{\Delta w}{w} = \frac{G^*\left[Y, i - \dfrac{\Delta P^e}{P}, 1 + \dfrac{\Delta P^e}{P}, \dfrac{w}{P}\left(1 + \dfrac{\Delta w^e}{w}\right)Nu\right]}{w/P} - 1 = g(\cdot) \quad \textbf{2.5.4}$$

showing w/P and $\Delta w/w$ do not have perfectly symmetrical effects, as in say $f(\cdot)$, where:

$$\frac{\partial f}{\partial w/P} = \frac{\partial f}{\partial \Delta w^e/w} \cdot \frac{1 + \Delta w^e/w}{w/P} \qquad \textbf{2.5.5}$$

Rather,

$$\frac{\partial g}{\partial \Delta w^e/w} = G_4^* = \frac{G_4}{w_1} = \frac{\partial w_2 \Big/ \partial \dfrac{\Delta w^e}{w}}{w_1} > 0 \qquad \textbf{2.5.6}$$

$$\partial g/\partial w/P = g_{w/P} = \frac{w/P\, G_4^*(1 + \Delta w/w^e) - G^*}{(w/P)^2}$$

$$= \frac{1}{w/P}\left[G_4^*(1 + \Delta w/w^e) - \frac{G^*}{w/P}\right] \qquad \textbf{2.5.7}$$

$$= \frac{1}{w/P}\left[G_4^*(1 + \Delta w/w^e) - (1 + \Delta w/w)\right]$$

Appendix 1, section 2, shows G_4^* is very likely less than unity; and thus if $\Delta w/w$ is approximately equal to $(\Delta w/w)^e$, then $g_{w/P}$ is negative.

---

32 Chapter 6 discusses policy towards growth in terms of AQ.

2.6. A Further Discussion of the Behavior of the Firm

This chapter has established two functions telling how prices and wages will change and three functions telling how firms desire quantity variables to change. Since firms can set prices and wages, desired changes in these variables always come about. But firms can be wrong about how much they will be able to sell and how many workers they will attract next period at the prices and wages they establish. If firms underestimate next period's demand, they will be able to sell everything they had planned and still face unfulfilled demand. If they overestimate, though, they find themselves with the capacity to produce more than can be sold. In the same way, if the labor supply curve is lower than expected, firms have more people seeking work than they want to hire at the wage rates they have announced. If firms overestimate labor supply, they cannot hire all they want and consequently cannot produce all they want. When the firm reacts to any such shortage or excess by changing prices or wages, the model moves from period 2 to period 3.

In times of positive excess demand, the typical firm cannot get all the investment goods it wants. The firm must then adjust both its price and its wage offer for next period to reflect the fact that it cannot invest as much as it would like this period. Chapter 4 deals with this case.

The firm learns of any failure to accumulate as much capital as desired before it announces its wage and price policies. But assume that the firm does not learn of any such failure of its wage and price policies in time to adjust its hiring. If there is excess capacity, the firm does not learn of this soon enough to reduce its hiring, at the wage rate it has already determined, to a level below what it had planned. If there is excess demand in the product market, assume that the firm does not learn of this in time to take advantage of any slack which it had not anticipated in the labor market.

Recall the assumption that there are no inventories in the model. Assume that when capacity is greater than demand, the firm either (1) produces only enough to meet demand, or (2) produces up to capacity and any unsold output wastes away before next period. (1) and (2) produce the same result.[33]

Finally, as long as the firm does not plan to disinvest in period 2, the assumption that there are markets for used capital goods is innocuous. If the firm believes there are markets and is wrong, it does not try to use them and does not find its error.

---

33 Assumptions (1) and (2) produce the same result in the absence of depreciation. Introduction of wear and tear on machines makes firms prefer (1).

3 A SIMPLE MACRO MODEL WITH EXCESS CAPACITY

Chapter 2 developed functions showing how firms change prices and wages and how they want to change investment, output, and hiring. These functions have real aggregate demand, Y_1^d, and the interest rate, i_1, as arguments. This chapter completes the system by showing how Y_1^d and i_1 are determined, and then derives comparative statics results.

To do this, it uses the *IS-LM* apparatus for the case in which price is fixed. The intersection of the *IS* and *LM* curves determines Y_1^d and i_1, if the intersection is not beyond the economy's capacity (the case Chapter 4 considers).

3.1. A Simple *IS-LM* Model

Take a very simple *IS-LM* model as a first approximation to the more complicated model of Chapter 7. Let real consumption depend only on real disposable income, with a positive marginal propensity less than unity; and let the flow demand for real balances depend only on current real income, the nominal rate of interest, and current holdings of real balances. Further, to be consistent with the model of Chapter 2, business holds no cash balances.[1]

These assumptions are straightforward. Relating real consumption only to real disposable income is very common, primarily because it lends simplicity to deriving results.

The assumption has an interesting implication in light of Chapter 2, section 2's discussion of the firm's discount rate. It implies that, given real disposable income, any increase in business savings is exactly matched by a decrease in household savings. The consumption function is:

$$C^d = C(Y - T), 0 < C_y < 1 \qquad\qquad 3.1.1$$

where Y is current real income and T is net taxation of households. The household sector's budget constraint is:

[1] This also simplifies the analysis, but Chapter 7 shows that policy recommendations are not much different when business demands money.

$$Y - S_b = C^d + S_h^d + T \qquad\qquad \textbf{3.1.2}$$

where S_h^d is real household savings and S_b is real business savings.[2] Substituting equation 3.1.1 into equation 3.1.2,

$$Y - S_b = C(Y - T) + S_h^d + T \qquad\qquad \textbf{3.1.3}$$

or

$$S^d \equiv S_h^d + S_b = (Y - T) - C(Y - T) \qquad\qquad \textbf{3.1.4}$$

where S^d is total desired private savings. Holding $(Y - T)$ constant,

$$dS_h^d/dS_b = -1 \qquad\qquad \textbf{3.1.5}$$

This is a common, though often unmentioned, result in Keynesian models.[3] It says that there is a given amount of real saving which the household sector desires to do out of real disposable income. Part of this saving is done for the household sector by the business sector, and part by households. If business changes the share it does for households, households merely offset this change. An implication of this interpretation is that it does not matter how much business saves; that is, it does not matter how business finances its investment. This is consistent with the spirit of the micro model of Chapter 2.

Chapter 2's model of the firm is fairly rigorous, but is slanted very much toward production rather than financial problems. Indeed, Chapter 2, section 2, explores two possible cases: (1) the neoclassical world where there is no "financial" problem per se; for the given interest rate is all that matters, the method of financing being irrelevant; and (2) the concept of the cost of capital where any problems of financing are assumed to be resolved, the resolution producing a discount rate to be used independently of the question of finance. There are some worlds—for example, where the Modigliani-Miller propositions hold—in which the mode of finance can be ignored, even without perfect certainty.[4] In worlds in which financial decisions cannot be

2 Equation 3.1.2 is a budget constraint relating households' desired consumption and savings to net income, $Y - S_b$, and holds whether or not business actually makes its savings take on the value business desires. Hence equation 3.1.2 holds whether or not S_b has the superscript d for desired, as it does in Chapter 4, section 2.

3 Joseph McKenna, *Aggregate Economic Analysis* (3d ed.; New York: Holt, Rinehart & Winston, 1970), makes a great distinction between S_h and S_b, totally ignoring the considerations of the next two paragraphs.

4 Franco Modigliani and Merton Miller, "The Cost of Capital, Corporation Finance, and the Theory of Investment," *American Economic Review*, Vol. XLVIII (June, 1958), pp. 261–97, show how the firm's cost of capital can be independent of its leverage; and in "Dividend Policy, Growth, and the Valuation of Shares," *Journal of Business*, Vol.

ignored, assume that the firm makes the "right" financing decision. That is, the firm makes the one decision in which it does not matter whether the M-M propositions hold or not. For example, assume there is an optimal method of financing the firm's activities, and the firm chooses this method. Then, treat the cost of capital the firm finds as if it existed in an M-M world, so it is just as if the firm faces this cost of capital independently from how it finances.

Thus, the assumption that private savings do not depend on how they are split between business and household savings turns on the world's being either one in which the method of financing is irrelevant, or one in which business always chooses the optimal method. In this latter world, private savings do not depend on business savings just because business always finances optimally. If the business sector were to change its financing pattern, the household sector would experience wealth effects and would presumably change its savings pattern. Therefore, the consumption function in equation 3.1.1 has hidden behind it some strong assumptions about the nature of capital markets or the firm's financing practices.

The government's issuance of money over the period is the flow supply of money. The household sector's flow demand for money depends on its current holdings of money for two reasons. First, given the stock desired for the end of the period, the larger the stock held at the start of the period, the smaller is the flow demand. Second, other things being equal, an increase in the stock held at the start of the period is an increase in wealth. If both present consumption and the services of real balances in the next period are superior goods, the net effect of such an increase is a decrease in flow demand, but by an amount less than the increase in the real value of the initial stock.

Real income and rate of interest are conventional entries in the money demand function. The interest rate represents the opportunity cost of transferring wealth from this period to the next in the form of money rather than bonds, thus allowing use of money services. The current interest rate, in conjunction with expected future rates, may also induce a conventional speculative demand for money.

This book views real income as solely a wealth variable in the flow money demand function; Y_1 influences money demand as does any other component of wealth.[5] This is distinct from Keynesian models in which current real income is a proxy for current transactions which must be made using money, and hence necessitates a current demand

XXXIV (October, 1961), pp. 411–33, how the cost of capital can be independent of dividend policy. These pioneering articles stimulated much further work. See, for example, Joseph Stiglitz, "A Re-Examination of the Modigliani-Miller Theorem," *American Economic Review*, Vol. LIX (December, 1969), pp. 78–93.

5 The only components of real wealth considered through Chapter 6 are real income and real balances. Chapter 7 considers wealth and wealth effects more generally.

for money. In this book, current income is a part of total wealth; and out of this total, one may decide to consume money services next period. Of course, current income may be a predictor of future income. Given the close relationship between future income and expenditures, one may then view an increase in current income as generating an increase in transaction demand for real balances, which must be accumulated this period, in order to make transactions next period.

A business flow demand for money would have to be motivated by the need to make transactions next period. Optimal holdings of money at the start of period 2 would presumably depend on revenue during that period and the way this revenue is used to pay the wage bill, to buy capital goods, $P_{K,2}\Delta K_2$, to pay dividends, and to accumulate money itself. Thus, in the most general case, decisions on ΔK_2 will influence decisions on MB_2^d, desired business money holdings at time 2.[6] But decisions on ΔK_2 $(=K_3 - K_2)$ are really also decisions on K_3. As is easily seen, this progression makes it impossible to decompose the firm's system of marginal conditions to solve just for period 2's variables. Instead, all variables K_t, N_t, MB_t $(t = 2,h)$ must be solved for at once, thus destroying most hope of comparative statics results.

But this is not the worst, for this model which sacrifices comparative statics results is very limited. Ideally, the problem of the firm's money holdings involves the question of corporation finance. Deeply involved in this question is the fact that firms can make transactions which individuals cannot—or not as cheaply. Firm and individual portfolios interact, and included in these portfolios is money. This money is there, of course, because it would cost its holder more than it would earn to place it elsewhere between transactions. Still, to discuss intelligently society's demand for money requires examination of this interaction, a problem too broad for this book.

However, Chapter 7 introduces a simple hypothesis about businesses' demand for money, which allows derivation of comparative statics results and is plausible. Chapter 7 considers wealth effects on the household sector, and adding a business demand for money barely affects the analysis of the model with only wealth effects. The simple model used until then is difficult enough to understand without wealth effects and business demand for money, and policy results derived from the simple model are little different from those of Chapter 7.

3.2. The Structure of the Macro Model

The model has four goods—output, bonds, money, and labor services. The one produced good, output, may be either consumed or added to

---

6 And hence decisions on ΔMB_1^d, since $MB_2^d = MB_1 + \Delta MB_1^d$.

the stock of capital to yield capital services. Ignore a firm's accumulation of inventories of its own output by assuming it desires to hold none, and any unsold output wastes completely by the end of the period.[7] Another interpretation, equivalent to complete wastage, is that business hires workers and buys capital to fulfill expected demand; and if the demand does not materialize, the firm allows its plant and workers to be idle rather than build up inventories, presumably because carrying costs make inventories unprofitable.

There is one security, the bond. Interpret this as literally one kind of security, or as an aggregate of many security types. Even taking the latter interpretation, the following discussion ignores all problems of aggregation; so it is as if there were only one kind of security. The second financial asset, money, is solely government fiat money.

These three goods are linked together in the following way: Whatever is the value of real income, equal to the value of real output, the sum of the nominal values of the excess demands for output, bonds, and money must equal zero.[8]

The price of output is the price level P, with the dimensions of dollars per unit. One unit of money, the dollar, sells for one dollar. The price of a bond, P_b, and the interest rate, i_1, may be related in different ways, depending on the "standard" bond. If the bond is a promise to pay the buyer one dollar during the next period, the price of the bond and the current one-period market rate of interest, i_1, are related by:

$$P_b = \frac{1}{1 + i_1} \qquad \textbf{3.2.1}$$

If the bond is a perpetuity paying one dollar per period, i_1, interpreted as the yield, is found from:

$$P_b = \frac{1}{i_1} \qquad \textbf{3.2.2}$$

Between these alternatives are different lengths of time over which the bond seller pays a certain amount, and this amount need not be one

---

7 An alternative treatment is to assume the firm always desires zero inventories, presumably because of carrying costs. Its desired production in period 2 equals desired sales in period 2 less any inventory inadvertently accumulated in period 1 because demand falls short of sales. (Marginal cost in period 2 runs along the Q axis from zero to the amount of inventory; there jumping to a positive value. The typical firm operates in the second range.) Any parametric change affecting desired sales, but not inventories, in period 2 has exactly the effects as in the text. In fact, given output (see Chapter 4 on capacity), only variations in period 1's aggregate demand can affect inventories; and the effect on inventories merely reinforces aggregate demand's other effects. For example, an increase in Y_1^d increases future expected demand and hence increases ΔN^d. But it also reduces inventories, again increasing ΔN^d.

8 Chapter 4 proves this well-known law.

dollar nor need it be constant over time. The particular assumption does not matter.[9]

Current output is produced with labor services and the capital services yielded by the existing stock of capital. There is a market for labor services, which need not clear, but no market for capital services per se. Each worker has one unit of labor service per period which he may sell, and the price he currently gets for this unit is w_1—if he desires to sell it and can find a buyer.

Each unit of capital generates one unit of capital services during every period in which the unit exists at the start of the period. There is, however, no market for capital services per se. Instead, as Chapter 2 discussed, the firm buys a unit of capital in one period to have its services in the next. In period t, the firm views the marginal factor cost of capital services next period as the current price level (thus, $P = P_K$) times the difference between the current interest rate and the expected rate of inflation,

$$P_t \left(i_t - \frac{\Delta P_t^e}{P_t} \right)$$

The firm decides in one period on the labor it desires to hire in the next period. Thus, hiring in one period is dependent on conditions in the preceding period. Chapter 5 discusses this at length. Meanwhile, view current employment as independent of current conditions. Think of current employment as something like the capital stock in the short run—it is what it is for this period. This interpretation gives an unambiguous measure of capacity output for this period. Output can never be above what can be produced by the stock of capital and the number of employed workers, and both are given for the period.

3.3. Some Comparative Statics Results. The II, AQ, NN, Δw, and ΔP Curves are Derived

Consider the effects of parametric changes on Y_1^d and i_1. Parametric changes affect business decisions first directly and secondly indirectly through i_1 and Y_1^d. There is a vital distinction between the case in which more output can be produced during the period and the case in which the system is already at capacity. This chapter studies the first case of excess capacity, postponing to Chapter 4 the case where society is already at capacity output.

---

9 Chapter 7 works with the first alternative. It has the virture of giving a short term interest rate, the one period yield, which does not have to be figured out laboriously from some term structure or set of expected future rates.

In what follows, the slope of a curve in the (i, Y) plane is denoted $\frac{di}{dY}$ followed by parentheses with the name of the function. For example, the slope of the LM curve is $\frac{di}{dY}$ (LM) and the slope of the IS curve is $\frac{di}{dY}$ (IS). The vertical shift of such a curve with respect to a parameter α is $\frac{di}{d\alpha}$ followed by parenthesis with the name of the function. For example, the upward shift in the IS curve when government spending, G, increases is $\frac{di}{dG}$ (IS). Throughout the book, assume that $\frac{di}{dY}(LM)$ is positive and finite, and that the IS curve has a smaller slope than the LM curve. The system of the IS-LM equations is:

$$I^d + G - S^d - T = 0$$

$$-\frac{\Delta M^s}{P} + \phi\left(Y, i, \frac{M}{P}\right) = 0 = -\frac{\Delta M^s}{P} + \frac{\Delta M^d}{P} \qquad \textbf{3.3.1}$$

$$\phi_y > 0, \ \phi_i < 0, \ \phi_{M/P} < 0; \ I_y - S_y = I_y - (1 - C_y) \gtreqless 0$$

Table 3-1 lists the standard effects on Y_1 and i_1 of increases in G, T, the average propensity to save (APS), ΔM^s, M, and ΔM^d.

No parameter in Table 3-1 directly enters the business behavior functions. Thus, the results of these parametric changes on business decisions are straightforward, since from equations 2.5.3:

$$f_y = 0, f_i > 0$$

$$sgn \ (g_y) = -sgn \ (g_i) > 0$$

$$sgn \ (H_y) = -sgn \ (H_i) > 0 \qquad \textbf{3.3.2}$$

$$sgn \ (I_y) = -sgn \ (I_i) > 0$$

$$sgn \ (AQ_y) = -sgn \ (AQ_i) > 0$$

The sign of the induced change in $\Delta P/P$ is always unambiguous, but only when Y_1^d and i_1 move in opposite directions are the signs of changes in $\Delta w/w$, ΔN^d, I^d, and AQ also unambiguous. Definition of some new curves—the II, AQ, NN, Δw, and ΔP curves—gives a better understanding of the causes of the ambiguity.

TABLE 3–1

SOME COMPARATIVE STATICS RESULTS: EXCESS CAPACITY

	Y_1	i_1 $\dfrac{di}{dY}(IS) < 0$	i_1 $\dfrac{di}{dY}(IS) > 0$
G	+	+	+
T	−	−	−
APS	−	−	−
ΔM^s	+	−	+
M	+	−	+
ΔM^d	−	+	−

The first is the *family* of II curves in the i_1, Y_1^d plane. For any given level of investment, hold constant $(\Delta P/P)^e$, w/P, $(\Delta w/w)^e$, and Nu, and trace out the locus of combinations of Y_1^d and i_1 which hold investment at this level—this is an isoinvestment curve, and the family of II curves is a family of isoinvestment curves. An II curve goes through the IS-LM intersection. From equations 3.3.2, each II curve has a positive slope—as in Figure 3–1. To see why the slope is positive, consider the investment demand functions in Figure 3–2. There is one function for $Y_1^{d'}$ and a higher function for the larger $Y_1^{d''}$. To hold I_1^d at $I_1^{d'}$ when Y_1^d rises from $Y_1^{d'}$ to $Y_1^{d''}$, i_1 would have to rise from i_1' to i_1'' $(I_y > 0, I_i < 0)$. From Figure 3–2, if Y_1^d is given—at, say, $Y_1^{d'}$—the lower is i_1, the larger is I_1^d. That is, movements vertically downward in the i_1, Y_1^d plane encounter II curves with larger and larger investment demand levels. Also from Figure 3–2, horizontal movements to the right in the i_1, Y_1^d plane encounter II curves with larger and larger indices.

Finally, a change in $(\Delta P/P)^e$, w/P, $(\Delta w/w)^e$, or Nu is a parametric change that shifts the entire family of II curves. For example, an increase in Nu increases investment demand for any pair i_1, Y_1^d. The investment demand functions shift to the right, because $I_{Nu} > 0$ in equations 2.5.3. (the partial derivatives in these equations are important in the following discussion). Thus, to hold I_1^d at $I_1^{d'}$ when Y_1^d remains at $Y_1^{d'}$, i_1 must rise. That is, the II curve for the level $I_1^{d'}$ shifts up in the i_1, Y_1^d plane, as Figure 3–3 shows, when the II curve for the initial level of investment demand shifts from II_1 up to II_2. Both curves represent the same level of I_1^d, but II_2 does so for the new higher value of Nu. Clearly, all the other II curves shift in the same way, so the whole family shifts up.

The family of AQ curves is a family of isoaggregate planned output curves, constructed in a manner exactly analogous to the II curves.

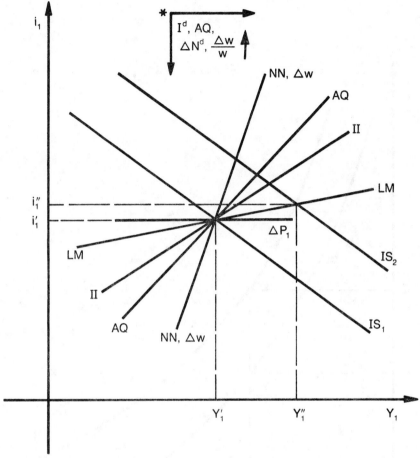

*Interpret this sort of arrow, in all figures, as follows. A movement to the right or down in the plane (an increase in Y_1^d or a fall in i_1) *increases* I^d, AQ, ΔN^d and $\Delta w/w$. The ΔP curves are horizontal: increases in Y_1^d do not affect $\Delta P/P$, while increases in i_1 raise $\Delta P/P$.

FIGURE 3-1

AN INCREASE IN G

Since both AQ and I^d are positively related to Y_1^d (AQ_y, $I_y > 0$) and negatively to i_1 (AQ_i, $I_i < 0$), AQ curves have positive slopes; and the higher an AQ curve, the lower the value of aggregate planned output it represents. There is an AQ curve through any IS-LM intersection, as in Figure 3-1. A change in $(\Delta P/P)^e$, w/P, $(\Delta w/w)^e$, or Nu shifts the entire family of AQ curves, just as with the II curves. Since an increase in Nu positively affects both the AQ and I^d functions (AQ_{Nu}, $I_{Nu} > 0$), the family of AQ curves shifts up in Figure 3-3 as the II curves do. AQ_1 and AQ_2 represent the same value of aggregate planned output,

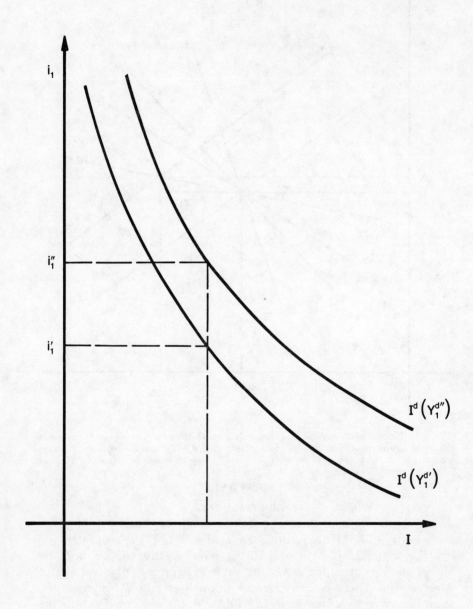

FIGURE 3-2

THE INVESTMENT FUNCTION AND THE *II* CURVE

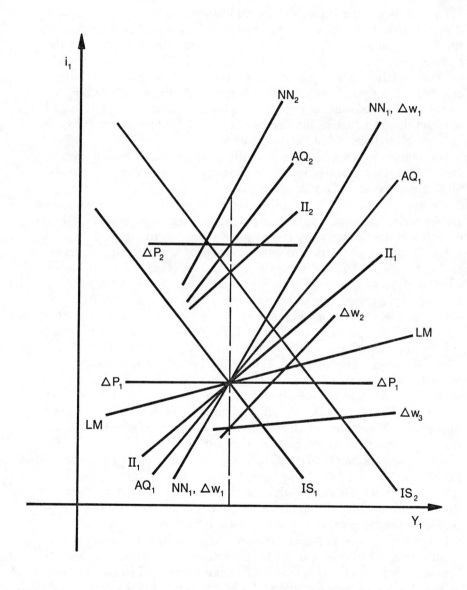

FIGURE 3-3

AN INCREASE IN *Nu*

but AQ_2 does so for a larger value of Nu. The next section discusses why the increase in Nu causes a larger vertical shift in the AQ than the II curves.

The AQ is steeper than the II curve through the IS-LM intersection. Along II, increases in Y_1^d cause the typical firm's marginal revenue product of capital ($MRP_{K,2}$) curve to rise just enough to balance the reduced demand for capital caused by raising i_1. The marginal revenue product of labor ($MRP_{N,2}$) curve rises due to the increase in Y^d, but i_1 affects labor demand only to the extent that K_2^d varies. Therefore, the rise is i_1 which offsets the rise in Y_1^d and keeps K_2^d constant is too small to offset the influence of the rise in Y_1^d on N_2^d. It would take an increase in i_1 which reduces K_2^d to keep N_2^d constant.[10]

The family of NN curves is a family of iso-planned hiring curves, constructed in a manner exactly analogous to the II and AQ curves. Since both ΔN^d and I^d are positively related to Y_1^d ($H_y, I_y > 0$) and negatively to i_1 ($H_i, I_i < 0$), NN curves have positive slopes; and the higher an NN curve, the lower the value of planned hiring it represents. There is an NN curve through any IS-LM intersection, as in Figure 3-1.

The family of Δw curves is a family of iso- wage inflation curves, and is closely related to the family of NN curves. Each Δw curve shows combinations of i_1 and Y_1^d which hold constant the percentage rate of change of wage—or the rate of wage inflation—given $(\Delta P/P)^e$, w/P, $\Delta w/w$, and Nu. Since w_1 has already been set, $\Delta w/w$ depends only on w_2. But the quantity of labor a firm plans on using in period 2 (N_2^d), and hence planned hiring, depends on w_2 from the labor supply curve. Combinations of i_1 and Y_1^d that hold constant $\Delta w/w$ and hence w_2, also hold constant N_2^d and hence planned hiring. Thus, the families of NN and Δw curves are identical. Since NN curves have positive slopes, so do Δw curves. Higher NN curves represent lower rates of hiring and thus lower wage increases to attract workers. Higher Δw curves represent lower rates of wage inflation.

When the parameters $(\Delta P/P)^e$, w/P, $(\Delta w/w)^e$, or Nu change, the families of the NN and Δw curves shift, just as with II curves. Since both ΔN^d and I^d functions are positively related to Nu ($H_{Nu}, I_{Nu} > 0$), the family of NN curves shifts up in Figure 3-2 as the II curves do. NN_2 and NN_1 represent the same value of planned hiring, but NN_2 does so for a larger value of Nu. The next section discusses why the increase in Nu causes a larger vertical shift in the NN than in either the II or AQ curves.

Notice that when the parametric change—here an increase in Nu—affects the labor supply relation, the NN and Δw families do not shift together. In this example, the Δw_1 curve shifts down to Δw_2, because Nu has opposite effects on the functions for planned hiring and

10 The argument is made more formal in Appendix 1, section 7.

the rate of wage inflation ($H_{Nu} > 0$, $g_{Nu} < 0$). Thus, Δw_2 represents the same rate of wage inflation as Δw_1 but is associated with more hiring than NN_1 and NN_2 represent—the higher is unemployment, the more hiring it takes to keep the same rate of wage inflation. A change in $(\Delta P/P)^e$ does not affect the labor supply relation as do changes in w/P, $(\Delta w/w)^e$, and Nu; and hence the families of NN and Δw curves shift exactly together, as Figure 3–4 shows.

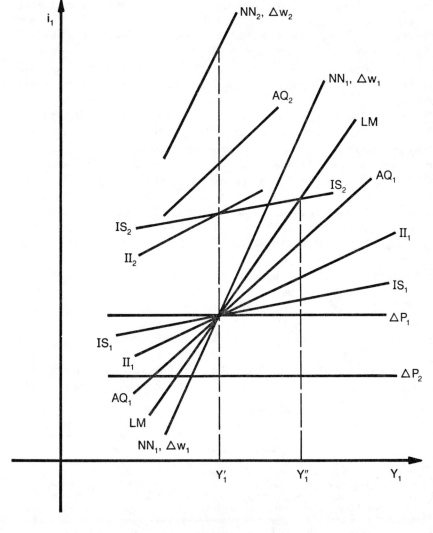

FIGURE 3–4

AN INCREASE IN EXPECTED INFLATION

To see that the NN is steeper than the AQ curve through any point, say, the IS-LM intersection, move upward along the NN curve, keeping labor demand constant. Increases in aggregate demand raise the typical firm's $MRP_{N,2}$ curve, increasing the number of workers wanted. Along the NN curve, increases in the interest rate decrease the firm's demand for capital, lowering the $MRP_{N,2}$ curve enough to reduce the demand for labor back to its old level. The increase in i_1 which keeps labor demand constant lowers investment demand, or the increase is more than the change which would keep I^d constant. Thus, the NN curve is steeper than the II curve. But the change in i_1 which keeps N_2^d constant lowers desired capital, and this implies a decline in desired output. Thus, the change in the rate of interest which keeps N_2^d constant lowers aggregate planned output and is larger than the change which keeps aggregate planned output unchanged. Thus, the NN curve is steeper than the AQ curve.[11]

The final family of curves is the family of iso-price inflation curves, the ΔP curves. Along a given ΔP curve in the i_1, Y_1^d plane, the percentage rate of change of the price level is constant. Since increases in Y_1^d are assumed to shift each firm's expected period 2 demand curve isoelastically relative to the price axis, the increase in Y_1^d causes no change in the profit-maximizing P_2 and hence none in $\Delta P/P$ ($f_y = 0$). Thus, the ΔP curves are all horizontal. But an increase in i_1 raises the cost of capital services and marginal cost in period 2, and thus raises P_2 and $\Delta P/P$ ($f_i > 0$). Higher ΔP curves represent higher rates of price inflation. There is some ΔP curve through any IS-LM intersection.

An increase in $(\Delta P/P)^e$, w/P, $(\Delta w/w)^e$, or Nu shifts the entire family of ΔP curves. For example, an increase in Nu affects the price inflation function negatively ($f_{Nu} < 0$), meaning an increase in i ($f_i > 0$) is required if $\Delta P/P$ is not to fall. Thus, the ΔP map shifts up, as in Figure 3–3 where ΔP_2 represents the same $\Delta P/P$ as ΔP_1 but for a higher value of Nu.

It is easy, now, to see the effects of a change in, say, G in Figure 3–1.[12] The ambiguous effects depend on whether the NN, AQ, and II curves

11 The argument is made more formal in Appendix 1, section 7.

12 Everywhere in this essay, all government spending is for privately produced output of goods and services. None of the changes in G are for hiring government employees. The primary reason for this assumption is to avoid conceptual problems and analytical difficulties.

If government hires workers, national income accounting treats the real value of their wage payments as part of national income. This does not alter the equation of the IS curve. Either the real value of government hiring, G_N, is treated analytically as affecting the labor market but not the product market (and hence $Y = C^d + I^d + G$ is still the equation of the IS curve); or it is treated as producing services of equal value for the output market. Government demand for such services exactly matches supply, so:

$$-(Y + G_N) + C^d + I^d + (G + G_N) = -Y + C^d + I^d + G = 0$$

is still the IS curve equation.   (footnote continued)

are steeper than the *LM* curve. If they are, an increase in *G* raises ΔN^d, *AQ*, and I^d.

Using Table 3–1 and equations 2.5.3,

$$\frac{d(\Delta P/P)}{dG} = f_i(di/dG) > 0 \qquad\qquad \textbf{3.3.3}$$

and

$$dAQ/dG = A\overset{+}{Q}_y(\overset{+}{d}Y/dG) + \overset{-}{A}Q_i(\overset{+}{di}/dG)$$

$$= -AQ_i(dY/dG)(-AQ_y/AQ_i - di/dG \cdot 1/dY/dG) \;\; \textbf{3.3.4}$$

$$= -AQ_i(dY/dG)[di/dY\,(AQ) - di/dY\,(LM)] \gtreqless 0$$

Thus, the change in *AQ* (chosen as an example) depends on whether the *AQ* is steeper than the *LM* curve. Clearly, in the case illustrated in Figure 3–1—an increase in *G*, and/or decrease in *T* or *APS*—I^d, *AQ*, ΔN^d, and $\Delta w/w$ all rise.

However, government wage payments to households are a part of real disposable income which now equals $\{Y - (T - G_N)\}$. But to be consistent with the treatment of government spending on privately produced goods and services, G_N should be considered analytically as a *transfer payment*, so net taxation T_N equals $(T - G_N)$. Rather than some right wing ploy, this is the serious question of the effect of government activity on private consumption.

Assume that the labor market is quite slack, so government hiring does not affect private hiring (see below for the relevance of this assumption). The question concerns the different effects of hiring ten men versus paying the same amount of money as transfers. In either case, household money income rises by the same amount. But in the first case, measured income also rises by that amount; for by the rules of national income accounting, any government funds disbursed to employees automatically generate an equal amount of national product. If the transfer is made to men who spend eight hours per day at recreational hole-digging, the only effect of hiring these men for the same money to dig the same holes is artificially and statistically to increase income and reduce transfer payments. This "increase" in income does not induce any multiplier effects, of course, and the excess demand for output is unchanged.

This experiment may resemble the balanced budget multiplier, but it is very different. If i_1 is held constant and *G* and *T* increase by one unit, then national income rises by one unit and consumption demand does not change, the increase in *Y* balancing the increase in *T* just as above. But the *IS* curve shifts to the right here unlike above. Thus, changes in *G* affect excess demand in the product market as changes in G_N do not. And changes in G_N affect excess demand exactly as do changes in transfer payments.

Now, the assumption that C^d depends only on $(Y - T)$ within the relevant range says increases in *G* do not influence private consumption, either because such increases are merely thrown away, or because they are "neutral". How does more national defense change the intertemporal path of private consumption? In the same way, hiring the hole-diggers is alternatively "wasteful" or "neutral". Clearly, government employees or government purchases of goods and services can be used to influence private consumption in any desired fashion. (1) Government provision of beach lifeguards may be a perfect substitute for private purchases of such services—the kind of case in mind in Martin Bailey, *National Income and the Price Level* (2d ed.; New York: McGraw-Hill Book Co., 1971). (2) Failure to provide law enforcement to ensure safety in the city may

Note that the pump-priming effects of fiscal policy depend on the slopes of the AQ and II curves relative to the LM curve's. The slope of the II curve depends on the ratio of the income elasticity to the interest elasticity of investment. Given the former, the less interest elastic is investment, the steeper are the II and AQ curves and the better the chance fiscal policy has of priming the pump.[13] Clearly, if the LM curve is very inelastic, the effects of fiscal policy are likely to be in the

---

either induce saving to flee to suburban safety or reduce it by encouraging purchase of a safe house; and beginning to provide such safety may reduce saving or consumption. (3) Tyranny involving internal police and electronic spying, G_N and G, may encourage either saving for horrible contingencies or consumption because there is no tomorrow. Because the influence on consumer welfare and behavior of government spending—and especially changes in it—is so unsure, some authors simply assume no such spending. See Boris Pesek and Thomas Saving, *Money, Wealth, and Economic Theory* (New York: Macmillan Co., 1967). Others assume it has no effect on private consumption—the assumption here, and the typical, implicit Keynesian assumption. Still others assume government is so expressive of the public will that government activity is a perfect substitute for private activity (leaving a doubt about capital punishment; but see Bailey, *op. cit.*, Chapter 10).

The assumption that the activities of government employees have no effect on consumption is the perfect parallel to the assumption that G has no effect. Thus, the effect of G_N on excess demand for output is exactly the same as transfer payments.

This leaves the equally important questions of how G_N affects total employment and, through this, the private provision of goods and services. As for total employment, the answer anticipates Chapter 5. If the current labor market is slack enough, government recruiting does not affect availability of workers to industry and, on this score, raises total employment by the amount of government hiring. If the labor market is somewhat tighter, government recruiting interferes, to some extent, with private efforts; so the net increase in current employment is less than the increase in government hiring. If the labor market is very tight, government hiring merely replaces private hiring, and current unemployment is unaffected.

Aside from the effect of the activities of new government employees on society's welfare, such hiring affects private hiring, and through the change in private hiring, affects society's welfare. For example, suppose the labor market is very tight, and the output of any worker is readily demanded. Then, an increase in government hiring decreases private hiring by the same amount and lowers society's real wealth by the amount of output these workers could have produced. Thus, the government work of these employees must be worth at least this foregone output or there is a negative effect on wealth.

13 The AQ is always steeper than the II curve. Branson points out that if I^d is positively related to Y, a family of iso-I^d curves can be constructed in the (i, Y) plane; and fiscal policy stimulates I^d if and only if the initial iso-I^d curve is steeper than the LM curve. See William Branson, *Macroeconomic Theory and Policy* (New York: Harper & Row, Publishers, 1971), p. 224.

The relationship between the interest elasticity of investment and the slope of II is easily seen. The income elasticity of investment is:

$$E_y = \frac{\partial I}{\partial Y} \frac{Y}{I} = I_y \frac{Y}{I}$$

while the interest elasticity of investment, treated as a positive number, is:

$$E_i = -\frac{\partial I}{\partial i} \frac{i}{I} = -I_i \frac{i}{I}$$

(footnote continued)

wrong direction, reducing future labor demand and aggregate supply.

Figure 3–5 shows the effects of an increase in ΔM^s, a decrease in ΔM^d, or an increase in M/P. Since the NN, AQ, and II curves are necessarily steeper than the IS curve, any move along the IS curve to the right will increase I^d, AQ, ΔN^d, and $\Delta w/w$.[14]

Increases in either G or ΔM^s increase current output. Increases in ΔM^s also increase aggregate planned output. Fiscal policy increases aggregate planned output only when the LM curve has a smaller slope than the AQ curve; and even so, there is, in addition, the possibility of stultifying effects on growth due to reduced investment if the LM is steeper than the II curve.

3.4. Further Comparative Statics Results

Consider parametric changes in $(\Delta P/P)^e$, $(\Delta w/w)^e$, Nu, and w/P. The LM curve does not shift with these parameters, so parametric variations merely move the system on the unchanged LM curve.[15] The change in Y_1 due to such a change depends on how the IS curve shifts, and hence on how the investment demand function changes.

The ratio of the two is:

$$\frac{E_y}{E_i} = \frac{I_y(Y/I)}{-I_i(i/I)} = \frac{-I_y}{I_i}\frac{Y}{i}$$

and

$$\frac{di}{dY}(II) = -\frac{I_y}{I_i} = \frac{E_y}{E_i}\frac{i}{Y}$$

Thus,

$$\frac{d[di/dY(II)]}{dE_i} = -\frac{E_y}{(E_i)^2}\frac{i}{Y} < 0$$

14 The slope of the II curve is:

$$\frac{di}{dY}(II) = -\frac{I_y}{I_i}$$

while that of the IS is:

$$\frac{di}{dY}(IS) = -\frac{(-1 + C_y + I_y)}{I_i}$$

$$= \frac{1 - C_y}{I_y} + \frac{di}{dY}(II) < \frac{di}{dY}(II)$$

15 In a more sophisticated economic model, the LM curve should depend on $(\Delta P/P)^e$ —see Chapter 7 for one such possible model.

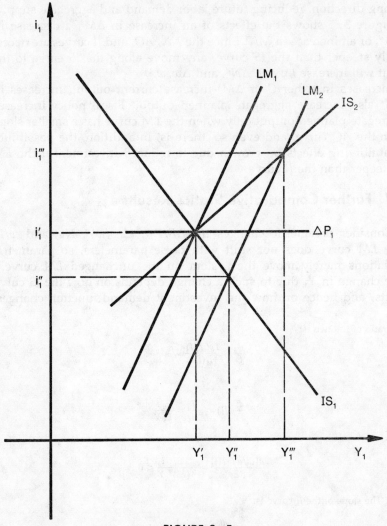

FIGURE 3–5

AN INCREASE IN ΔM^s

These parametric changes shift the IS and II curves vertically exactly the same distance.[16]

16 The vertical shifts in the two curves with respect to, say, $(\Delta w/w)^e$ are:

$$\frac{di}{d(\Delta w/w)^e}(IS) = -\frac{(I_{\Delta w}e_{/w})}{I_i} = \frac{di}{d(\Delta w/w)^e}(II)$$

Both curves shift only because the investment function shifts.

Take the example of an increase in Nu in Figure 3–3. Recall from the preceding section's discussion that introduced the families of II, AQ, NN, Δw, and ΔP curves that an increase in Nu shifts the families of curves. From equations 2.5.3, an increase in Nu shifts up the initial curves II_1, ΔP_1, AQ_1, and NN_1 to II_2, ΔP_2, AQ_2, and NN_2. di/dNu is positive for I^d, $\Delta P/P$, AQ, and ΔN^d. II_2 represents the same value of I^d as II_1, but for a higher value of Nu, and similarly for the other curves. The NN shifts farther than the II curve, for the increase in i_1 that holds I^d and hence K_2^d constant keeps the MRP_N curve of the firm constant; and in the face of a rightward shift of the labor supply curve, N_2^d rises. The AQ shifts up more than the II and less than the NN, for somewhere between these two the decrease in K_2^d and increase in N_2^d just balance for AQ. The AQ and ΔP shift the same vertical distance; for if AQ is unchanged, so is P_2.[17] As noted above, the II and IS curves shift the same vertical distance.[18] The initial Δw_1 curve falls to Δw_2 or Δw_3. Since the Δw may be more or less steep than the LM curve (Δw_2 versus Δw_3), the effect on $\Delta w/w$ is ambiguous (Δw_2 is steep enough to make $\Delta w/w$ rise). Intuitively, the rightward shift in the typical firm's labor supply function stimulates the economy, increasing I^d, AQ, and ΔN^d, and may, but need not, so stimulate the economy that $\Delta w/w$ rises in the face of increased labor supply. The reduction in labor costs tends to reduce $\Delta P/P$: if the IS curve has a negative slope, as drawn, $\Delta P/P$ falls; but if the IS slope is positive, $\Delta P/P$ may rise or fall. Figure 3–3 also serves to illustrate a decrease in $(\Delta w/w)^e$.

Table 3–2 summarizes the comparative statics results for this simple model with excess capacity, including the results of the preceding section. Variations in $(\Delta P/P)^e$, $(\Delta w/w)^e$, and w/P cause reactions similar to Nu's.

Increases in expected inflation, $(\Delta P/P)^e$, shift up the curves II_1, AQ_1, NN_1, and Δw_1 to II_2, AQ_2, NN_2, and Δw_2 in Figure 3–4, as is clear from the partial derivatives in equations 2.5.3. As in the preceding example, the NN shifts more than the AQ curve, which in turn shifts more than the II curve. Under relatively weak conditions, the ΔP_1 curve shifts down to ΔP_2.[19] Then I^d, ΔN^d, $\Delta w/w$, and $\Delta P/P$ all rise. Notice that this is so, even though the IS curve is drawn with a positive slope, but a slope smaller than that of the LM curve.

Finally, Figure 3–6 shows that an increase in w/P shifts the initial IS, II, AQ, NN, and ΔP curves down, causing I^d, AQ, and ΔN^d to fall and $\Delta P/P$ to rise. If the IS curve has a positive slope, the new IS-LM intersection may be below ΔP_2, causing $\Delta P/P$ to fall. But there is no

17 For relative shifts of the curves, see Appendix 1, section 7.
18 See footnote 14, page 43.
19 See Appendix 1, sections 2 and 7.

other ambiguity, since the II is steeper than IS curve. The initial Δw_1 curve falls more than the II curve, to Δw_2, implying $\Delta w/w$ falls. To see this last result, recall that the initial impact on $\Delta w/w$, $g_{w/P}$, is negative from equations 2.5.3; and the second effect of a fall in N_2^d must also work to lower $\Delta w/w$.[20]

TABLE 3-2

SUMMARY OF COMPARATIVE STATICS RESULTS: EXCESS CAPACITY

Parameters				Variables					
	Y	i_1	i_1	$\frac{\Delta P}{P}$	$\frac{\Delta P}{P}$	AQ	ΔN^d	$\frac{\Delta w}{w}$	I^d
		$\frac{di}{dY}(IS) < 0$	$\frac{di}{dY}(IS) > 0$	$\frac{di}{dY}(IS) < 0$	$\frac{di}{dY}(IS) > 0$				
G	+	+	+	+	+	?	?	?	?
T	−	−	−	−	−	?	?	?	?
APS	−	−	−	−	−	?	?	?	?
ΔM^s	+	−	+	−	+	+	+	+	+
M	+	−	+	−	+	+	+	+	+
ΔM^d	−	+	−	+	−	−	−	−	−
Nu	+	+	+	−	?	+	+	?	+
$\frac{\Delta P}{P}e$	+	+	+	+	+	+	+	+	+
$\frac{w}{P}$	−	−	−	+	?	−	−	−	−
$\frac{\Delta w}{w}e$	−	−	−	+	?	−	−	?	−

This completes the comparative statics of the macro model when aggregate demand is less than capacity. The next step is to use this knowledge to discuss policy questions. Before turning to policy, though, Chapter 4 examines the workings of the system when aggregate demand exceeds capacity. Chapter 5 discusses the determination of actual employment, as opposed to the desired change in employment, ΔN^d, already discussed. After this, Chapter 6 turns to policy issues.

20 The initial impact of a rise in Nu or a fall in $(\Delta w/w)^e$ is to reduce $\Delta w/w$, but the second effect, a rise in N_2^d, works in the opposite direction, implying ambiguity.

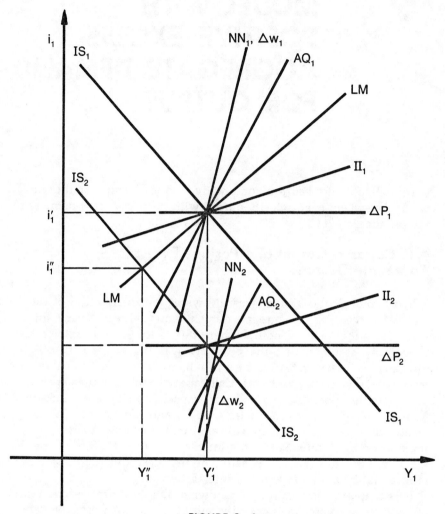

FIGURE 3-6

AN INCREASE IN w/P

4

A SIMPLE MACRO MODEL WITH POSITIVE EXCESS AGGREGATE DEMAND FOR OUTPUT

This chapter derives the comparative statics results for the model when the system is at capacity output with positive excess demand in the product market.

4.1. Capacity Output and Positive Excess Aggregate Demand

In Chapter 3, the system was always at the intersection of the IS and LM curves. Hence aggregate demand equalled real income, for the IS curve is the locus of points where this is so. Such an intersection specifically assumed that the economy was below capacity output. This chapter investigates the case in which the IS and LM curves intersect beyond capacity output. Call capacity real output for period 1 Y_1^c, where the superscript c stands for "capacity." (The determination of Y_1^c is taken up shortly.) In Figure 4–1, IS_1 and LM_1 induce i_1', Y_1'. Increases in real government spending raise the IS curve. A large enough increase would locate IS_2 and the intersection at i_1'', Y_1''. Since Y_1^c is the maximum amount that can possibly be produced this period, the system cannot be at this IS and LM intersection.

This chapter considers the system when the IS-LM intersection is at a real income greater than capacity output. It first discusses the nature of the capacity constraint. The model assumes that the economy produces capacity output when the IS and LM intersection is beyond capacity—the system is on the Y_1^c curve. It then discusses the determination of the rate of interest, develops a graphical analytical apparatus, and gives comparative statics results.

Capacity output for period 1 depends on the aggregate production function:

$$Y_1 = Y(K_1, N_1) \qquad \textbf{4.1.1}$$

This is the function from which, on a macro level, the aggregate supply function is derived. Where the aggregate supply function is obtained

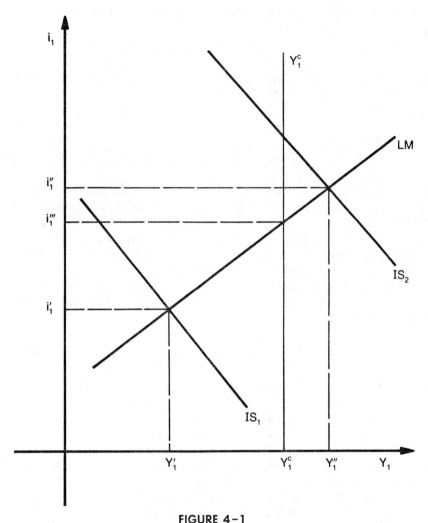

FIGURE 4-1

CAPACITY OUTPUT AND EXCESS DEMAND

from aggregating individual firms' output responses, the aggregate production function is conceptually obtained by aggregating firms' production functions. Equation 4.1.1 tells the maximum output which can be produced this period given the stock of capital and the number of workers. The stock of capital during any period is what it is, in the sense that it equals last period's stock plus last period's investment. Current actions in the form of investment affect next period's capital stock.

The Keynesian unemployment analysis assumes that current employment can be affected this period, or that N_1 is determined endogenously in this period. For example, if real government spending were higher than otherwise, N_1 would be higher.

In the present model, N_1 is not influenced by this period's variables, but depends on the previous period's endogenous variables. The explanation anticipates Chapter 5. The number of workers business wants to hire next period is determined this period in light of this period's conditions, as Chapter 2 showed when developing the function:

$$\Delta N^d = H[Y, i - (\Delta P/P)^e, (\Delta P/P)^e, w/P(1 + \Delta w^e/w), Nu, N] \quad \textbf{4.1.2}$$

The number of people who seek work next period is also determined in this period. The number of workers actually employed next period depends only on how many workers business wants to hire and how many workers want jobs. Thus, the two influences on employment in one period, demand and supply of labor, depend only on variables from the previous period and not on current variables.

The number of people seeking jobs next period depends, by assumption, only on exogenous population and next period's real wage rate $(w/P)_2$. But,

$$\left(\frac{w}{P}\right)_2 = \left(\frac{w}{P}\right)_1 \cdot \frac{1 + (\Delta w/w)}{1 + (\Delta P/P)} \quad \textbf{4.1.3}$$

Now, $(\Delta P/P)$ and $(\Delta w/w)$ are determined this period on the basis of this period's variables. Thus, $(w/P)_2$ depends on the variables of period 1 and not period 2; and hence labor supply next period is not influenced by any of next period's variables. Assuming that only labor demand and supply determine a period's employment, then, since period 2's demand and supply are both independent of that period's variables, period 2's employment is not endogenous to that period. Employment, then, is what it is. The relevant decisions with regard to employment are decisions about changes in employment between periods. N_1 is given; and from equation 4.1.1, so is capacity output, Y_1^c.

By hypothesis, the IS and LM curves intersect beyond capacity output. The system "wants" to be at an output higher than capacity. In such a case, the model assumes the system produces capacity output. Thus, the system is somewhere on the Y_1^c curve, and the rate of interest remains to be determined.

4.2. The Rate of Interest and Three Laws of Excess Demand

To discuss the determination of the rate of interest requires a digression on three identities involving excess demands. The model assumes that the interest rate adjusts to make the excess demand for money equal zero in the sense of the third identity, but not necessarily in the sense of the first two.

The first identity, Walras' Law, states that the sum of the values of excess demand for all goods and services must equal zero—the labor market is explicitly included—or,

$$PExD_Q + ExD_m + P_BExD_B + wExD_N = 0 \qquad \textbf{4.2.1}$$

where ExD_Q, ExD_m, ExD_B, and ExD_N are, respectively, the excess demand for output, money, bonds, and labor; and P the price level, P_B the price of bonds, and w the wage rate. Walras' Law always holds. To derive the excess demands in equation 4.2.1, confront each actor in the system with a vector of prices and allow him to maximize utility (household) or profit (business) subject only to his budget constraint (household) or production function (business). Note in particular that each person chooses his income by choosing the number of hours he desires to work, and each firm chooses its profit by choosing the amount to produce.

A second accounting identity, standard in macroeconomics, says that given the value of real income and thus real output, the sum of the values of the excess demands for output, money, and bonds must equal zero; or:[1]

$$P\overline{ExD}_Q + \overline{ExD}_m + P_B\overline{ExD}_B = 0 \qquad \textbf{4.2.2}$$

The experiment here is to tell each person how much he may work (and hence his labor income), and what his non-labor income will be, and then allow him to maximize utility; and to tell each firm how much it can produce. Notice that this differs from Walras' Law in that households and firms no longer choose their income and output. Income is given.

These excess demands are barred because, for the same vector of prices, they are different from those in Walras' Law. Subtract equation 4.2.1 from equation 4.2.2 to find:

1 This is often called Walras' Law, as, for example, in Warren Smith, *Macroeconomics* (Homewood, Ill.: Richard D. Irwin, 1970), p. 249n. Don Patinkin, *Money, Interest, and Prices* (2d ed.; New York: Harper & Row, Publishers, 1965), asserts Walras' Law holds in his system, when in fact, because income is included, equation 4.2.2 holds. Martin J. Bailey, *National Income and the Price Level* (1st ed.; New York: McGraw-Hill Book Co., 1962), misunderstands Patinkin's error and asserts a third "version" of Walras' Law different from equations 4.2.1 and 4.2.2. Robert Clower, "The Keynesian Counterrevolution: A Theoretical Appraisal," *The Theory of Interest Rates*, edited by F. Hahn and F. P. R. Brechling (New York: Macmillan Co., 1965), gives a brilliant discussion of Walras' Law and other laws of excess demand and their implications for analysis.

$$P(\overline{ExD}_Q - ExD_Q) + (\overline{ExD}_m - ExD_m) +$$

$$P_B(\overline{ExD}_B - ExD_B) = wExD_N \qquad \textbf{4.2.3}$$

which says that the two kinds of excess demands in each market may equal each other only if:

$$ExD_N = 0 \qquad \textbf{4.2.4}$$

If equation 4.2.4 holds, the two laws are in fact the same; for an individual's demand for a given good is invariant, whether he chooses his own income or whether he is told his income, provided the specified income is the one he would choose anyway. A household earns just the labor income it desires when the economy is on the labor supply curve, and a firm maximizes profits when it is on its labor demand curve. Now, if all households are told the number of hours of work possible and firms told the output they may produce, desired income and output equal actual income and output—the household earns as much as it wants and the firm produces exactly what it wants—just in the event that the labor market clears at the given price vector. In this case, not only may the Walrasian and the single-barred excess demands be equal, they must be; for the levels of output and income to which firms and households are constrained are the levels they would choose if unconstrained.

The budget constraints of the household, business, and government sectors imply the second law. The household sector's budget constraint is:

$$Y - S_b^d = C^d + S_h^d + T \qquad \textbf{4.2.5}$$

or real income (equals real output) minus desired real business savings, S_b^d, equals desired real consumption (on the basis of Y) plus desired real household savings, S_h^d (equal to the real value of desired money accumulation, $\Delta M^d/P$, plus the real value of desired bond purchases, $P_B \Delta B^d/P$) plus real net taxation, T(which equals gross taxation less transfer payments). The business sector's constraint is:

$$I^d = \frac{P_B}{P} \Delta B_{bus}^s + S_b^d \qquad \textbf{4.2.6}$$

or business plans to finance desired investment with its flow supply of bonds, ΔB_{bus}^s, and its real desired savings. Government's constraint is:

$$G - T = \frac{P_B}{P} \Delta V^s + \frac{\Delta M^s}{P} \qquad \textbf{4.2.7}$$

which says that government finances its deficit with its flow supplies of money and bonds, ΔV^s. Finally, define the value of the demand for output as:

$$PY^d \equiv PC^d + PI^d + PG \qquad\qquad \textbf{4.2.8}$$

and the value of the single-barred excess demand for output as:

$$P(Y^d - Y) \equiv P\overline{ExD}_Q \qquad\qquad \textbf{4.2.9}$$

Then from equation 4.2.8 and equation 4.2.9,

$$P\overline{ExD}_Q - P(C^d + I^d + G - Y) = 0 \qquad\qquad \textbf{4.2.10}$$

From the household sector's budget constraint, equation 4.2.5,

$$PY = PC^d + PS_h^d + PT + PS_b^d \qquad\qquad \textbf{4.2.11}$$

and so from equation 4.2.10,

$$P\overline{ExD}_Q + P[-(C^d + I^d + G) + C^d + S_h^d + T + S_b^d] = 0$$

$$P\overline{ExD}_Q + P[-(I^d + G) + S_h^d + T + S_b^d] = 0$$

$$P\overline{ExD}_Q + P[S_h^d + (S_b^d - I^d) + (T - G)] = 0$$

$$P\overline{ExD}_Q + PS_h^d - P_B\Delta V^s - \Delta M^s - P_B\Delta B_{bus}^s = 0$$
$$\textbf{4.2.12}$$

$$P\overline{ExD}_Q + \Delta M^d - \Delta M^s + P_B(\Delta B^d - \Delta V^s - \Delta B_{bus}^s) = 0$$

$$P\overline{ExD}_Q + \overline{ExD}_m + P_B\overline{ExD}_B = 0$$

The third law states that given the level of real income and output, and given the method of rationing output, the sum of the values of the excess demands for money and bonds equals zero, or:

$$\overline{\overline{ExD}}_m + P_B\overline{\overline{ExD}}_B = 0 \qquad\qquad \textbf{4.2.13}$$

where the excess demands are double-barred because, for the same price vector, they are different from those in the first and second laws. In addition to units having specified incomes or outputs, as with the second law, the third law also specifies amounts of output they can buy or sell. For example, imagine that when there is excess demand for output, a rule divides the given output among the competing households and firms which demand output. In this case, a household draws up demands on the basis of its budget constraint, its given real income, and the maximum amount of output it is allowed to demand or forced to buy; while a firm draws up its demands on the basis of its production function, the given amount it is allowed to produce, and the maximum amount of output it is allowed to demand or forced to buy.[2]

Given the rationing rule, the household sector, business sector, and government sector budget constraints are, respectively,

$$Y - \tilde{S}_b^d = \tilde{C}^d + \tilde{S}_h^d + T = C^d + \frac{\Delta \tilde{M}^d}{P} + \frac{P_B}{P} \Delta \tilde{B}^d + T \qquad 4.2.14$$

$$\tilde{I}^d = \tilde{S}_b^d + \frac{P_B}{P} \Delta \tilde{B}_{bus}^s \qquad 4.2.15$$

and

$$\tilde{G}^d - T = \frac{P_B}{P} \Delta \tilde{V}^s + \frac{\Delta \tilde{M}^s}{P} \qquad 4.2.16$$

where the "~" indicates the variables are desired given Y and the rationing scheme.

Now, the rationing scheme ensures:

$$Y = \tilde{C}^d + \tilde{I}^d + \tilde{G}^d \qquad 4.2.17$$

that output is exactly divided among demanders. Thus, using equation 4.2.14 and equation 4.2.17,

$$P(Y - Y) = P[\tilde{C}^d + \tilde{S}_h^d + \tilde{S}_b^d + T - (\tilde{C}^d + \tilde{I}^d + \tilde{G}^d)] = 0$$

$$= P[T - \tilde{G}^d + (\tilde{S}_b^d - \tilde{I}^d) + \tilde{S}_h^d] = 0$$

$$= -\Delta \tilde{M}^s - P_B \Delta \tilde{V}^s - P_B \Delta \tilde{B}_{bus}^s + \Delta \tilde{M}^d + P_B \Delta \tilde{B}^d = 0 \qquad 4.2.18$$

$$= \overline{\overline{ExD_m}} + P_B \overline{ExD_B} = 0$$

This law has a simple interpretation. Each unit knows its income and the amount it can or must spend on output. Now, for society as a whole

---

2 Formally, the same kind of thing can be done for any good. Tell each unit its income or output and that a particular good it wants—output, money, or bonds—is being rationed. Taking money as an example, tell each unit its income or output and the number of dollars it is allowed to accumulate. Then, given real income and the rationing rule for money accumulation, the sum of the value of the excess demands for output and bonds equals zero. The text argues, however, that economic units always act to set the excess demands for money and bonds equal to zero.

when rationing is in effect, total planned—given the rationing—spending on output equals total income; and the only way to demand extra money is by supplying bonds of equal value. Society spends all its income on output, so any demand for money is financed by bonds; and the double-barred excess demand for money equals the value of the double-barred excess supply of bonds.

Chapter 2 assumed no inventories, any unsold output wasting away completely by the end of the period. This implies that when aggregate demand is below capacity, actual real output and income equal aggregate demand. Hence, the inventory assumption implies that, though the third law is valid whatever the sign of excess demand for output, the allocation rule for rationing when demand is different from output is applicable in this model only when there is positive excess demand for output.[3] The inventory assumption implies that when there is not positive excess demand for output, the second and third laws are identical. The first and second laws are identical just when:

$$ExD_N = 0 \qquad\qquad \textbf{4.2.19}$$

Thus, all three laws are identical if equation 4.2.19 holds and aggregate demand does not exceed capacity.

4.3. The Rate of Interest Sets the Double-Barred Excess Demand for Money Equal to Zero

Assume that when excess aggregate demand for output is positive, the rate of interest adjusts to set:

$$\overline{\overline{ExD_m}} = 0 \ (= \overline{\overline{P_B ExD_B}}) \qquad\qquad \textbf{4.3.1}$$

In other words, if there is positive excess demand for output, then the rate of interest adjusts to ensure that there is zero double-barred excess demand for money. That is, on the basis of the given level of real income (equal to real output) and the given way real output is rationed, each unit can buy or sell as many bonds as it desires, and can accumulate or expend as many dollars as it likes.

This assumption seems to be a good representation of the real world. Intuitively, one can always go back and forth between money and

---

3 An alternate inventory assumption is that desired inventories are always zero, but unsold output is transferred intact to the next period. A natural application of the third law is to assume that any unsold output is undesired inventory accumulation. If business holds no money balances, then rationing does not affect any demander or supplier of money; and $\overline{ExD_m} = \overline{ExD_m}$. The analysis proceeds exactly as before in Chapter 3, though inventory is now an argument in the business behavior functions, as shown in footnote 7, Chapter 3, page 31.

securities, regardless of the state of excess demands in other markets. The only way to achieve this is to assume equation 4.3.1.

Such an assumption agrees well with the facts of the real world. There is the trivial point that anyone may accumulate any quantity of dollars short of his income. But more important is the fact that anyone may dispose of his financial assets very quickly, and thus accumulate any quantity of dollars short of his wealth.[4]

Finally, there is a case for viewing the financial markets as adjusting so that anyone who wants to borrow may do so at some price. The stumbling block before any such interpretation is credit rationing. Some people are told flatly that they may not have a loan. But there may be other sources from which they could borrow, where the interest rates—or credit terms—are so bad they do not wish to borrow. There is the possibility—really rather narrow, when all sources such as pawnshops are considered—of someone not being able to borrow at all. In this case, the interest rate is infinite to him. This is not just a verbal trick. Lenders could ensure that he not borrow merely by demanding an infinite rate of interest. If for some reason they prefer to achieve the effects on borrowing of an infinite rate of interest without employing that measure, they nevertheless achieve the effects. On an aggregated level, with i to represent all credit conditions, it seems reasonable to say that i adjusts so that all who wish to borrow may do so.

4.4. Business Bears All Excess Demand for Output

There must be some rationing rule. When the real world is in a state characterized by positive aggregate excess demand, output gets rationed in a number of ways; for example, by queueing, favoritism, nepotism, influence peddling, and the exercise of various governmental powers to preempt output. For every possible rationing scheme, there is a double-barred *LM* curve showing the locus of combinations of the interest rate and aggregate demand at which the double-barred excess demand for money equals zero. Presumably, each such *LM* curve has the same properties as a normal, conventional *LM* curve drawn up for single-barred excess demands; that is, it has a positive slope, and increases in the flow supply of money lower the curve.

Variations in the rationing rule usually lead to different double-barred excess demands for money and bonds, and to a different rate of interest to set these equal to zero. Units benefiting from variations in rationing rules change their demands for bonds and money, as do units who suffer; and there is no reason to suppose these changes exactly offset each other.

4 On the aggregated level of this model, the representative bond is equivalent to a government bond and is hence very liquid. But almost any financial asset can be disposed of very quickly at some price, and the length of the period in any sensible macro model is great enough for most financial assets to be liquid.

Out of the infinity of double-barred *LM* curves associated with the infinity of rationing processes, the present model assumes that the government and household sectors can always buy as much output as they desire.[5] This throws all the burden of unfulfilled demands on the business sector. The difference between aggregate demand and actual output is equal to the difference between desired investment and actual investment. Here as elsewhere, inventories are ignored because their inclusion must either be so trivial as to be uninteresting; or if interesting, must render the comparative statics ambiguous.

This rationing assumption allows use of the normal, conventional *LM* curve. To see this, note that business holds no cash balances, and only the household and government sectors demand and supply money. Now, rationing affects the demand and supply of money—given real income—just as the household or government sector is affected by rationing. But the model assumes they are not, and thus the demand for money and the supply of money are unaffected. The locus of points where money demand equals supply is the conventional, single-barred *LM* curve; and the double-barred excess demand for money equals zero when the system is on the conventional, single-barred *LM* curve. Since society is on the Y_1^c curve, equation 4.3.1 and the assumption that business bears all rationing imply that the system is at the intersection of the Y_1^c and *LM* curves, with output at capacity and the rate of interest adjusted to set the double-barred excess demand for money equal to zero.[6]

If rationing sometimes did deprive households of the output they demand, then presumably they would accumulate money with some of the revenues freed by the inability to consume. This would shift the *LM* curve up, showing that it would take a higher rate of interest to make consumers accumulate the bonds business sells to finance the extra investment the new scheme allows.

4.5. The *IS'* Curve

In Chapter 3, the system was always at a point at which aggregate demand equalled real income. Here, the intersection of the *LM* and Y_1^c curves is below the *IS* curve (see Figure 4-2), and there must be positive, single-barred excess demand for output. It is vital for comparative statics to know the magnitude of aggregate demand.

5 Appendix 2 discusses the rationing assumption in detail, offering alternatives and showing the sensitivity of results to such changes. It concludes that the text's assumption is relatively unobjectionable.

6 Notice that under this rationing scheme,

$$\overline{\overline{ExD_m}} = \overline{ExD_m}$$

which allows the use of the usual, conventional *LM* curve.

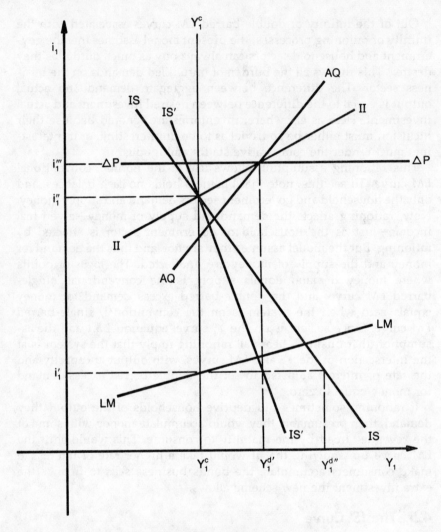

FIGURE 4-2

THE *IS'* CURVE AND EXCESS DEMAND

Determination of aggregate demand requires an important behavioral distinction between the household and business sectors. The household sector bases its behavior on real income, not on aggregate demand. Simply put, you do not spend demand, you spend income. The business sector, though, bases its behavior on aggregate demand, not real income. Recall that the demand a firm faces today depends positively on current aggregate demand, and the demand the firm expects to face next period depends positively on the demand it faces this period. Thus, the higher is current aggregate demand, the higher each firm expects its demand to be next period.[7] In planning for next period, it does not matter to the firm whether it is currently supplying exactly what is demanded. Naturally, it would like to be on this period's demand curve; but if it is not, there is nothing to be done, and the firm must get on with its plans. It is only the state of demand that matters for planning purposes. Simply put, in running a regression on past demand to estimate future demand, it does not matter whether these historical demands were fulfilled or not.

In this chapter, real income is always equal to capacity output. Thus, the expression for aggregate demand is:

$$Y^d = C^d(Y^c_1 - T) + I^d(Y^d, i, \ldots) + G^d \qquad \textbf{4.5.1}$$

This emphasizes the behavioral distinction just discussed: desired consumption depends on actual real income; desired investment depends on aggregate demand.

The IS' curve, a new relation similar to the IS curve, interacts with the interest rate to determine aggregate demand. The IS curve is the locus of points at which the equation,

$$Y^d = C^d(Y^d - T) + I^d(Y^d, i, \ldots) + G^d \qquad \textbf{4.5.2}$$

holds. The slope of the IS curve in the (i, Y) plane, is:

$$\frac{di}{dY^d}(IS) = -\frac{-1 + C_y + I_y}{I_i} \qquad \textbf{4.5.3}$$

A new relation, the IS' curve, may be defined as the locus of (i, Y^d) points at which equation 4.5.1 holds. This specifically holds C^d constant at the value induced by $(Y^c_1 - T)$. The slope of the IS' curve is:

$$\frac{di}{dY^d}(IS') = -\frac{-1 + I_y}{I_i} \qquad \textbf{4.5.4}$$

Assume this slope is negative, implying I_y is less than unity.

The IS' curve depends on $(\Delta P/P)^e$, $(\Delta w/w)^e$, w/p, Nu (since desired investment depends on these) and on Y^c_1, G, T, and APS. Given the IS' curve, the interest rate determines the level of aggregate demand. Thus, in Figure 4–2, aggregate demand is $Y^{d'}_1$, since the IS' curve gives this value of aggregate demand for the interest rate i'_1 that sets the double- and single-barred excess demand for money equal to zero

7 See Chapter 2, section 4.

when the system is at capacity output. To justify the assumption that $di/dY^d(IS')$ is negative—I_y is less than unity—note that if it is not, aggregate demand is infinite.

The IS' curve is steeper than the IS curve when the latter has a negative slope, or:

$$\frac{di}{dY}(IS) - \frac{di}{dY}(IS') > 0 \qquad \textbf{4.5.5}$$

From equation 4.5.3 and equation 4.5.4,

$$\frac{di}{dY}(IS) - \frac{di}{dY}(IS') = -\frac{-1 + C_y + I_y}{I_i} + \frac{-1 + I_y}{I_i} = -\frac{C_y}{I_i} > 0 \qquad \textbf{4.5.6}$$

It is interesting to interpret the IS' curve in terms of multiplier effects. A decrease in the interest rate induces an increase in investment demand. Along the IS curve, this increase in investment increases equally both aggregate demand and real income. Increased aggregate demand stimulates investment demand, and increased real income stimulates consumption demand. Both of these increases further stimulate aggregate demand and real income. The process goes on in the usual multiplier way.

Along the IS' curve, the decrease in the interest rate stimulates investment demand, and this increase in investment demand implies an increase in aggregate demand. Real income, however, is constant at Y_1^c, by hypothesis. Thus, this increased aggregate demand stimulates investment demand; but since real income is unchanged, consumption demand is unchanged. The increase in investment demand raises aggregate demand; and the aggregate demand multiplier works itself out, but without any household multiplier effects. In Figure 4-2, this is why going from i_1'' (where Y^d equals Y_1^c) to i_1' increases aggregate demand to $Y_1^{d'}$ and not $Y_1^{d''}$. For aggregate demand to rise to $Y_1^{d''}$, real income has to increase to $Y_1^{d''}$, not remain constant at capacity.[8]

4.6. The Graphical Analytical Apparatus

With the IS' curve, it is possible to develop a graphical apparatus to derive comparative statics results in this chapter and policy recommendations in Chapter 6. Recall that business bears all the burden of unfulfilled demand and thus,

8 It may be argued that before the multiplier can work itself out very far, business will make new decisions and the system thus will move on to the next period. Note that this questions the adequacy of the IS-LM framework and not this essay's theory of business behavior, particularly as embodied in the business behavior functions in equations 2.5.3.

$$Y_1^d - Y_1^c = C^d + G^d + I^d - (C^a + G^a + I^a) = I^d - I^a \qquad \textbf{4.6.1}$$

(a means actual). Now, when actual is less than desired investment, it is actual investment that business must consider. Business' decisions with regard to prices and wages and desired output and hiring depend on actual investment, and not on whether desired equals actual investment. The marginal revenue product of labor depends on the stock of capital, not on whether the stock was chosen freely or under a rationing scheme. Similarly, planned output—and thus price—depends on actual capital and employment, not on whether the stock of capital was freely chosen.

Given Y_1^c, real output and real income are the same at $(i_1', Y_1^{d'})$ and (i_1'', Y_1^c) in Figure 4–2. At both points, consumption and government demand are the same. Thus, actual investment is the same at (i_1'', Y_1^c) and $(i_1', Y_1^{d'})$.[9] At (i_1'', Y_1^c), actual equals desired investment, for the system is on the IS curve on which excess demand for output is zero. The II curve running through (i_1'', Y_1^c) shows values of the interest rate and aggregate demand for which desired investment equals what actual investment is at both (i_1'', Y_1^c) and $(i_1', Y_1^{d'})$. Now, at $(i_1''', Y_1^{d'})$, desired investment just equals what actual investment is at $(i_1', Y_1^{d'})$. As noted above, business' decisions on pricing and output and wages and employment made at $(i_1', Y_1^{d'})$ depend on I^a and not on whether I^a equals I^d. Given I^a, these decisions are the same at $(i_1', Y_1^{d'})$, with desired greater than actual investment, as they would be at $(i_1''', Y_1^{d'})$ with I^d equal to I^a.[10] To see this, recall that actual investment is the same at both points. The only difference as far as the business sector is concerned is that i_1' is less than i_1'''. At i_1', business demands more investment goods than at i_1'''; and if the sector could get them, it would want to hire more workers at a higher wage and produce more output to sell at a lower price. But business cannot get more investment at $(i_1', Y_1^{d'})$ than at $(i_1''', Y_1^{d'})$. I^a is exactly the same at both points. Under rationing, the difference between i_1' and i_1''' is irrelevant for wage, employment, pricing, and output decisions.

Thus, the index on the AQ curve through $(i_1''', Y_1^{d'})$ tells the value of desired future aggregate supply generated by the point $(i_1', Y_1^{d'})$ when I^a is limited to the amount just desired at $(i_1''', Y_1^{d'})$. The indices of the ΔP, NN, and Δw curves through $(i_1''', Y_1^{d'})$ are similarly interpreted.

While reasoning with these aggregate curves is plausible and gives perfectly correct results, real understanding requires consideration of the effect on the individual firm of rationing of investment goods. On

---

9 Desired investment is higher at the second point, since the rate of interest is lower and the level of aggregate demand higher than at the first point.

10 Appendix 1, section 3, proves these assertions rigorously.

the micro level, rationing prevents the firm from investing to reach a K_2 above, say, K_2^* in Figure 4-3. For low enough Q_2's, rationing is ineffective, because the firm wishes to use a stock of capital smaller than K_2^*. At Q_2's above Q_2^*—the Q_2 associated with K_2^*—the firm uses labor to make up for the capital it cannot get and hence uses inoptimal combinations—given labor supply, $P_{K,1}$, $\Delta P_{K,1}^e/P_{K,1}$ and i_1—of labor and capital. Thus, the marginal cost curve has a positive slope beyond Q_2^*. One effect of rationing is that isoelastic (relative to the price axis) increases in expected demand induced by increases in Y_1^d now raise P_2 (see Figure 4-3), while with no rationing P_2 is unchanged. (The MRP curve for each factor shifts up as before.) Thus, f_y is now positive, and not zero as before in equations 2.5.3.

In Figure 4-4, a rise in i_1 such that K_2^d still exceeds K_2^* affects only I_1^d—down from $I_1^{d'}$ to $I_1^{d''}$. But since K_2^* is unchanged, $MRP_{N,2}$ is unchanged, and so are N_2^d and w_2. MC, when Q_2 is below Q_2^*, rises, and Q_2^* shifts to the right, showing that, at a higher i_1, the firm wishes to use less capital than before. Hence the K_2^* constraint becomes effective only at a higher Q_2; but as long as K_2^d exceeds K_2^*, Q_2^s exceeds Q_2^*, so P_2 and Q_2^s are unchanged. Thus, the business sector's functions, save for I^d, now have zero partials for $i - (\Delta P/P)^e$, or:

$$f_i = g_i = AQ_i = H_i = 0 \qquad \text{4.6.2}$$

K_2^* is a new parameter. Before, every partial with respect to K_2 was zero, for business could freely choose K_2. Now, an increase in K_2^* caused by a rise in I^a raises $MRP_{N,2}$ (by assumption).[11] Hence it raises N_2^d and w_2 and lowers MC, beyond Q_2^*, which shifts rightward, thus raising Q_2^s and lowering P_2 (see Figure 4-5). Therefore,

$$f_{I^a} < 0; g_{I^a}, H_{I^a}, AQ_{I^a} > 0 \qquad \text{4.6.3}$$

$$I_{I^a}^d = 0$$

The signs of all other partials of the business behavioral functions are unchanged, as Figures 4-3 through 4-5 show.[12]

4.7. The Comparative Statics Results

The comparative statics with positive excess aggregate demand are closely related to those of Chapter 3. Where previously a change led to an increase in real income and aggregate demand, the two being

---

11 Variations in K_1 are not considered.
12 See Appendix 1, section 3, for a mathematical demonstration.

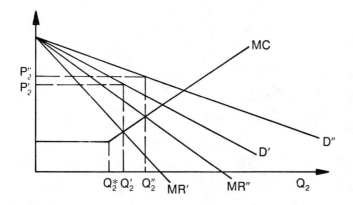

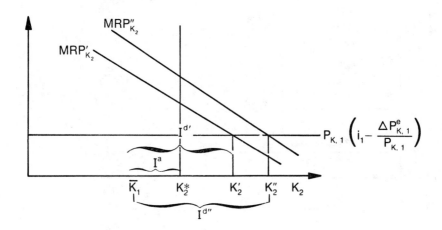

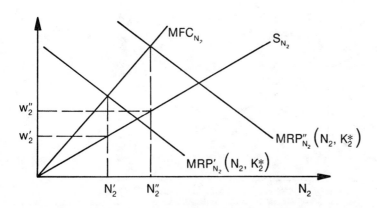

FIGURE 4-3

EXPECTED DEMAND AND RATIONING

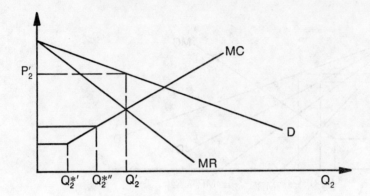

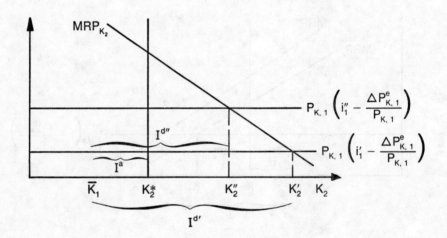

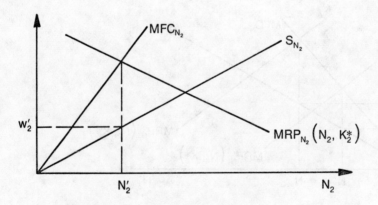

FIGURE 4-4

THE INTEREST RATE AND RATIONING

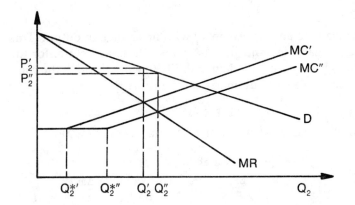

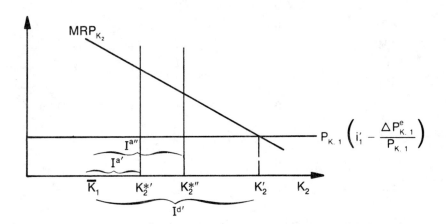

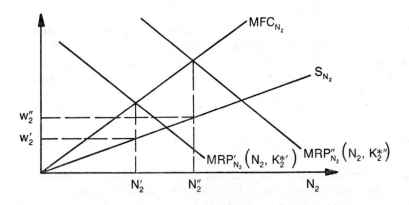

FIGURE 4-5

ACTUAL INVESTMENT AND RATIONING

equal, it now leads to an increase in Y_1^d with no change in output. This increase in aggregate demand has the same effects as before, for the most part, though they are muted by inability to work through the complete multiplier. Table 4-1 summarizes the results.[13]

TABLE 4-1

SUMMARY OF COMPARATIVE STATICS RESULTS: EXCESS DEMAND

Parameters				Variables			
	Y^d	i_1	$\dfrac{\Delta P}{P}$	AQ	ΔN^d	$\dfrac{\Delta w}{w}$	I^d
G	+	0	+	?	?	?	+
T	−	0	−	?	?	?	−
APS	−	0	−	?	?	?	−
ΔM^s	+	−	+	+	+	+	+
M	+	−	+	+	+	+	+
ΔM^d	−	+	−	−	−	−	−
Nu	+	0	?	+	+	?	+
$\dfrac{\Delta P}{P}e$	+	0	+	+	+	+	+
w/P	−	0	?	−	−	−	−
$\dfrac{\Delta w}{w}e$	−	0	?	−	−	?	−

The system is always at the intersection of the Y_1^c and LM curves. Changes in Y_1^c are not considered, so the rate of interest changes only through a change in the LM curve.

Any burden of excess demand is borne entirely by the business sector. From equation 4.6.1, the difference between aggregate demand and output, $(Y_1^d - Y_1^c)$, is equal to the excess of desired over actual investment, $(I^d - I^a)$. As the previous section argued, it is I^a, not the interest rate, that matters for decisions about $\Delta P/P$, $\Delta w/w$, ΔN^d, and AQ. Now,

$$I^a = Y_1^c - C^d - G^d \qquad 4.7.1$$

so any parametric change not affecting Y_1^c, C^d, or G^d has no effect on I^a.

Consider first the effects of variations in parameters that do not enter the business sector's functions. In Figure 4-6, an increase in ΔM^s

---

13 Note there is only one interest-rate column, since it does not matter what the IS curve's slope is—the IS' curve has a negative slope.

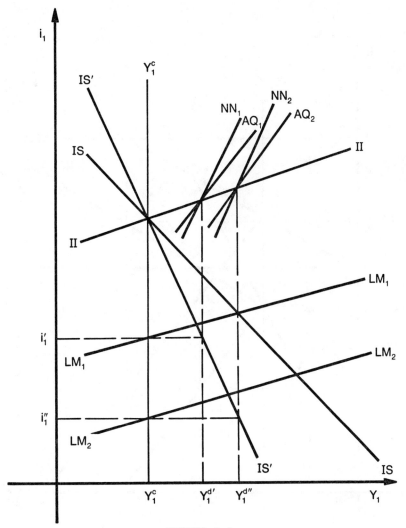

FIGURE 4-6

ΔM^s AND EXCESS DEMAND

or M^s, or a decrease in ΔM^d, shifts the LM curve down, lowering i_1 to i_1''. A decrease in i_1 along the given IS' curve raises Y_1^d to $Y_1^{d''}$, but, from equation 4.7.1, has no effect on I^a, since C^d and G^d are unchanged. Such a parametric change then raises ΔN^d, $\Delta w/w$, AQ, and $\Delta P/P$ through its effect on Y_1^d (the indices on the curves through II at $Y_1^{d''}$ are higher), and raises I^d through its effect on Y_1^d and i_1.

In Figure 4-7, an increase in G or decrease in APS or T raises the IS' curve and, from equation 4.7.1, reduces I^a. With i_1 unchanged, Y_1^d

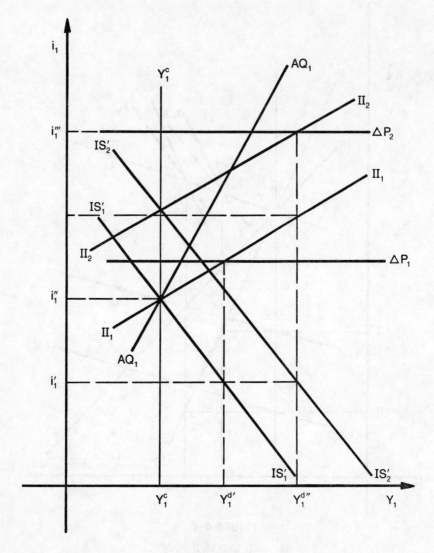

FIGURE 4–7

G AND EXCESS DEMAND

increases to $Y_1^{d''}$, as can be found from equation 4.5.1. Since from the preceding section,

$$f_y > 0, f_{I^a} < 0, g_y > 0, g_{I^a} > 0$$

$$H_y > 0, H_{I^a} > 0, AQ_y > 0, AQ_{I^a} > 0$$

4.7.2

the effects on $\Delta w/w$, ΔN^d, and AQ are ambiguous; but the effects on inflation are not.

I^a falls as the government and household sectors acquire a larger share of the fixed Y_1^c. Comparing the indices on II_1 and II_2—the family if II curves has not shifted—gives the change. At the new lower I^a in Figure 4–7, business makes the same decisions it would if it could invest as much as it liked at i_1''' and $Y_1^{d''}$. The index on the AQ curve through i_1''', $Y_1^{d''}$ shows the new level of AQ, which may be higher or lower than before the parametric change depending on the steepness of the curve AQ_1. (A similar analysis holds for ΔN^d and $\Delta w/w$.) The interpretation of the ambiguous change in AQ is that the increase in Y_1^d tends to increase AQ, but the fall in I^a tends to decrease it. A fall in I^a is like an increase in i_1 when business can invest as much as it likes. If output decisions are very sensitive to Y_1^d and insensitive to i_1, and thus to I^a, AQ_1 is very steep (as drawn), the Y_1^d effect dominates, and AQ rises (the point i_1''', $Y_1^{d''}$ is below AQ_1). Inflation rises, for the effects of I^a and Y_1^d are in the same direction.

Now consider changes in parameters entering the business sector's functions. An increase in $(\Delta P/P)^e$ or Nu, or a decrease in $(\Delta w/w)^e$ or w/P, raises the IS' curve by increasing I^d; and at the unchanged i_1 causes an increase in Y_1^d. Since neither C^d or G^d vary, I^d is unchanged. Thus, changes in these parameters give results of the form:

$$\frac{d\Delta P/P}{d\alpha} = f_y \frac{dY^d}{d\alpha} + f_\alpha \qquad \textbf{4.7.3}$$

Consequently, there is ambiguity only when the effect of Y_1^d (f_y $(dY^d/d\alpha)$ in this example) is opposite to the initial impact on the function concerned (f_α). From Table 4–1, and equations 2.5.3, this is so in the cases:

$$g_{Nu}, f_{Nu} < 0$$

$$f_{w/P} > 0 \qquad \textbf{4.7.4}$$

$$f_{\Delta w^e/w} > 0; \; g_{\Delta w^e/w} > 0$$

Chapter 6 uses these results to discuss the policy implications of the model. But first Chapter 5 discusses the determination of actual employment—as opposed to desired hiring, which Chapters 2–4 covered—and the rate of unemployment.

5

LABOR SUPPLY, THE LEVEL OF EMPLOYMENT, AND THE RATE OF UNEMPLOYMENT

Chapters 2 and 4 discussed the determination of the rate at which business desires to adjust its employment. Chapters 3 and 4 showed how this rate varies in response to parametric changes. This chapter discusses the determination of the supply of labor, and shows how demand and supply conditions interact to determine the actual rate of employment change and the rate of unemployment.

5.1. The Actual Rate of Change of Employment

Given ΔN^d, what determines the actual value of ΔN?

The firm, feeling perfectly certain about its expectations, announces a wage at which it expects to hire exactly the number of workers it wants. This may not always come about. There is a certain finite period, determined by the firm, during which the firm does not change prices or wages.[1] During this period, if the firm was mistaken about labor supply conditions, it does not find out soon enough to change either its price or wage policy. If the firm can hire only fewer workers than anticipated, it hires these at the wage it has announced. If more workers are available than the firm had supposed, it still takes only the number it had planned; and because it does not yet know it can, the firm does not attempt to get this number at a lower wage. Figure 5–1 illustrates this. The firm expects the supply curve S. If supply is really S', the firm hires OA workers and is disappointed by the amount $AN^{d'}$. If the supply curve is S'', the firm hires $ON^{d'}$ workers, though it could hire OB workers.

This has a serious macroeconomic implication. Firms desire a particular change in employment, $\underline{\Delta N^d}$. By deciding on prices and wages, they fix the real wage rate at $\overline{(w/P)}$. If the number of workers seeking

---

1 This period is, in fact, the period of the model. Section 3 of this chapter discusses the determination of this period.

employment, ΔN^s, depends only on w/P, then $\overline{(w/P)}$ fixes ΔN^s, and ΔN depends on the interaction of the two given quantities ΔN^d and ΔN^s.

Consider the interaction of demand and supply. Let the household and business sectors decide on values of ΔN^s and ΔN^d. Then, suppose:

$$\Delta N = \theta(\Delta N^d, \Delta N^s)$$

$$1 \geq \theta_1 > 0 \text{ if } \Delta N < \Delta N^s$$

$$\theta_1 = 0 \text{ if } \Delta N = \Delta N^s$$

$$1 \geq \theta_2 > 0 \text{ if } \Delta N < \Delta N^d \qquad\qquad \textbf{5.1.1}$$

$$\theta_2 = 0 \text{ if } \Delta N = \Delta N^d$$

$$\text{for some } \Delta N^s > \Delta N, \ \theta_1 = 1$$

$$\text{for some } \Delta N^d > \Delta N, \ \theta_2 = 1$$

The assumptions are reasonable when workers do not know which firms have openings at the current wage structure. If there is one opening and one job seeker, he may not stumble on the firm with the opening. If there are two job seekers, there is a greater chance one of them will find the firm with the opening. As the number of job seekers increases, so does the likelihood of some one of them finding the job. When there are so many job seekers that the probability of one of them finding the opening is virtually unity, further increases in the number of workers will do no good.

With one job seeker, the probability of his finding an opening increases as the number of openings increases. When the probability of his finding a job reaches unity, increases in openings are ineffectual.

Furthermore, workers are looking not only for an opening, but for a "good" opening. If it is known that the going wage—the "average wage" or the "market wage"—is $\overline{(w/P)}$, some workers will turn down one or several openings in search of an above-average offer. Suppose that workers differ in their propensity to do this. Then, the more job seekers there are, the more who will have a chance to refuse a given job this period, and the more likely it is that the firm will be found by a job seeker with such a low propensity to seek that he will take the job. The more openings there are, the more likely is a worker with a low propensity to search to find and accept an opening.

Figure 5-2 illustrates the model. ΔN equals $\Delta N^{d\prime}$—which also equals $\Delta N^{s\prime}$—for any combination of ΔN^d and ΔN^s on the curve $FBCAE$, and similarly for $\Delta N^{d\prime\prime}$ and $F'B'C'A'E'$ (ignore curve $B''C''A''$ until section 3).

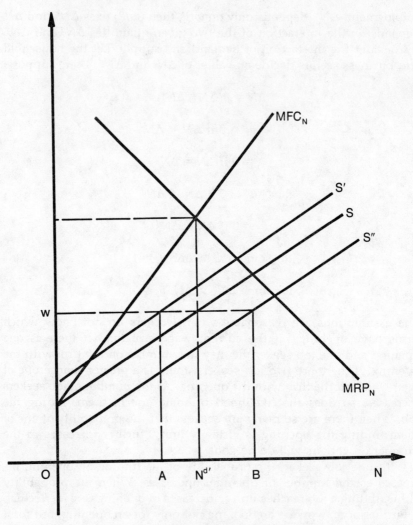

FIGURE 5–1

THE MICROECONOMICS OF EMPLOYMENT

At C, an increase in either ΔN^d or ΔN^s causes an increase in ΔN. At A, an increase in ΔN^s has no effect on ΔN. At B, an increase in ΔN^d has no effect on ΔN. At F, an increase in ΔN^s from $\Delta N^{s'}$ to $\Delta N^{s''}$ increases ΔN equally. At E, an increase in ΔN^d from $\Delta N^{d'}$ to $\Delta N^{d''}$ increases ΔN equally. (BCA may be convex near the 45° line, but differentiability of the iso-ΔN curves implies BCA becomes concave as it smoothly becomes congruent with $F\Delta N^{s'}$ or $\Delta N^{d'}E$.)

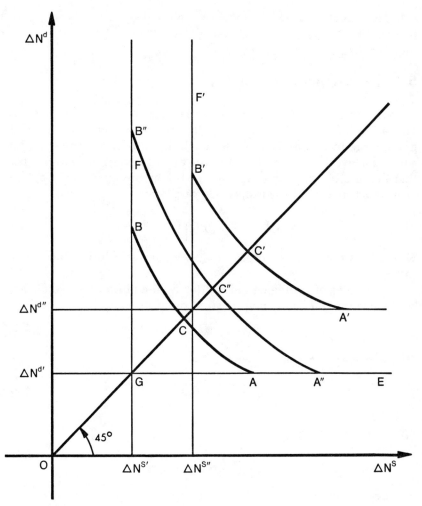

FIGURE 5-2

THE INTERACTION OF AGGREGATE DEMAND AND SUPPLY OF LABOR

Let the business sector plan on $\Delta N^{d'}$ at $\overline{(w/P)}$. If ΔN is to equal $\Delta N^{d'}$, there must be frictional unemployment equal to GA. If the system is at E, then AE is unnecessary unemployment. For these workers, there is no job, corresponding on the micro level to $N^{d'}B$ in Figure 5–1.[2] Further, offering to take a cut in wages will do them no good, for business has decided on ΔN equal to $\Delta N^{d'}$.

_____

2 The sum of all $N^{d'}B$ in the economy equals AE if the average job seeker applies at one firm per period. It equals $2AE$ if each applies at two firms per period, etc.

If ΔN^d equals $\Delta N^{d'}$ at $\overline{(w/P)}$, then the business sector is acting as if it thought ΔN^s were equal to exactly $\Delta N^{d'}A$, not $\Delta N^{d'}E$. Business has incorrect beliefs about labor supply.

5.2. The Supply of Labor

Now consider ΔN^s. Suppose that the number of people who will take a job if offered depends on $\overline{(w/P)}$ and what workers think is the going wage in the market. Ignore this last point for a moment and assume that workers think $\overline{(w/P)}$ is the average wage. Suppose further that the number of people willing to work at any given real wage rate grows each period at the exogenous percentage rate g. Thus:

$$L_t = (1 + g)^t L_o\left[\left(\frac{w}{P}\right)_t\right] \qquad \text{5.2.1}$$

where L_t is the number of people who want a job during the period t to $t + 1$.

The number of people employed during the period $t - 1$ to t is N_{t-1}, so the change in employment desired by workers is:

$$\Delta N^s_{t-1} = L_t - N_{t-1} \qquad \text{5.2.2}$$

Define percentage unemployment, Nu, as:

$$Nu_t \equiv \frac{L_t - N_t}{N_t} = \frac{L_t}{N_t} - 1 \qquad \text{5.2.3}$$

From equation 5.2.3,

$$L_t = N_t(Nu_t + 1) \qquad \text{5.2.4}$$

From equation 5.2.1,

$$L_{t+1} = (1 + g) L_t\left[\left(\frac{w}{P}\right)_{t+1}\right] \qquad \text{5.2.5}$$

and expanding the expression about $(w/P)_t$,

$$L_{t+1} = (1 + g)\left\{L_t\left[\left(\frac{w}{P}\right)_t\right] + L'_t\left[\left(\frac{w}{P}\right)_{t+1} - \left(\frac{w}{P}\right)_t\right]\right\} \qquad \text{5.2.6}$$

Then, from equations 5.2.2, 5.2.4, and 5.2.6,

$$\Delta N^s_1 = L_2 - N_1 = (1 + g)\left\{L_1\left[\left(\frac{w}{P}\right)_1\right] + L'_1\left[\left(\frac{w}{P}\right)_2 - \left(\frac{w}{P}\right)_1\right]\right\} - N_1$$

$$= (1 + g)\left\{N_1\left(Nu_1 + 1\right) + L'_1\left[\left(\frac{w}{P}\right)_2 - \left(\frac{w}{P}\right)_1\right]\right\} - N_1 \qquad \text{5.2.7}$$

Equation 5.2.7 says that whatever the real wage is in period 2, more people want to become employed the higher is Nu_1, unemployment in period 1. This provides a rationale for firms reacting to Nu_1 when planning their policies in period 1 for period 2.[3]

5.3. Frictional Unemployment and Reservation Demand

Section 1 of this chapter explained frictional unemployment on the basis of lack of information about which firms have job openings and about differences in wages among firms. If laborers in the market had complete knowledge of this kind, the equi-ΔN curves would be right angles, such as FGE in Figure 5-2.

Frictional unemployment is aggravated by the number of workers currently employed who resign to seek work elsewhere, retire, or are fired. In any of these cases, for a given net number of positions, say $\Delta N^{d'}$, more people are in the market who do not know where the jobs are—where the "good" jobs are. When a worker quits, he does not know which other firms are offering jobs. His old job is now open, but no one else knows this. Figure 5-2 portrays an increase in the retirement rate, given L_2, or the rate at which people quit or are fired, by shifting BCA to $B''C''A''$, resulting in an increase in frictional unemployment.[4] These last three additions to frictional unemployment account for the fact that, in the stationary state, there is still frictional unemployment.

The model displays unemployment through lack of information, not faulty information on the part of workers. So far, misinformation is unmentioned. Recall the actual real wage rate is $\overline{(w/P)}$. A worker has faulty information when he believes $\overline{(w/P)}$ is not the going market rate. If offered a job at $\overline{(w/P)}$, some workers reject it in favor of searching for a job at the supposedly higher market rate. Figure 5-3 illustrates this, showing the labor supply function for period 2. The curve LL shows the number of workers who will accept a job at any real wage rate if they think it is the going rate. The number who will accept jobs increases at higher real wage rates. Fewer are willing to accept a job if they think the market rate is higher than the rate offered.

For example, if workers think the going rate is $(w/P)'$, they move along BDA; and if offered $(w/P)''$, only $(w/P)''D$ take a job. If people believe $(w/P)'$ is the going market rate, $(w/P)'A$ take work at $(w/P)'$. The labor supply curve, given that $(w/P)'$ is believed to be the going rate, is $BDAL$. The effect of $(w/P)^e$, the rate people believe is the going

3 See Chapter 2, section 3. Firms need not know the numerical value of Nu. They see slacker labor markets currently the higher is Nu and expect slacker labor markets in the future. Equation 5.2.7 says this is reasonable.

4 Assume that the decision to quit or to fire a worker is not based on and does not entail production considerations. Thus, an increase in either quitting or firing does not have to be reflected in some change in the production function.

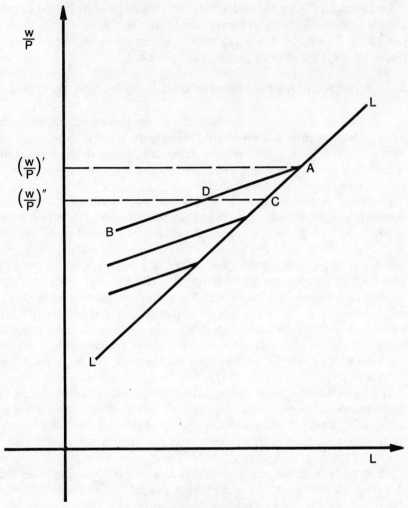

FIGURE 5-3

LABOR SUPPLY WITH RESERVATION DEMAND

rate, is to decrease the number of people who will take a job when $(w/P)_2^e$ exceeds $(w/P)_2$. This is a reservation demand based on faulty information.

In Figure 5-2, there are two ways to treat this reservation demand. One way is to say that those who will not accept an offer at $(\overline{w/P})$ are not to be counted in ΔN^s. This leaves Figure 5-2 as before. If the system is at point A, then GA is frictional unemployment. Empirically, though, ΔN^s seems larger, say by AE, since there is no way of telling how much of observed unemployment is due to misinformed reservation demand.

The alternative is to shift the curve BCA to the right at all points ($B''C''A''$ rather than BCA). The interpretation is that the more misinformed reservation demand, the smaller the ΔN a given observed couple, (ΔN^d, ΔN^s), produces.

Misinformed reservation demand explains some part of unemployment, but it is not necessary to the explanation of the existence of unemployment. Neither is it sufficient. This problem is difficult, though, and involves the fundamental microeconomic causes of aggregate unemployment.

As section 1 of this chapter showed, firms set wage rates to attract a certain number of workers. In conjunction with prices, these decisions establish a structure of real wage rates and a total aggregate desired hiring. If business is to achieve its desired hiring, $\Delta N^{d'}$, given that every potential worker is perfectly correct in his beliefs about the wage structure, then the number of people seeking employment, ΔN^s, must exceed $\Delta N^{d'}$ by a certain minimum amount, say GA as in Figure 5–2. GA is *frictional* unemployment, workers so unlucky as never to find a firm with an opening or a firm with an opening at the above-average wage sought. If ΔN^s is $\Delta N^{d'}E$, then AE is unnecessary unemployment, and on the micro level corresponds to $N^{d'}B$ in Figure 5–1.[5] For the length of the period of the model, over which wage rates are unchanged, there are AE people who want jobs which business does not offer. For the length of the period of the model, then, there is unemployment— even beyond frictional unemployment—even though workers are correct in their beliefs about going wage rates. The problem is to explain why a firm will spend a finite period of time off its labor supply curve; that is, why there is more than the easily understood frictional unemployment.[6] The natural question is why the firm does not immediately adjust its wage offer to return instantly to its supply curve, thus eliminating nonfrictional unemployment.

Recent works give a number of reasons why a firm should not immediately change price. All of these reasons concern problems of information and its costs. Phelps argues that, over the long run, a firm can expect lower labor supply prices by providing its workers with the security implicit in not adjusting wage rates immediately to equate quantities demanded and supplied.[7] There are setup costs involved in taking a new job, such as moving expenses. Other things being equal, a worker prefers to be employed by a firm promising some stability so that he does not have to shift to other opportunities, and hence endure

5 See footnote 2, page 73.

6 It will become obvious that the explanation for why the firm spends time off its labor supply curve is also an explanation for why the firm spends time off its demand curve—the other aspect of disequilibrium.

7 See Edmund Phelps, "Money Wage Dynamics and Labor Market Equilibrium," in Edmund Phelps *et al. Microeconomic Foundations of Employment and Inflation Theory,* (New York: W. W. Norton & Co., 1970), pp. 133–34.

these setup costs. This implies a preference to work for an employer promising some stability in his wage offers, and hence implies a willingness to work at a discount.

From the firm's point of view, frequent wage changes lead employees to quit to pursue other opportunities, forcing the firm to undertake the costs of hiring, training, and integrating new workers. If the firm wants an average work force of a given size, it may well find that the setup costs it saves by not changing wages "too often" are greater than the savings made by always being on its supply curve.

Alchian gives a more fundamental analysis, which includes Phelps's as a subcase.[8] Alchian contends that knowledge of a firm's prices— the price at which it sells output, or the price it pays for labor services— is valuable information. The more frequently a firm changes its price variables, the more expensive it is to have correct information about these variables. The more frequently a firm changes its price variables, the more frequently it destroys the valuable information of what its prices are. Buyers will pay a premium to a firm with stable prices in order to avoid the costs of acquiring and acting on information about the more volatile prices of other firms. Thus, there is an inherent tendency toward not adjusting prices and wages instantly whenever information is costly.

Beyond the foregoing reasons, and on the same order of precision, are two others. First, information that a decision was wrong is not necessarily information about what the right decision is. For example, Chapter 2 assumed that rivals' price increases shift the firm's demand curve isoelastically relative to the quantity axis, while increases in aggregate demand shift the demand curve isoelastically relative to the price axis. If the quantity demanded is smaller than expected, has the demand curve shifted relative to the quantity or price axis? In the first case, the optimum response is a price cut; but in the second, the optimum response is no change in price if the marginal cost curve is horizontal, or a price increase if marginal costs are declining. Until it accumulates data on others' prices, the firm has no rational way of deciding on a price change; and with decreasing marginal costs, no probabilistic argument makes a price cut the best interim solution.

A second reason for varying prices infrequently is that the firm not only is selling output at its current price, it is generating information about how many units are demanded at that price, given the length of time for which the price is maintained. Within limits, the longer the length of time over which a price is maintained, the more widespread becomes knowledge of this price. The larger the number of people who

---

8 See Armen A. Alchian, "Information Costs, Pricing, and Resource Unemployment," in Edmund Phelps *et al. Microeconomic Foundations of Employment and Inflation Theory,* (New York: W. W. Norton & Co., 1970).

know the price, the larger the number of people who can act on this price. Suppose the firm charges one price for two months and a different price for one month. The price-quantity data thus generated cannot be compared, in the sense that, if the prices had been the same during each period, different quantities would have been found, since one period allowed more time for information to spread. Drawing up a demand curve for prices which were maintained for widely different lengths of time is meaningless.

Consider a firm which has many observations of quantities bought when price is maintained for four weeks. Suppose it has maintained a price for three weeks and is sure that the price is too high. If it lowers price now, it will raise profits. But it will also lose a data point, for it cannot compare the 3-week quantity with the 4-week quantities. If it keeps the current price for one more week, it will have another comparable price-quantity observation. In a world in which information such as this is valuable, firms will sometimes purchase such information by foregoing the immediate profits to be gained by an immediate price change.

Firms, then, will not adjust prices and wages instantly because of the information problems involved.[9] This gives a periodic structure to the model of the firm. The model itself, however, makes no direct use of information problems beyond having the implied periodic structure. This is because of the analytical difficulty of working with uncertainty, search, and estimation. The model assumes away these many problems in order to derive comparative statics results.

A point about the interpretation of "unnecessary" unemployment needs elaboration. Unnecessary unemployment, such as AE in Figure 5-2, results when there are more applications for jobs at the wage rates firms offer than the number necessary to fulfill the firms' planned hiring. Thus, the labor supply curve the typical firm faces is lower than expected. One might naively suppose this means that the "solution" to

9 This means firms are sometimes off their labor supply curves, and this, together with the search behavior of workers, can lead to more-than-frictional unemployment. Frictional unemployment has long been numbered with the traditional explanations of aggregate unemployment, which also include: (1) government intervention (for example, minimum wage laws, fair price laws, pegged foreign exchange rates); (2) oligopolistic and oligopsonistic power (which are supposed to make adjustment difficult, even if they provide little in the way of a static explanation for unemployment); (3) unions; (4) long term contracts, leases, and agreements that hinder rapid adjustment; (5) financial collapse that simply closes up firms and makes adjustment much more difficult; and (6) deficient aggregate demand. This chapter shows that explanations (1) through (4) are not necessary to explain unemployment; and this is just as well, for their empirical relevance and theoretical foundations are often denied. (5) is an important influence in deep depressions but, following too prevalent custom, is not treated here. This chapter's discussion of unemployment is obviously unsympathetic to the Keynesian model's explanation in terms of (6), deficient aggregate demand. However, the next paragraph in the text and Chapter 6 both show how mismanagement of monetary and fiscal policy can aggravate macro problems, including unemployment.

unemployment is lower wages. This is not so. Unnecessary unemployment means that the current set of all prices is not an equilibrium set. There is no presumption at all that only one subset, wages, is not at equilibrium values. To see this, suppose in Figure 5–4 that the *IS* curve has a negative slope and that the economy is at a general equilibrium with no excess capacity, no inflation, and no unnecessary unemployment this period or next. Then, let the government raise the interest rate by reducing the flow supply of money (the *LM* curve rises to LM_2).

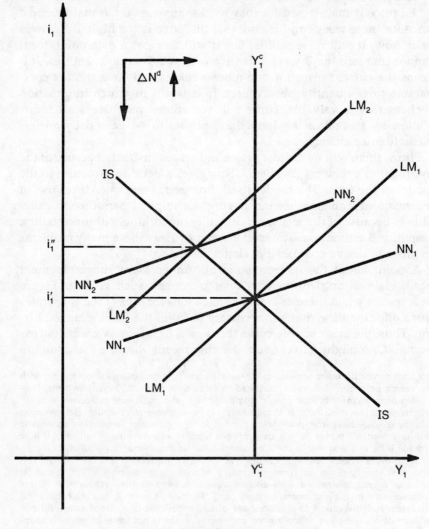

FIGURE 5–4

UNEMPLOYMENT AND THE PRICE OF BONDS

This adversely affects next-period's hiring (NN_2 versus NN_1), not because wages are wrong, but because the current price of bonds is wrong.

5.4. Involuntary Unemployment

Discussions of involuntary unemployment are notoriously unfruitful. This chapter's theory of employment and unemployment depends in part on lack of information about which firms have openings, including which firms have openings at above-average wages. Other models based on information and search display no involuntary unemployment.[10] Hence it may be worthwhile to point out the sense in which workers are involuntarily unemployed in the present model.

In this model, the notion of involuntary unemployment depends on the distinction between type 1 and type 2 job searchers. In a type 1 job search, the worker does not ask a prospective employer if a job is available, but asks only what the terms are. The worker goes from one prospective employer to another, seeking the "best" terms possible, including nonpecuniary benefits, rejecting job offers to continue the search, and ceasing his search when the expected present value of further search and consequent higher income just equals the earnings foregone to continue the search. Until the searcher accepts one of the offered jobs, he is unemployed. But this unemployment is voluntary because he chooses the length of his search, that is, the length of his unemployment.

This book particularly emphasizes the type 2 job search, in which the worker goes from one prospective employer to another, asking if there is a job available at the set wage rate the employer pays.[11] There is no bickering or bargaining between employer and employee.[12] The employer announces a wage, and the job searcher's only decision is to take

10 See Alchian, *op. cit.*; and Armen A. Alchian and William R. Allen, *University Economics: Elements of Inquiry* (3d ed.; Belmont, California: Wadsworth Publishing Co., 1971). Dale Mortenson, "A Theory of Wage and Employment Dynamics," in Edmund Phelps *et al. Microeconomic Foundations of Employment and Inflation Theory,* (New York: W. W. Norton & Co., 1970), assumes a worker need only find a firm to find a job.

11 Alchian, *op. cit.*; Alchian and Allen, *op. cit.*; and Mortenson, *op. cit.*, all assume a worker can have a job with any firm he finds (with any "contacts," as Mortenson puts it). Alchian in his book and Alchian and Allen in theirs assume this is so because there is some low enough wage rate at which the firm will hire anyone (but see pages 82–84). Mortenson assumes the firm announces a wage rate at which it expects to get a certain number of employees. He does not specify at all how the firm reacts when more workers apply than expected, though this possibility is nontrivial since his theory is based on stochastic foundations.

12 Alchian, *op. cit.*; and Alchian and Allen, *op. cit.*, couch much of their discussion in terms of a worker taking a sufficient wage cut to preserve employment, or demanding a tolerable (to the employer) wage increase.

the job or not—if there is an opening at that particular firm. The preceding section showed why a firm in the present model does not instantly adjust wages to create an opening for anyone who wants one, and thus why a perfectly qualified searcher may be rejected at every firm he tries. The earnest job searcher who goes from one employer to another all day long, eager, willing, and able to work at the wages paid his lucky peers with jobs, but who finds no opening, is likely enraged when told he is voluntarily unemployed.[13]

Part of the issue of involuntary unemployment, then, is a quantitative matter of what ratio of the unemployed are engaged in type 1 versus type 2 job-search.[14] Intuitively, financial executives used to a certain salary and beyond a certain age, as well as film directors on the way up or way down, and ballet dancers of a certain promise, are much more likely to spend time in a type 1 job search than are members of the International Association of Machinists, or farm workers, or janitors living near a commercial center. Employers will do a good deal more bargaining with uniquely skilled job searchers; whereas, with prospective employees having only standard skills, employers will more likely estimate the labor market, make a take-it-or-leave-it general offer, and rely on market forces to fill vacancies.[15]

Uniqueness is not entirely a question of innate, specific capabilities, but also depends on the cost of attaining information. Every inhabitant of a town of 500 may be economically unique in the others' eyes; though to an outsider, the town and its residents seem virtually interchangeable with many others.

A frustrated type 2 job searcher cannot find work by announcing in a personnel office that he will work for 10% less than they are paying though they are not hiring. The going wage was set to attract on an average the number of workers desired; and until beliefs are shown to be erroneous, the firm feels the current excess of applications for jobs is transitory, and a 10 percent cut now will shortly have to be reinstated. The previous section showed how such instability is costly. If a firm has not previously adopted a strategy of price instability, this one additional worker is unlikely to make it seem profitable.

13 The great frustration unemployed workers report in depressions is perhaps due to type 2 job searching, where the unlucky searcher is "just like anyone else"—except he does not have a job.

14 The number of unsuccessful type 2 job searchers has no necessary relationship to what sections 1 and 3 of this chapter called unnecessary unemployment (AE in Figure 5-2). Suppose the economy is on $FBCAE$ above the 45° line; then, the vacancies left unfilled exceed the workers left unhired. But some are unhired because, by bad luck, they found only firms in that minority of firms which had a larger supply than anticipated. A type 2 searcher who is solely a part of frictional unemployment (GA on $FBCAE$ in Figure 5-2) may earnestly claim to be involuntarily unemployed.

15 Although the worker with only standard skills may not be able to bargain for his job originally, he may be able to bargain for a raise after proving himself superior in his job.

But will not the firm hire just the single individual, paying him 10 percent less than his fellow workers? Presumably not, unless the firm is already practicing discriminating monopsony. Two economic forces militate against such price discrimination. First, it may be very costly to do with any efficiency. The costs of erring on the low side, losing the worker, and having to train a replacement may make it unprofitable; and the costs of acquiring information so as not to err may be quite high. Secondly, every worker prefers to work for a nondiscriminator; for he is then sometimes paid above his opportunity cost, while a price discriminator always tries to pay only opportunity costs. If a worker is to take a job with the price discriminator instead of the non-discriminator, the former must offer an expected present value of wages at least equal to the latter's offer. But there is always the risk the discriminator will later find the worker's opportunities have worsened and take advantage of this, where the nondiscriminator would not.[16] To compensate for this risk, the price discriminator must pay a premium. A firm initially chooses the nondiscriminatory strategy because it finds the premium too high, and is unlikely to change due to one worker's offer to take a cut.

Some analysts deny workers are involuntarily unemployed when the economy's vacancies exceed unemployment. But this depends to an extent on the unemployed's knowledge of the exact location of the vacancies. Newspaper ads and employment bureaus provide such information, but sometimes all they provide is an opportunity to apply for a job that is possibly available in the future. With vacancies exceeding unemployment and every major city running newspaper listings for dishwashers, even in the severest modern recessions, it is true no one person need be unemployed; and with sufficiently dispersed information on vacancies perhaps there need be no aggregate unemployment.[17] The frustrated type 2 job searcher may perhaps still quarrel with being designated "voluntarily unemployed" merely because he does not take any available job listed in the newspapers at a positive wage.[18]

If frustrated type 2 job searchers are labelled "involuntarily unemployed," what percent of unemployment do they constitute? Statistics do not tell, but the implicit test is whether the worker is actively seeking jobs for which personnel departments find him in all ways qualified, but receives no offer of employment because firms just are

16 For example, a serious illness in the worker's family may drain liquid resources and make it less feasible to quit and search for a new job; so the price discriminator takes advantage of this by cutting wages, or more likely, by increasing wages at a slower pace.

17 Beyond those unemployable because of age, minimum wage laws, health, etc. See footnote 14, page 82, for comments on the relationship of vacancies to job searchers and involuntary unemployment.

18 Any job searcher with a dime who does not buy an apple and becomes a self-employed entrepreneur in the corner apple stand industry is "voluntarily" unemployed.

not hiring, though he would take such an offer at the wages the firms are paying.

5.5. The ΔN^s, $\Delta N \Delta N$, and $NuNu$ Curves

The workers' desired change in employment, ΔN^s, the actual change in employment, ΔN, and the unemployment rate Nu, remain to be integrated into the graphical apparatus of Chapters 3 and 4.

Each ΔN^s curve is a locus of (i_1, Y_1^d) points that holds ΔN_1^s at a given value. Since ΔN_1^s varies endogenously only with period 2's real wage rate, the ΔN^s curve is an iso-$(w/P)_2$ locus. Starting at $(i_1', Y_1^{d'})$ in Figure 5–5, horizontal movements to the right increase $\Delta w/w$ and hold $\Delta P/P$ constant, and since:

$$\left(\frac{w}{P}\right)_2 = \left(\frac{w}{P}\right)_1 \cdot \frac{1 + \Delta w/w}{1 + \Delta P/P} \qquad 5.5.1$$

$(w/P)_2$ rises. To keep $(w/P)_2$ constant requires some increase in i_1 to raise $\Delta P/P$ and restrain $\Delta w/w$. Thus ΔN_1^s curve in Figure 5–5 has a positive slope, and horizontal rightward movements intersect ΔN^s curves with ever higher labor supply indices. The slope of ΔN_1^s is less than that of NN_1; for moving up along NN_1, $\Delta w/w$ is constant (NN_1 is the initial Δw_1 curve) and $\Delta P/P$ is rising, so $(w/P)_2$ falls.

If the system is in a region where increases in either ΔN^d or ΔN^s increase ΔN (θ_1, θ_2 both positive in equation 5.1.1), then the locus of points giving the same value of ΔN as (i_1', Y_1') lies between the NN_1 and ΔN_1^s curves. Moving between these curves raises ΔN^d and lowers ΔN^s, and the curve $\Delta N \Delta N_1$ is the locus where the forces balance. Thus the $\Delta N \Delta N_1$ curve is steeper than the ΔN_1^s curve.

Moving rightward along ΔN_1^s holds $(w/P)_2$ constant, meets lower and lower NN and $\Delta N \Delta N$ curves—both are steeper than ΔN^s curves—and increases ΔN^d; and thus ΔN increases. The lower the $\Delta N \Delta N$ curve, then, the higher its employment index. Moving rightward along ΔN_1^s, ΔN^s is constant and ΔN rising; so period 2's unemployment rate must be falling. Call the locus of (i_1, Y_1^d) points that generates a given value of Nu for period 2 an $NuNu$ curve. Then, rightward movements along ΔN_1^s intersect $NuNu$ curves with lower and lower period 2 unemployment indices. When such rightward movements have increased ΔN^d enough, all who want work can find it. ΔN^s equals ΔN and further increases in ΔN^d bring no change in ΔN (θ_1 equals zero). At such a point, the $\Delta N \Delta N$ curve with the same index as the ΔN_1^s becomes congruent with the ΔN_1^s curve; and the curve $NuNu_0$ with a zero index goes through the point. Leftward movements along NN_1 increase ΔN^s; and at some point, such increases cease to have an effect on ΔN. The

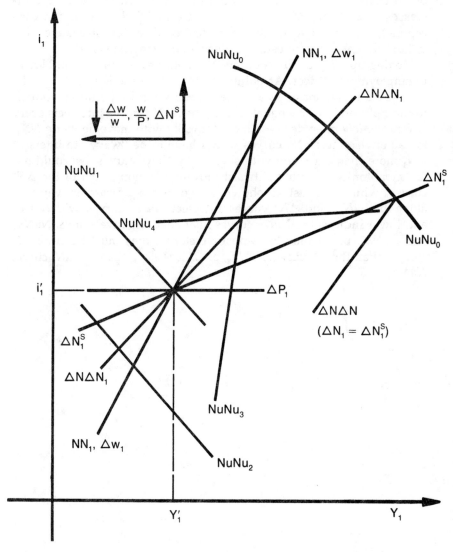

FIGURE 5-5

THE ΔN^s, $\Delta N \Delta N$, AND NuNu CURVES

$\Delta N \Delta N$ curve with the same index as NN_1 becomes congruent there with NN_1.

The *NuNu* curve's slope is indeterminate. Consider the *NuNu* curve through some point on NN_1. Horizontal rightward movements increase both ΔN^d and ΔN^s, and hence ΔN. Since both ΔN and ΔN^s increase, the effect on *Nu* is ambiguous; and it may require an increase, decrease, or no change in i_1 to return to the initial $NuNu$ curve. Given the increases in ΔN^d and ΔN^s with an increase in Y_1^d, θ_1, and θ_2 can conceptually be varied to require any desired direction of change in i_1 to hold Nu constant. Indeed, the $NuNu$ curve may be vertical.

Moving up NN_1, one encounters $NuNu$ curves with lower and lower unemployment indices. At points far enough to the left on NN_1, ΔN^s is large enough to make Nu as large as desired, and at points far enough to the right on NN_1, Nu equals zero. (The $NuNu_0$ curve intersects every NN curve.) Nu must decrease monotonically with movements up NN_1, for otherwise the $NuNu$ curves would have to be "wavy" to intersect NN_1 more than once; and with such wavy $NuNu$ curves, Nu could not fall monotonically with rightward movements along each of the ΔN^s curves, which it must as shown above. Since upward movements along both NN and ΔN^s curves intersect $NuNu$ curves with lower and lower indices, the $NuNu$ curves may have negative slopes, $NuNu_1$ and $NuNu_2$; but if they have positive slopes, they must be either (1) steeper than the NN curve, $NuNu_3$, or (2) less steep than the ΔN^s curve, $NuNu_4$.

6 MACROECONOMIC POLICY IMPLICATIONS OF THE MODEL

Chapters 2, 3, and 4 built the general, short-run macro model from its micro foundations.[1] The purpose was to show how the system determines macroeconomic variables and to use the model to show how policy may make the system generate more satisfactory values of the variables. This chapter discusses policy questions.

6.1. A Review of the Excess Capacity Case

As a preliminary to the discussion of policy, this section reviews the model when there is excess capacity.

The business sector behavior functions developed in Chapter 2 are fundamental to the model. These aggregate functions are built from a fairly general micro model of the firm. Their partial derivatives show how the percentage rate of change of prices, $\Delta P/P$, the percentage rate of change of wages, $\Delta w/w$, the rate of change of the size of the work force the business sector wants, ΔN^d, the level of current investment the business sector desires, I^d, and the aggregate planned output firms desire to produce next period, AQ, vary with parametric changes in current aggregate demand, Y_1^d, the current rate of interest, i_1, business's expectations of percentage price and wage changes, $(\Delta P/P)^e$ and $(\Delta w/w)^e$, the current percentage rate of unemployment, Nu, and the current real wage rate, w/P.

These five functions are used in a simple IS-LM model. In Figure 6-1, the IS curve is the locus of combinations of i_1 and Y_1 where excess demand for output equals zero. The IS curve satisfies the equation for zero excess demand for output,

$$I^d + G = S^d + T \qquad\qquad 6.1.1$$

or desired real investment plus government spending must equal desired real private savings plus real taxation. Since the IS curve depends on I^d, and I^d depends on $(\Delta P/P)^e$, $(\Delta w/w)^e$, Nu, and w/P, a different IS curve results for a change in the values of any of these four

---

1 The path to the long run is a series of changing short runs. This chapter's policy prescriptions refer to the short run, and it is a willfull misinterpretation to apply them to the long run or criticize them because they are not long run. Nevertheless, the model obviously has something to say about the system's path to the long run.

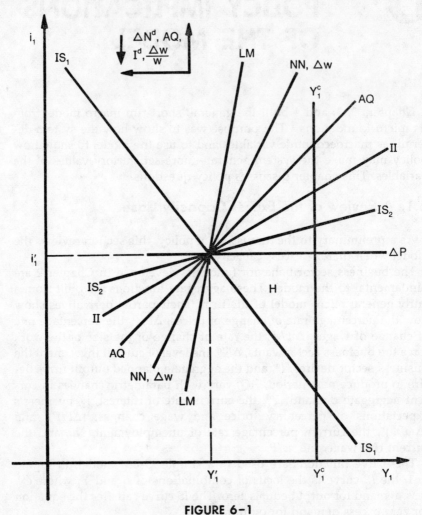

FIGURE 6-1

THE *IS*, *LM*, ΔP, Δw, NN, AQ, AND *II* CURVES

parameters.[2] Assume that total private savings depend positively only on real disposable income.[3] Differentiating equation 6.1.1 to find the slope of the *IS* curve in (i_1, Y_1) space, $di/dY(IS)$, yields:

$$\frac{di}{dY}(IS) = -\frac{I_y - S_y}{I_i} \left(= -\frac{-1 + I_y + C_y}{I_i} \right)$$ 6.1.2

$$I_y, S_y, C_y > 0, C_y = 1 - S_y$$

2 See Chapter 3, section 4.
3 See Chapter 3, section 1.

This derivative may be negative, IS_1, or positive, IS_2, depending on whether an increase in output and demand so stimulate investment demand that i_1 must rise to keep the demand-induced increase in investment demand plus the income-induced increase in consumption demand from exceeding the increase in output.[4]

The LM curve is the locus of points in the (i_1, Y_1) plane where the excess demand for money equals zero. It is drawn up for a given initial stock of real balances, M/P, and a given flow supply of real balances, $\Delta M^s/P$. The LM curve satisfies the condition for zero excess demand for money,

$$\frac{\Delta M^s}{P} = \frac{\Delta M^d}{P} = \phi(Y_1, i_1, M/P); \phi_y > 0, \phi_i < 0, \phi_{M/P} < 0 \quad \textbf{6.1.3}$$

The slope of the LM curve is:

$$\frac{di}{dY}(LM) = -\frac{\phi_y}{\phi_i} > 0 \qquad \textbf{6.1.4}$$

Assume throughout that the LM is steeper than the IS curve, even if the IS curve has a positive slope.[5]

Assume that the system is always at the intersection of the IS and LM curves—unless the intersection is beyond capacity output. In Figure 6–1, the IS and LM curves intersect to the left of the curve Y_1^c which indicates capacity output for this period, and thus the system is at (i_1', Y_1'). Section 3 of this chapter reviews the nature of the capacity constraint, and the case in which the constraint is effective.

Several families of curves helpful in discussing policy alternatives are the ΔP, Δw, NN, AQ, and II curves.[6] Consider the curves through (i_1', Y_1'). The IS curve depends on the parametric values of $(\Delta P/P)^e$, $(\Delta w/w)^e$, Nu, and w/P for this period. Hold these parameters at the values which generated (i_1', Y_1'). Then insert the values Y_1' and i_1' into the business sector behavior functions to find $\Delta P/P$, $\Delta w/w$, ΔN^d, AQ, and I^d.

The ΔP curve through (i_1', Y_1') is the combinations of i_1 and Y_1^d which generate the same value for $\Delta P/P$ as do (i_1', Y_1').[7] Its slope,

$$\frac{di}{dY}(\Delta P) = -\frac{f_y}{f_i} \qquad \textbf{6.1.5}$$

is zero since Y^d-induced increases in expected demand are isoelastic to the price axis and generate no price changes as long as the system is

4 See Chapter 3, section 3.
5 See Chapter 3, section 3.
6 See Chapter 3, section 3.
7 See Chapter 3, section 3.

below capacity.[8] Since f_i is positive, movements above the ΔP curve increase inflation.

Along the Δw curve through (i'_1, Y'_1), the percentage rate of change of wages has the same value.[9] Its slope is:[10]

$$\frac{di}{dY}(\Delta w) = -\frac{g_y}{g_i} > 0; \, g_y > 0, \, g_i < 0 \qquad \qquad 6.1.6$$

From the partials, movements to the right or down increase the rate at which wages increase. (See Figure 6-1.)

The NN curve through any point, showing the locus of (i_1, Y_1^d) combinations where ΔN^d maintains a given value, lies on top of the Δw curve through that point.[11] Movements along an NN curve imply no change in ΔN^d; and given the labor supply function, this means no change in next period's wages. Δw_1 is also NN_1, the locus of points where the value of ΔN^d generated by i'_1 and Y'_1, and the parameters which determine i'_1 and Y'_1, is constant.

Each II curve is the locus of (i_1, Y_1^d) combinations where I^d takes on a given value, and the AQ curve is the locus where the aggregate planned output which business desires for next period takes on a given value. Each curve is drawn by taking $(\Delta P/P)^e$, $(\Delta w/w)^e$, w/P, and Nu as given; and different curves result if any one of these parameters changes. Figure 6-1 shows the AQ, II, NN, and Δw curves through (i'_1, Y'_1). Chapter 3, section 3, explained why the NN is steeper than the AQ curve, which is steeper than the II curve. Since:

$$I_y, \, AQ_y, \, g_y, \, H_y > 0$$

and

$$I_i, \, AQ_i, \, g_i, \, H_i < 0$$

all four curves have positive slopes, and movements to the right or downward from them imply increases in I^d, AQ, ΔN^d, and $\Delta w/w$.[12]

Figure 6-1 shows the LM curve as steeper than the II, NN, and AQ curves, but there is no a priori reason why this should be so. Given the finite slopes of the II, NN, and AQ curves, the partial derivative of the

---

8 For the partial derivatives of the business sector behavior functions, see Chapter 2, sections 4 and 5.

9 See Chapter 3, section 3.

10 For the partial derivatives of the business sector behavior functions, see Chapter 2, sections 4 and 5.

11 See Chapter 3, section 3.

12 For the partial derivatives of the business sector behavior functions, see Chapter 2, sections 4 and 5.

flow demand for money with respect to income (interest) can conceptually fall (rise) and rotate LM clockwise through (i'_1, Y'_1) until it is less steep than the other curves.[13] But the II curve is always steeper than the IS curve, even when the IS curve has a positive slope.[14] Consider an increase in Y_1. The II curve shows the increase in the rate of interest which leads to no change in desired investment. But the IS curve shows the smaller increase in i_1 that allows I^d to increase by the positive difference between the increase in Y_1 and the smaller increase in consumption.

Thus, considering an IS-LM intersection: (1) the IS curve may have a positive or negative slope, and the ΔP curve has a zero slope; (2) the NN curve is steeper than the AQ, which is steeper than the II, which in turn is steeper than the IS curve; and (3) the LM may be more or less steep than the NN, AQ, or II curves, but is steeper than the IS curve by assumption.

6.2. The Policy Implications—Excess Capacity

The present model generates some policy suggestions at odds with those currently accepted, though the degree of divergence is to some extent an empirical question.[15]

Current views on macroeconomic policy are conveniently summarized by the policies proposed to remedy any particular ill.[16] "Unacceptably" high *unemployment* can be reduced through combinations of increased government expenditure, reduced taxation, and increases in the money supply. *Inflation* can be reduced by decreases in government spending, increases in taxation, and decreases in the money supply. A high rate of *growth* can be achieved by keeping the economy close to capacity output with little unemployment, though it is recognized that expansionary fiscal policy close to capacity output may deprive the business sector of some investment goods which get diverted to the government or household sector. *Excess capacity* can be reduced by increasing government expenditures, decreasing taxation, and increasing the money supply; while *excess demand* for output can be reduced by reversing these policies.

In the light of coming recommendations, it is worthwhile to note the common view that high interest rates do not "cause" inflation. It is pointed out that interest rates are endogenous and, far from "causing" anything, are themselves "caused". Or, it is asserted that lowering interest rates through monetary policy means more inflation, and hence even higher interest rates in the future as the nominal rate rises to keep

13 See Chapter 3, section 3.
14 See Chapter 3, section 3.
15 See also footnote 1, page 87.
16 The discussion is restricted, as all along, to a closed economy.

the real rate of interest on financial assets from falling due to inflation. In contrast with these views, this section argues that lowering the rate of interest, in part through monetary policy, is a policy against inflation, though the magnitude of the effect depends on the size of f_i, the partial derivative of the inflation function. Since monetary policy that lowers the rate of interest also decreases the rate of inflation in this section's case of excess capacity, such monetary policy creates no inflationary upward force on the nominal rate of interest. On the contrary, it reduces inflationary pressure.[17]

Suppose policy makers find projected unemployment and inflation "unacceptably" high and growth "unacceptably" low while there is currently excess capacity. This poses an awkward choice since conventional policies likely to decrease unemployment and increase growth are also likely to increase inflation, according to the views just summarized. And anti-inflationary policies are considered likely to increase excess capacity while hurting both employment and growth.[18]

While some choices are inevitable, the awkward ones proposed can often be avoided, and the painful results of difficult choices mitigated. Suppose the economy is at the intersection of the curves IS_1 and LM in Figure 6-1. Assume that the index on the curve ΔP is "unacceptably" high, projected unemployment is "unacceptably" high, and the index on AQ is "too low". Realistically, business is likely to be unhappy with the excess capacity in the economy ($Y_1' < Y_1^c$).

Allow the government to control real government spending, G, real taxation of households, T, and the flow money supply, ΔM^s.[19] These variables effectively allow the government to control perfectly the IS and LM curves; and this in turn implies perfect control of i_1 and Y_1, since they are determined by the intersection of the IS and LM curves.[20] If the government selects a (i_1, Y_1) point to the right of (i_1', Y_1') and below ΔP, the economy experiences less inflation and business desires to

17 Clearly this is a short-run proposition, for in the long run the rate of monetary expansion determines inflation. The proposition deals with the path to the long run. See Milton Friedman, "The Optimum Quantity of Money," *The Optimum Quantity of Money & Other Essays* (Chicago: Aldine Publishing Co., 1969); and Harry G. Johnson, "The Neo-Classical One-Sector Growth Model: A Geometrical Exposition and Extension to a Monetary Economy," *Economica*, Vol. XXXIII (August, 1966), pp. 265-87. Further, in the case of positive aggregate excess demand for output, discussed in sections 3 and 4 of this chapter, reductions in the rate of interest through monetary policy are inflationary.

18 Part of this conventional awkward choice is captured in the Phillips Curve, where lower unemployment means higher wage and hence price inflation.

19 The government is assumed not to change the tax structure that business faces. Business taxation and the effects of changes in such taxation have been ignored throughout. One reason is that there is enough to handle already. More fundamentally, a sensible model of business reaction to taxation must also be a model of corporate finance; and this is a very complicated question, much too broad to be tackled here.

20 Again, assume that the economy does not run into the capacity constraint Y_1^c. Of course, governments never know in advance the precise consequences of their policies. This book is merely following the convention of a nonstochastic discussion of policy—just as do most Keynesian treatments.

increase employment more than at (i_1', Y_1'). In addition, next period's aggregate planned output increases, and the economy currently experiences less excess capacity than otherwise. (See point H in Figure 6-1.)

It is not clear how H affects next period's unemployment. Nu_2 may rise. The interpretation is that the decrease in the rate of interest reduces inflation. At the same time, the increase in income and decrease in the interest rate reinforce each other to induce an increase in the demand for labor and in the wage rate firms offer in order to attract more workers. Thus ΔN^d and $\Delta w/w$ rise. The increase in $\Delta w/w$ and decrease in $\Delta P/P$ raise $(w/P)_2$ so ΔN^s is higher than otherwise. The increase in ΔN^d tends to lower Nu_2 while the increase in ΔN^s tends to raise Nu_2, with no a priori way of knowing which force will predominate. But this interpretation makes the question of the effect on Nu_2 less pressing, since any hypothetical increase is due to an increase in ΔN^s in response to an improved $(w/P)_2$; for both ΔN^d and ΔN rise.[21]

Government can increase ΔN^d and AQ and decrease inflation and excess capacity because it can choose the (i_1, Y_1) point at which the IS and LM curves intersect. Exactly what policies are necessary to choose such a point? Consider expansion of the money supply and no change in fiscal policy. In terms of Figure 6-1, an increase in ΔM^s lowers the LM curve, and successive increases trace out the IS curve. Rightward movements along the IS curve imply increases in ΔN^d and AQ since the IS curve always has a smaller slope than the NN and AQ curves; and if the IS curve's slope is negative, these movements also decrease inflation, since the ΔP curve is horizontal.

Thus *expansionary* monetary policy can by itself raise both ΔN^d and AQ and lower inflation, if the IS curve's slope is negative; but whatever is ΔM^s, inflation is lower, the lower is the IS curve. Notice that a key element of the strategy is to lower the interest rate, in part, at least, through increasing the money supply.

Hold ΔM^s constant and try to achieve the goals by using fiscal policy alone. In Figure 6-1, expansionary fiscal policy—increases in G or decreases in T—moves the IS curve upwards and traces out the LM curve. This necessarily raises current income and reduces excess capacity. But notice that this necessarily implies increased inflation, as conventional wisdom assumes when there is already inflationary pressure.[22] In addition, if the LM curve is steeper than the NN and AQ

21 Moving from (i_1', Y_1') in Figure 5-5 to some point below and to the right may well put the system on a lower $NuNu$ curve, especially given the variety of possible slopes of such curves. But if the Nu index rises, it is only because so many people are lured into the work force by the aggreeable rise in $(w/P)_2$.

22 The present model implies increases in prices over what they would have been, whether the rate of inflation would have been positive or negative (deflation). Conventional policy prescriptions often predict a range where fiscal policy will cause no increase in prices.

curves, such fiscal policy reduces ΔN^d and AQ. Usual policy prescriptions show clearly that expansionary fiscal policy increases the demand for labor, though the expected effect on growth is unclear. Some see inflation as an indication that the system "must" be near capacity, implying that increases in demand by the household or government sector may deprive business of some investment, hence reducing growth.[23] But when there is a good deal of excess capacity, conventional wisdom seems to hold that increases in aggregate demand stimulate growth.[24]

If the LM is steeper than the NN and AQ curves, expansionary fiscal policy lowers ΔN^d and AQ. The interpretation is that the increase in Y_1 increases ΔM^d, and thus i_1 must increase if ΔM^d is to return to equality with an unchanged ΔM^s. If ΔM^d is not very sensitive to i_1, it takes a large increase to do this. If ΔM^d is very sensitive to changes in Y_1, i_1 must again take a large increase to bring ΔM^d back to equality with a given ΔM^s. To business, the increase in Y_1^d indicates more optimistic demand conditions next period, and it wants to increase employment and output. There is some increase in i_1 which would raise the cost of capital services enough to keep AQ constant, and a larger increase that would keep ΔN^d constant. The more sensitive are AQ and ΔN^d to the cost effects of interest, or the less sensitive they are to the demand effects of Y_1^d, the smaller are the necessary increases in the interest rate. It may well be that, given the responsiveness of ΔM^d, ΔN^d, and AQ to changes in Y_1^d, the responsiveness of ΔM^d to interest changes may be so relatively slight that the change which keeps the system on LM is larger than the changes which would keep the system on NN or AQ.

Consider *deflationary* fiscal policy. This policy moves the system to the left along the LM_1 curve and diminishes inflation—a conventional Keynesian policy prediction. Inflation falls no matter how steep the LM curve. While some monetarists make the alleged lack of sensitivity of money demand to the interest rate, making the LM curve practically vertical, a key argument for the futility of attempts to control aggregate demand with fiscal policy, such insensitivity makes fiscal policy an even more effective short-run weapon against inflation; for a given fiscal cut has more impact the steeper is the LM curve. If the LM curve is steeper than the NN and AQ curves, ΔN^d and AQ rise. Usual policy

---

23 Consider the many macro models where price changes depend on the difference between aggregate demand and full-employment output. See Alain C. Enthoven, "A Neo-Classical Model of Money, Debt and Economic Growth," appendix to John G. Gurley and Edward S. Shaw, *Money In A Theory of Finance* (Washington, D.C.: Brookings Institution, 1960); Jerome Stein, "Money and Capacity Growth," *Journal of Political Economy*, Vol. LXXIV (October, 1966), pp. 451–65, and "Monetary Growth Theory in Perspective," *American Economic Review*, Vol. LX (January, 1970), pp. 85–106.

24 Probably this induced growth does not stimulate inflation.

recommendations do not predict these possible short-run effects. Whatever the steepness of the LM curve, as long as the slope is not infinite, income declines and excess capacity increases—the conventional policy predictions.

Many configurations of the IS, LM, ΔP, NN, and AQ curves permit the government to move to the desired mixture of all goals only if both monetary and fiscal policy are used; since given the ΔP, NN, and AQ curves, there is no reason to believe that movements in either direction along some arbitrary IS or LM curve will lead to exactly the desired point in the (i_1, Y_1) plane.

The case professional economists currently find so unpleasant is "stagflation"—excess capacity, high inflation, high unemployment, and low growth. Conventional wisdom has a cure for any one of these ills taken separately and for some combinations of them (e.g., excess capacity and unemployment, but not inflation). But all of them taken together seem to force the policy maker to choose between inflation and unemployment, and this is a very hard choice. The choice is made more unpleasant by the empirical fact that having once decided to allow high unemployment in order to achieve low inflation, the policy maker may well get both high unemployment and high inflation.

The present model has an explanation for this failure of policy. In Figure 6-2, suppose the system is at (i_1', Y_1'). If government perversely wishes to increase an already severe inflation and to lower business demand for labor when there is already "too much" unemployment, all it need do is move the intersection of the IS and LM curves, whatever the IS curve's slope, somewhere above ΔP_1 and NN. For example, a decision to fight inflation by a restrictive monetary policy and expanded government spending to keep aggregate demand constant leads to IS_2, LM_2, and (i_1'', Y_1'). Aggregate demand is unchanged, but inflation increases and business demand for labor declines as does growth, AQ. Unemployment may decline, because as the demand for labor and wage offers fall, these lower offers combined with the higher inflation reduce $(w/P)_2$ and hence ΔN^s, perhaps by enough to offset the decline in ΔN^d.[25] Labor leaders are likely to find this an unsatisfactory way of fighting unemployment. As should be clear from the above analysis and Figure 6-2, a better policy might be to hold aggregate demand constant and lower the interest rate through restrictive fiscal policy and increases in the money supply.

The unhappy situation discussed above could be worse for the policy maker. Suppose the government "hardens its heart" and takes no fiscal action to offset the restrictive monetary policy's effects on aggregate

25 Unemployment falls if and only if the $NuNu$ curve through (i_1', Y_1') has a negative slope. See Chapter 5, section 5.

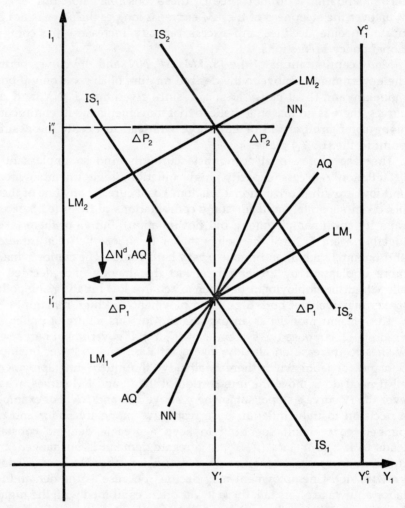

FIGURE 6-2

PERVERSE POLICY

demand. If the IS curve has a negative slope—a possibility but not a necessity—each decrease in the money supply increases inflation and decreases the business demand for labor and the growth rate. Thus, the more likely it is that the IS curve has a negative slope, the more likely it is that restrictive monetary policy will have perverse effects on inflation.

These examples show why a government may follow either a restrictive monetary policy or a restrictive fiscal policy or both and find disasterous consequences for employment and very poor results on inflation for the given sacrifices.

The best combination of policies depends on the exact positions and shapes of the *IS*, *LM*, ΔP, *NN*, and *AQ* curves. The model suggests some general policy guides. First, restrictive monetary policy will increase inflation if the *IS* curve has a negative slope, lowering real income and raising i_r. Second, holding income constant and raising i_1 as an anti-inflation move has positively perverse effects, though the magnitude of these effects is an empirical question of the influence of interest rates on costs. Holding Y_1 constant and lowering i_1 lowers inflation and increases growth and business demand for labor. Third, the deflationary effects of restrictive fiscal policy are mitigated to the extent that restrictive monetary policy does not allow the interest rate to fall, since decreases in the rate of interest reduce inflation. In the same way, the possibly harmful effects of restrictive fiscal policy on growth and employment are reinforced by the policy of keeping interest rates high, since low interest rates stimulate growth.

This completes the discussion of the policy implications of the model of Chapter 3, and the next section turns to the model of Chapter 4.

6.3. A Review of the Case of Positive Excess Aggregate Demand for Output

The last section discussed one "hard" case with excess capacity, "unacceptably" high inflation and unemployment, and a "low" growth rate. Now consider a second hard case where inflation and unemployment are again "too high" and growth "too low", but there is positive excess aggregate demand for output. This complicates the graphical analysis, as in Chapter 4, and changes some of the symptoms of macroeconomic ills and some of the pressures to cure them. When there is excess capacity, producers suffer from unpleasantly refuted expectations. The difference between Y_1^c and actual real income is a good measure of business overestimation of demand.[26] With positive excess demand for output, business has underestimated demand; and this is much more pleasant to sellers than overestimating demand. But if business enjoys a larger demand than expected, some demanders are frustrated in their attempts to buy. Positive excess demand for output may not lead business in its role of seller to pressure government as strongly as excess capacity does; but in its role as buyer, zero excess demand is obviously desirable. Further, since positive excess demand prevents consumers from buying what they wish, they want this excess demand eliminated.

This section reviews the model when there is positive excess demand for output. In Figure 6-3, the *IS* and *LM* curves intersect to the right of the Y_1^c curve that indicates maximum possible output for this period.

26 A good measure, but not precise. Business might not have been able to hire all the workers it wanted.

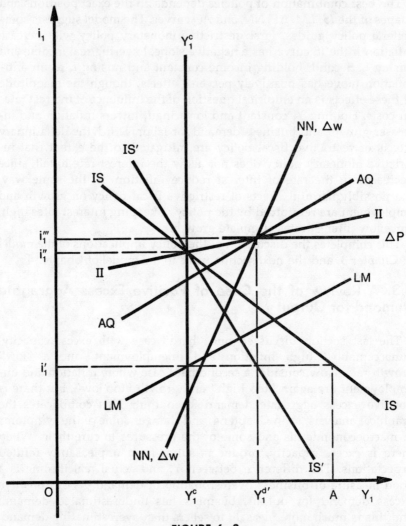

FIGURE 6-3

POSITIVE EXCESS AGGREGATE DEMAND

Actual output is Y_1^c. It cannot be as high as the system would "like."[27] Assume an aggregate production function relates maximum real output to the current stock of capital and current employment. The stock of capital depends only on past decisions, as does current employment in the sense that changes in this period's policy parameters affect next period's employment but not this period's. Current employment depends on the number of jobs business plans to fill at the start of the

27 See Chapter 4, section 1.

period and the number of people looking for jobs. The number of workers firms try to hire was decided last period and is independent of current variables. Likewise, firms are currently deciding how many workers to hire next period. The number of people seeking jobs this period depends on last period's unemployment—for these unemployed would like work—and on how the real wage rate has changed since last period. The change in the real wage rate depends on how firms have changed prices and wage offers since last period. But these changes were made at the start of this period on the basis of only what had gone on up until the end of last period. These decisions were unaffected by what is currently going on; for at the start of this period, business could only guess at what would happen during the period. Thus, both business's and workers' desired changes in employment are independent of current variables; and since current employment depends only on these desired changes, actual current employment is not endogenous to this period. Thus, capacity output for this period depends on past decisions and is exogenous to this period.[28]

The *IS* curve intersects the *LM* curve to the right of the Y_1^c curve (see Figure 6-3). Actual income equals Y_1^c, and there is excess demand for output. Excess demand for output requires some assumption of how actual output is rationed. Assume that the government and household sectors' demands are always satisfied, and thus only business suffers disappointed demands. This assumption simplifies further analysis of the excess demand for money.[29] Chapter 4 assumes that there is always zero excess demand for money given the extent of excess demand for output and no matter how output is rationed.[30] But continuing to assume that only households hold money and government issues it, excess demand for output and the consequent rationing affect the excess demand for money just when these two sectors are in fact subject to rationing. Having assumed they are not subject to rationing, the excess demand for money equals zero only on the conventional *LM* curve.[31] Since output is Y_1^c, the intersection of the Y_1^c and *LM* curves gives the rate of interest. This intersection is below the *IS* curve, implying positive excess aggregate demand for output.

Aggregate demand is not equal to *OA*, the level of real output for which excess demand equals zero at the interest rate i_1' in Figure 6-3. Begin at (i_1'', Y_1^c) with zero excess demand for output and lower i_1 to i_1'. This lower i_1 generates an increased investment demand, and this

28 See Chapter 4, section 1; and Chapter 5, sections 1, 2, and 5.

29 See Chapter 4, sections 2, 3, and 4.

30 This is the double-barred excess demand for money. See Chapter 4, sections 3 and 4.

31 In other words, the assumptions about rationing and who holds money imply that double-barred excess demand for money equals zero just when single-barred excess demand equals zero. See Chapter 4, section 4.

higher aggregate demand itself induces an increase in investment demand. If output can increase, this increase in output and real income generates an increase in consumer spending; and this increase in consumer spending generates another increase in income which generates yet another increase in consumer demand. The total multiplier effect depends on the marginal propensity to invest given a change in aggregate demand and the marginal propensity to consume out of changes in real income.[32]

Start at i_1'' and hold income constant at Y_1^c. Aggregate demand is:

$$Y^d = I[Y^d, \left(i - \frac{\Delta P^e}{P}\right), \frac{\Delta P^e}{P}, \frac{w}{P}\left(1 + \frac{\Delta w^e}{w}\right), Nu] + G + C^d(Y_1^c - T) \qquad 6.3.1$$

and clearly depends on the values of the parameters $(\Delta P/P)^e$, $(\Delta w/w)^e$, w/P, Nu, G, T, and the average propensity to save. The IS' curve goes through (i_1'', Y_1^c) and is the locus of points for which equation 6.3.1 holds, given income equals Y_1^c. The slope of the IS' curve is:

$$\frac{di}{dY}(IS') = -\frac{-1 + I_y}{I_i} \qquad 6.3.2$$

Comparing this to the slope of the IS curve in equation 6.1.2, the IS' curve omits the household multiplier effect. The IS' curve is the IS curve with consumption independent of current income and equal to $C(Y_1^c - T)$, and the IS' curve shows only the multiplier effects of business's reactions to changes in aggregate demand. Aggregate demand at the rate of interest i_1', then, is $Y_1^{d'}$, the level of aggregate demand which puts the system on IS' at i_1'.

Desired investment depends on i_1' and aggregate demand. Actual investment, however, is the difference between actual output, Y_1^c, and the sum of desired consumption plus real government spending. Desired consumption depends on $(Y_1^c - T)$, not on aggregate demand. Thus, actual investment is independent of any changes in aggregate demand which arise through changes in the interest rate.[33]

At the point (i_1'', Y_1^c), actual investment equals desired investment, and actual investment is the same as at $(i_1', Y_1^{d'})$. What rate of interest would make the actual investment available at $(i_1', Y_1^{d'})$ equal to desired investment at $Y_1^{d'}$? Along the II curve through (i_1'', Y_1^c), desired investment remains constant and equal to what actual investment is at either $(i_1', Y_1^{d'})$, where actual investment is less than desired, or (i_1'', Y_1^c), where actual equals desired investment. Thus at $(i'''', Y_1^{d'})$, business desires investment equal to the actual investment allowed at $(i_1', Y_1^{d'})$.[34]

---

32 See Chapter 4, section 5.
33 See Chapter 4, sections 6 and 7.
34 See Chapter 4, sections 6 and 7.

Recall that as far as price, output, wage, and employment decisions are concerned, whether the quantity of capital the firm uses is determined by the price of capital services or by some rationing procedure does not matter. That is, if the firm cannot buy as many units of capital services as it would like, there is some interest rate which would induce it to buy only the limited amount available; and at this new higher rate, exactly the same price, output, wage, and employment decisions as before would be made. In Figure 6–3, exactly the same decisions for $\Delta P/P$, AQ, $\Delta w/w$, and ΔN^d are made at $(i_1', Y_1^{d'})$ when there is excess demand for output as would be made at $(i_1''', Y_1^{d'})$ if business could invest as much as it likes. The values of $\Delta P/P$, AQ, $\Delta w/w$, and ΔN^d at $(i_1', Y_1^{d'})$ are given by the indices on the ΔP, AQ, and NN curves through $(i_1''', Y_1^{d'})$; and these curves aid the policy analysis which follows.[35]

Since the NN and AQ curves are steeper than the II curve, they intersect the Y_1^c curve below i_1''. It is impossible to say a priori whether they intersect the Y_1^c curve above i_1'. Figure 6–3 shows the NN curve intersecting Y_1^c below and the AQ curve above i_1'.

6.4. The Policy Implications—Positive Excess Aggregate Demand

Consider the second hard case. Conventional wisdom says that increasing taxation, decreasing government spending, or decreasing the supply of money reduces both excess demand for output and price inflation. Unfortunately, it is believed, these measures, alone or together, harm employment. It is generally felt that the restraint necessary to curb inflation will harm growth.

Consider first the effects of restrictive monetary policy in the present model. Decreases in the money supply raise the LM curve and hence the $Y_1^c - LM$ intersection. Thus, i_1 rises from i_1' to i_1'' in Figure 6–4. The IS' and IS curves are unchanged, so aggregate demand falls. Desired consumption does not change, so actual investment does not change. The interest rate that makes this unchanged level of actual investment equal desired investment at $Y_1^{d'}$ is i_1''', on the curve II_1 through the $IS' - Y_1^c$ intersection. Through $(i_1''', Y_1^{d''})$ are new NN, AQ, and ΔP curves, all carrying indices lower than the initial curves'. Aggregate demand is lower, so businesses expect poorer demand conditions next period. They cannot get any more capital than at $(i_1', Y_1^{d'})$. Cost conditions have not changed, but next period's anticipated demand has fallen; so $\Delta P/P$, $\Delta w/w$, ΔN^d, and AQ decline. Thus, every such reduction in excess demand for output and in inflation implies deterioration in business hiring and in growth.

35 See Chapter 4, sections 6 and 7; and Appendix 1, section 3.

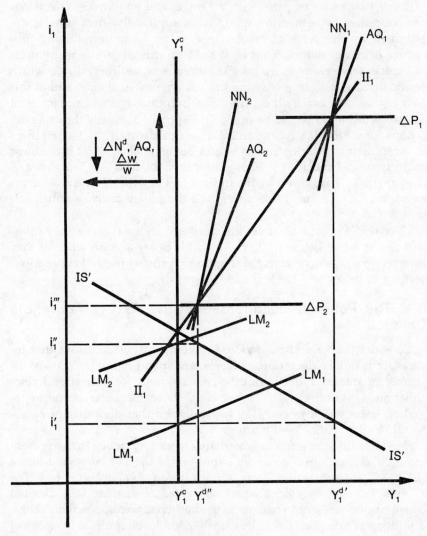

FIGURE 6-4

EXCESS DEMAND AND MONETARY POLICY

Nu_2 may rise or fall. ΔN^d, $\Delta w/w$, and $\Delta P/P$ all fall; but $(w/P)_2$ may rise or fall since both $\Delta P/P$ and $\Delta w/w$ fall. Thus, ΔN^s may rise or fall. ΔN^d falls, but ΔN^s may fall enough to offset this, so that Nu_2 falls. But this decrease is not very enjoyable, since it occurs only if $(w/P)_2$ falls so much that many job seekers leave the market.[36]

36 If the initial $NuNu$ curve has a negative slope, Nu_2 rises; but if it has a positive slope, Nu_2 may rise or fall. See Chapter 5, section 5.

Turn now to restrictive fiscal policy. If government lowers its spending or lowers consumer spending by raising taxes, the IS_1 and IS_1' curves shift down together in Figure 6–5 while the LM curve is unchanged.[37] Actual investment rises by the amount of the decline in government or household spending, the indices on II_1 and II_2 showing the increase in actual investment. The new IS' curve, IS_2', and the unchanged rate of interest, i_1', determine aggregate demand, Y_1^d falling to $Y_1^{d''}$. With the new government and household demands, actual investment would equal desired investment at $Y_1^{d''}$ if the interest rate were

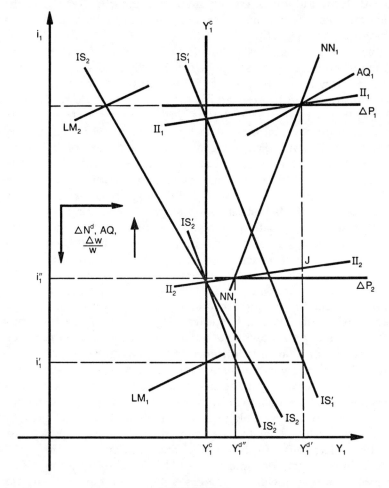

FIGURE 6–5

EXCESS DEMAND AND FISCAL POLICY

37 See footnote 14, Chapter 3, page 43.

i_1''. The effects on ΔN^d and AQ are ambiguous, contrary to conventional wisdom. Figure 6–5 illustrates this by assuming ΔN^d is unchanged and AQ rises. But with a less steep NN curve, ΔN^d would rise. Or, if the NN and AQ curves were very steep, both ΔN^d and AQ would fall. An interpretation is that actual investment rises, and this improves cost conditions; but demand conditions have worsened, and it is impossible to say which effect will dominate business hiring and output decisions. Again, what happens to unemployment is ambiguous.

To summarize: Restrictive monetary policy reduces excess demand and inflation, but hurts employment and growth. Restrictive fiscal policy reduces inflation and excess demand, but may or may not hurt employment and growth.

Once excess demand is eliminated, the effects of further doses of restrictive monetary and fiscal policy are exactly as described in Chapter 3 and section 2 of this chapter. Such continued doses of monetary restriction decrease desired and actual investment, ΔN^d, $\Delta w/w$, and AQ, and increase inflation as drawn. Continued doses of fiscal restraint lower inflation and real income, and have beneficial effects on investment, labor demand, and aggregate planned output only if the LM curve is steeper than the II, NN, and AQ curves. Perhaps this explains the transition from inflation, high growth, and positive excess demand to "stagflation"—inflation, low growth, and excess capacity. Starting with excess demand, restrictive fiscal policy may or may not hurt growth. But a combination of restrictive fiscal policy and monetary policy which keeps interest rates high or rising implies decreases in AQ and, once excess capacity is eliminated, provides a spur to further doses by causing little if any decrease in inflation. As more and more restrictive measures are taken, the economy moves from high growth and excess demand to low growth and excess capacity. (The $IS_2 - LM_2$ intersection is on ΔP_1 but has lower AQ and ΔN^d.) The transition is neither necessary nor inevitable, but arises from acceptance of the usual recommendation that inflation be stopped by tight budgets and tight money. Tight money alone is sufficient to cause the problem.

With excess demand, an alternative to either restrictive fiscal policy, restrictive monetary policy, or both is to use restrictive fiscal policy and expansionary monetary policy, or rather, restrictive fiscal policy and low interest rates. The drawbacks of restrictive fiscal policy are its possibly deleterious effects on ΔN^d and AQ, since the induced reduction in aggregate demand worsens business expectations. Raising the money supply lowers i_1, increases aggregate demand, and hence offsets the demand-reducing effects of fiscal restraint. Government might choose, for example, the point J in Figure 6–5. Here, there has been no decline in aggregate demand, and the rate of inflation is higher than it would be with fiscal restriction but no change in the money supply. Inflation, however, is lower than that implied by the ΔP_1 curve, and demand for labor and aggregate planned output are higher.

The danger, of course, is that expansionary monetary policy may more than offset fiscal policy, resulting in an increase in ΔN^d and AQ, but also in an increase in excess demand and inflation. Clearly, though, the economy is better off in all regards, save two, at point J, since ΔN^d and AQ rise and inflation falls. The two drawbacks are that excess demand is unchanged and that resources are diverted to the business sector from the public or household sectors. Households naturally want consumption as high as possible, and the public sector provides valuable services; so there are costs in diverting resources to business. But the decision to rely solely on restrictive monetary policy and not to divert any resources to the business sector can be based only on the belief that neither consumer nor government spending should be curtailed.

Indeed, where there is excess demand for output, the relevant trade is not between inflation and employment, but between nonbusiness spending and macroeconomic goals. If government is willing to use its spending and taxing powers, it can achieve low inflation, high employment, high growth, and zero excess demand for output. If there is excess demand for output, fiscal restraint diverts resources to investment and hence reduces inflation. Of course, even with zero excess demand for output, inflation may still be "too high", and employment and growth may be "unsatisfactory".[38] Government can then move down the Y_1^c curve by undertaking ever more restrictive fiscal policies while lowering the interest rate to stimulate investment demand and keep excess demand for output equal to zero. Moving down the Y_1^c curve, one encounters ΔP curves with ever lower indices of inflation, and NN and II curves with ever higher indices of labor demand, aggregate planned output, and investment. Again, the drawback is that the household and government sectors must sacrifice resources to business.

Figure 6-6 illustrates the above, arbitrarily drawing the curves NN_1 and AQ_1 so that the former intersects Y_1^c below and the latter above i_1'. Thus, with no change in monetary policy, restrictive fiscal policy generates zero excess demand for output by moving the IS_2 curve (not shown) down until it runs through i_1' on the Y_1^c curve. Investment and aggregate planned output increase, since II_2 and AQ_2 have higher indices than II_1 and AQ_1, and inflation is lower. But the demand for labor falls, since the system is above NN_1. Lowering both the IS and LM

---

38 Employment and growth could be perhaps more unsatisfactory than before the government undertook its restrictive policies, if labor demand and aggregate planned output suffer from fiscal restriction.

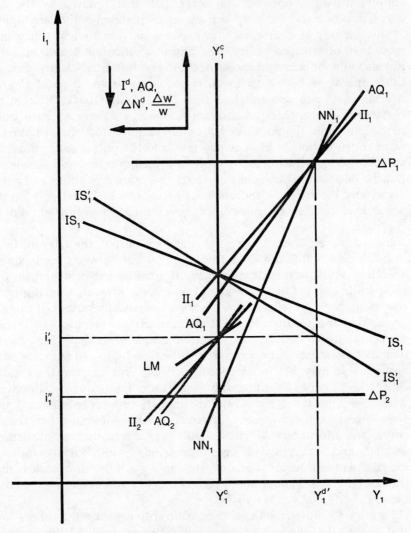

FIGURE 6-6

RESTRICTIVE FISCAL AND EXPANSIONARY MONETARY POLICY

curves along the Y_1^c curve below i_1' increases the demand for labor, desired investment, and aggregate planned output, and lowers inflation.

The present analysis, both when there is excess capacity and when there is positive excess demand for output, generates policy solutions which are sometimes at odds with current common policy prescriptions. It lays stress on the mixture of policies in a closed economy. It suggests that low interest rates are beneficial for high employment and growth and for fighting inflation in the short run.[39]

Policy recommendations often depend on knowing the positions and slopes of the IS, LM, ΔP, NN, AQ, and II curves; for a change in a single policy variable often leads to ambiguous results. For example, increasing real government spending when there is excess capacity increases inflation; but the effects on investment, aggregate planned output, and the demand for labor are unclear, depending as they do on the slope of the LM curve relative to the II, NN, and AQ curves. This suggests two considerations. The first is the usual plea for more empirical knowledge. It would be nice to know the relative slopes of the LM curve and the II, AQ, and NN curves, for example.

A second consideration is that the slope of the IS and ΔP curves may be rather similar "on the average", and the LM curve's slope may be rather close to the other three curves' "on the average". Indeed, the IS and LM curves may change their relationships to the other curves from period to period. This suggests that successful policy of either the crude, single variable variety, or the crude, conventional sort, may be very much a matter of luck. Thus, a decision to prime the pump and endure inflation may work because the LM curve happens by chance to be below the AQ curve for the relevant periods. Or a decision to use restrictive monetary policy to reduce inflation may work because by chance the IS curve has a positive slope.

Any such policies that work out could just as well have failed. While one cannot hope to escape the crowing politicians who preside over good fortune much as a sun-vain rooster, one might suppose that economists would only timidly suggest policy measures until they have worked out clearly the channels through which such measures work. The model here developed suggests some of these channels, and the policies the model suggests are different enough from the usual that conventional prescriptions are perhaps cast in doubt.

39 See footnote 1, page 87.

7 THE MODEL WITH WEALTH EFFECTS AND A BUSINESS DEMAND FOR MONEY

This chapter extends the models of Chapters 3 and 4. First, it introduces wealth effects on the household sector and then derives comparative statics results for the new system both in the case of excess capacity and in the case of positive excess aggregate demand for output. Second, it adds a business demand for money. Section 6 develops a simple micro demand for money in order to derive results from the model of the firm.

The macro comparative statics with both wealth effects and the business demand for money are virtually identical to those derived when there are wealth effects and no business demand for money. The policy implications of this extended model are little changed from those Chapter 6 derives by using the simpler models of Chapters 3 and 4. Thus, not very much is lost by using these simpler models.

7.1. The Meaning of Wealth Effects

It is difficult to put an interpretation on wealth effects. In a world of perfect certainty and perfect markets, an individual's wealth is the present value of his endowments from the present until the end of his life. Leaving such a world, there are various analogues to the meaning of wealth in the frictionless world. But any analogue is at best imprecise, if only because it is impossible to assign a unique interpretation to the rate of interest for any period.

Take future incomes, or their mathematical expectation, and discount them to find wealth, supposing the horizon is h' periods. Any discount rate used will pick up elements of uncertainty, transactions costs, and irreversibilities. For example, borrowing and lending rates differ, and the discount rate should be higher if the individual spends most of his time as a borrower. Another irreversibility is being unable to buy back for face value less principle payments a contract binding oneself to a schedule of payments. A change in tastes on the part of an individual can lead to his consuming less in every period, though he ends his life with the same net worth in either case—he need only begin to prefer those options laden with transactions costs and irreversibilities. Surely this is a diminution of wealth in any reasonable sense. Yet all opportunities stay the same. The discount rate must then be a construct which can move with no change in market rates.

Even if the market interest rate is taken as the appropriate discount rate, there is no way of knowing how future expected short rates move with a change in the current short rate. At the one extreme, they do not vary at all; and at the other, all short and long rates are equal and vary proportionately.

Consider the discounted future incomes. A change in the discount rate or a change in these incomes induces a wealth effect. Previous chapters ignored the effects of changes in wealth induced by parametric variations, save the change in current income, considering only the initial impact of such variations. It seems desirable that wealth effects not offset the initial effect on future income of a parametric change. Imagine a parametric change generates an increase in future incomes when wealth effects are ignored. Expanding the model to allow changes in wealth to affect behavior should not lead the parametric change which previously increased incomes now to diminish them. It seems silly to say that a change in a parameter increases wealth if society does a bad job predicting the effects, but decreases wealth if it does a good job.

How do expectations of future incomes change? They "should" change in the right direction—if a change ensures higher future income, the model's actors should believe this is so. But many kinds of expectations can look reasonable. For example, it may be reasonable that a change inducing higher current income also induces expectations of higher future incomes. But just as reasonably, higher income now may induce expectations of future depression. Bust does follow boom, with some evidence that policy makers see to the inevitability of it all. In the present model, many policy changes leading to a higher current income can lead to business producing less in the next period.

For simplicity, ignore any changes in future incomes beyond next period's. Further, assume that households base their expectations of future income on business's expectations. Coordination may be poor between the two sectors, but surely the household sector has some idea of what is expected by firms which it owns. And surely firms' predictions, backed by action, should be given some weight in households' estimation of future income.

Business's prediction of next period's real income is precisely aggregate planned output.[1] Thus, a parametric change which induces an increase in period 2's aggregate planned output thereby increases wealth,

---

1 Households anticipate real labor income equal to the real wage (they expect) times the actual employment expected, or $(w/P)_2^s N_2$ and (from business expectations) real nonlabor income of $[AQ_2 - (w/P)_2^d N_2^d]$, or total real income of $AQ_2 - [(w/P)_2^d N_2^d - (w/P)_2^s N_2]$. If the two sectors have approximately the same wage, price, and employment expectations, expected real income is approximately AQ_2. More importantly, if variations in the parameter α do not significantly influence $(w/P)_2^d N_2^d - (w/P)_2^s N_2$, the change in expected income with α is $\partial AQ/\partial \alpha$.

as Figure 7–1 shows. The intersection of IS_1 and LM_1 gives i'_1 and Y'_1. An increase in G, neglecting wealth effects, leads to i''_1 and Y''_1. As drawn, AQ

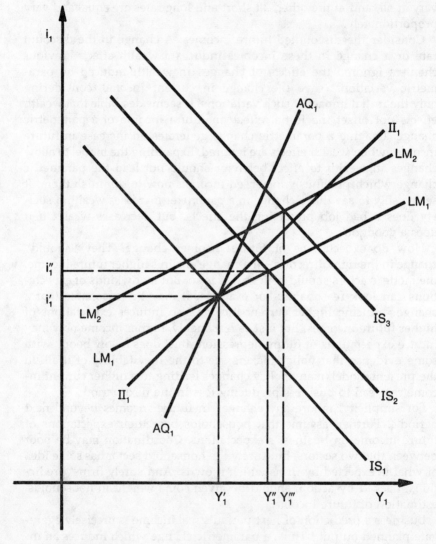

FIGURE 7–1

WEALTH EFFECTS AND AN INCREASE IN G

increases, causing a positive effect on wealth. Allowing for wealth effects shifts the IS_2 and LM_1 curves, but the new intersection must be somewhere in the angle given by IS_2 and AQ_1. Positive wealth effects shift both the IS and LM curves up.[2] But there will continue to be positive wealth effects only if the new equilibrium is to the right of AQ_1—say with IS_3 and LM_2—and this is assumed to be so.

A parametric change that affects AQ thereby induces a wealth effect. This wealth effect, in turn, leads to further shifts in the IS and LM curves. But these shifts will never, by hypothesis, reverse the change in AQ, for they themselves were induced by the change.

7.2. A Formal Definition of Wealth

Consider a formal definition of society's wealth. The definition is consistent with the preceding discussion in that it includes the discounted values of future aggregate supplies, though other definitions can also do this.[3]

Define nominal wealth, W_n, as:

$$W_n = P_1(Y_1 - I_1) - P_1 T_1 + M_1 + P_{b,1} V_1 + \sum_{t=2}^{h'} \frac{n_t(AQ_t - I_t)P_t^e - e_t T_t P_t^e}{\prod_{j=2}^{t} (1 + i_{j-1})}$$

$$= P_1(Y_1 - T_1) + M_1 + P_{b,1} V_1 + P_1 K_1 \qquad \textbf{7.2.1}$$

$$+ \sum_{t=2}^{h'} \frac{n_t[P_t^e AQ_t - P_{t-1}^e(i_{t-1} - \Delta P_{t-1}^e/P_{t-1}^e)K_t] - e_t T_t P_t^e}{\prod_{j=2}^{t} (1 + i_{j-1})}$$

where $(Y_1 - I_t)$ and $(AQ_t - I_t)$ are the net incomes business generates (the constraint alternately expressed by using the fact that I_t equals $\Delta K_t \equiv K_{t+1} - K_t$); P_1 is the current price level and P_t^e the price level expected to rule between t and $t + 1$; T_t is real net taxation expected in period t; M_1 is the money stock at time 1; V_1 is government bonds outstanding at $t = 1$, each paying one dollar interest per period, with $P_{b,1}$ their price per unit; and n_t and e_t $(t = 1, h)$ are nonnegative fractions less

---

2 See section 3 of this chapter.

3 One possibility is to give decreasing weight to future aggregate planned outputs to indicate they become more doubtful as they recede in time, or that it becomes doubtful that present members of society will live to enjoy them. The discount factor might also increase to indicate the same sort of thing and to indicate uncertainty over future rates. The opportunity cost of money services may be something less than the discount rate in recognition of money's liquidity. Other modifications are possible, but most are only more or less unsatisfactory devices for handling risk and uncertainty.

than or equal to unity.[4] The e_t are institutionally given and independent of the decisions of the actors in the model. For example, at age 65, each person now alive will receive another income tax deduction. The proportion of head taxes each pays declines as society grows. As for n_t, new workers enter the work force, and some of the aggregate planned output must go to compensate their labor.

Society makes intertemporal decisions subject to the constraint that nominal wealth, W_n, must equal the present value of nominal consumption of goods and money services, PV_{Cn}, or:

$$W_n - PV_{Cn} = 0 \qquad \textbf{7.2.2}$$

where

$$PV_{Cn} = P_1C_1 + \sum_{t=2}^{h'} \frac{C_tP_t^e + M_t i_{t-1}}{\prod_{j=2}^{t}(1 + i_{j-1})} \qquad \textbf{7.2.3}$$

and C_t is real consumption at time t, and M_t nominal cash balances held from time t to $t+1$. The expression $i_t M_{t+1}$ values money holdings during the period $t+1$ to $t+2$ at opportunity cost. There are, of course, no opportunity costs for using the services of whatever money one has on hand from $t=1$ to $t=2$—one controls flows during this first period, not the stocks with which one starts the period.

It is useful to make some substitutions into equation 7.2.2. First,

$$P_t^e = P_1 \prod_{j=2}^{t}\left[1 + \left(\frac{\Delta P}{P}\right)^e_{j-1}\right] \qquad \textbf{7.2.4}$$

$$M_t = m_t P_t \qquad \textbf{7.2.5}$$

where

$$m_t \equiv \frac{M_t}{P_t} \qquad \textbf{7.2.6}$$

4 This definition is but a step from calculating the present value of bond payments or a stream of dividends and is the natural analogue to the micro analysis of intertemporal utility maximization. Many macro discussions merely define real wealth as the sum of the capital stock, real government money, and some part of real government debt. See Jerome Stein, "Money and Capacity Growth," *Journal of Political Economy*, Vol. LXXIV (October, 1966), pp. 451–65. Equation 7.2.1 allows a firm's present value to exceed its capital stock and implicitly allows wealth to remain constant for a decrease in the stock of capital offset by an increase in the average productivity of labor. Pesek and Saving would argue that since this increases the ratio of human to nonhuman wealth, society feels less wealthy. See Boris Pesek and Thomas Saving, *Money, Wealth, and Economic Theory* (New York: Macmillan Co., 1967).

The horizon h' leaves some unanswered questions. If h' is the horizon at which the firm in Chapter 2 plans to go out of business, the value of $K_{h'}$ should be added to $AQ_{h'}$. Alternatively, h' may be so far in the future that society merely ignores possible incomes beyond it. If h' is many generations in the future, $n_{h'}$ is the nonlabor fraction of society's income and $e_{h'}$ is zero, for the dead are beyond both labor and taxation.

Then,

$$\frac{(W_n - PV_{Cn})}{P_1} = (Y_1 - I_1 - T_1 - C_1) + \left(\frac{M_1}{P_1} + \frac{P_{b,1}}{P_1}V_1\right)$$

$$- \sum_{j=2}^{h'} [C_t + m_t i_{t-1} - n_t(AQ_t - I_t) - e_t T_t] \cdot \frac{\prod_{j=2}^{t}[1 + (\Delta P/P)^e_{j-1}]}{\prod_{j=2}^{t}(1 + i_{j-1})}$$

$$= (Y_1 - T_1 - C_1) + \left(\frac{M_1}{P_1} + \frac{P_{b,1}}{P_1} + K_1\right) \qquad\qquad 7.2.7$$

$$- \sum_{j=2}^{h'} \left\{ C_t + m_t i_{t-1} - n_t \left[AQ_t - \frac{i_{t-1} - (\Delta P^e_{t-1}/P^e_{t-1})}{1 + (\Delta P^e_{t-1}/P^e_{t-1})}K_t \right] - e_t T_t \right\}$$

$$\cdot \frac{\prod_{j=2}^{t}[1 + (\Delta P/P^e_{j-1})]}{\prod_{j=2}^{t}(1 + i_{j-1})}$$

As Hicks and Leijonhufvud have made clear, the wealth effect of a parametric change in α is not a matter of finding $\partial(W_n)/\partial\alpha$ or $\partial(W_n/P)/\partial\alpha$.[5] Rather it is a matter of finding $\partial[(W_n - PV_{Cn})/P]/\partial\alpha$ while holding constant $C_t(t = 1, h)$ and $m_t(t = 2, h)$. If $\partial[(W_n - PV_{Cn})/P]/\partial\alpha$ equals zero, society can just consume exactly the same bundle as before; if it is positive, society can consume more in every period; and if it is negative, society must reduce its consumption in every period if it keeps the ratio the same between consumption in various periods.

A significant simplifying assumption is to ignore all changes in interest charges due to variations in K_2^d. Intuitively, the effect of AQ_2 must surely dominate such changes, and the ambiguity found below for $I_1^d(= K_2^d - K_1)$ makes the assumption important for ease in deriving results.

Now consider several effects on wealth. First, an increase in AQ_2 gives:

---

5 See J. R. Hicks, *Value and Capital: An Inquiry into Some Fundamental Principles of Economic Theory* (2d ed.; London: Oxford University Press, 1946), especially Chapter 14 and its Appendix B and Chapter 18. Also see Axel Leijonhufvud, *On Keynesian Economics and the Economics of Keynes: A Study in Monetary Theory* (London: Oxford University Press, 1968), Chapter 4, section 3. Notice that $(\partial W_n/P)/\partial i_1$ is negative whereas equation 7.2.9 is positive, an indication of the sophistication and power of this method relative to the usual macroeconomic effort.

$$\frac{\partial(W_n - PV_{Cn})/P_1}{\partial AQ_2} = \frac{1 + (\Delta P/P)_1^e}{(1 + i_1)} > 0 \quad (n_2 = 1) \qquad 7.2.8$$

Second, an increase in i_1, but no other short rate, yields:

$$\frac{\partial(W_n - PV_{Cn})/P_1}{\partial i_1} = \frac{1}{1 + i_1}\left(\frac{P_{b,1}\Delta B_1^d}{P_1}\right) > 0 \qquad 7.2.9$$

which is positive if private sector net bond purchases are positive.

When expected future prices rise, then the number of dollars one was saving will now be inadequate for planned future consumption. From equation 7.2.4, increases in P_1 and $(\Delta P/P)_1^e$ raise expected future prices,

$$\frac{\partial(W_n - PV_{Cn})/P_1}{\partial P_1} = \frac{-1}{P_1^2}(M_1 + P_{b,1}V_1) < 0 \qquad 7.2.10$$

and

$$\frac{\partial(W_n - PV_{Cn})/P_1}{\partial(\Delta P/P)_1^e} =$$

$$\frac{[Y_1 - I_1 - T_1 - C_1 + (M_1/P_1) + (P_b/P_1)V_1]}{1 + (\Delta P/P)_1^e} < 0. \qquad 7.2.11$$

where the expression in equation 7.2.10 is negative if the private sector holds net positive claims on the government; and the expression in equation 7.2.11 is negative if, in addition, household savings are positive. As usual,

$$1 = \frac{\partial(W_n - PV_{Cn})/P_1}{\partial Y_1} = -\frac{\partial(W_n - PV_{Cn})/P_1}{\partial T_1} \qquad (e_1 = 1)$$

Finally, suppose that all short rates are equal to each other at all times, and let i_1 rise. Then:[6]

6 See Hicks, *op. cit.*; and Leijonhufvud, *op. cit.* As these authors point out, the sign of inequality 7.2.12 depends on the intertemporal patterns of consumption relative to income. (Note that assuming all expected rates of inflation are equal generates an analogue to inequality 7.2.12 rather than inequality 7.2.11. This analogue strengthens the results of the effect of expected inflation in sections 4, 5, and 6 of this chapter.)

Note that if C_t becomes zero long before h' (current members of society die before their nonlabor income ceases) and if AQ and n are large "enough," inequality 7.2.12 is likely negative and large. This is analogous to Leijonhufvud's demonstration that Keynes' strong negative relation between i and C has a price-theoretic basis when capital is long-lived (as Keynes believed).

Pesek and Saving, *op. cit.*, derive the analogue of inequality 7.2.12 for the single individual, as Hicks did almost thirty years before. Hicks made a specific assumption about reaction times (Hicks, *op. cit.*, Chapter 18) to derive a negative relationship, while Leijonhufvud made a specific assumption about capital's longevity. Pesek and Saving, however, argue (Chapter 16) that it does not make sense to ask how i affects C^d on the aggregate level without asking why i changes—seeming to confuse the inadmissibility of asking how equilibrium price changes in a demand and supply diagram (price is not a parameter) with the perfectly good question of what is the slope of the demand curve with

$$\frac{\partial(W_n - PV_{Cn})/P_1}{\partial i} = \sum_{t=2}^{h'} [C_t + m_t i - n_t(AQ_t - I_t) - e_t T_t] \cdot$$

$$\frac{(t-1) \prod_{j=2}^{t} [1 + (\Delta P/P)^e_{j-1}]}{(1+i)^t} - \sum_{t=2}^{h'} \frac{m_t}{(1+i)^{t-1}} \gtreqless 0 \qquad \textbf{7.2.12}$$

7.3. The Consumption Function and Household Demand for Money

Changes in household consumption and hoarding depend on these partials and the market rates of transformation. Foregoing one unit of consumption now and investing the saved P_1 yields $(1 + i_1)P_1$ at the start of period 2, which is expected to buy:

$$\frac{(1 + i_1)P_1}{P_2} = \frac{1 + i_1}{1 + (\Delta P/P)^e_1} \qquad \textbf{7.3.1}$$

of consumption goods in that period. Giving up one unit of consumption now and instead accumulating P_1 in dollars yields:

$$\frac{P_1}{P_2} = \frac{1}{1 + (\Delta P/P)^e_1} \qquad \textbf{7.3.2}$$

in real balances for next period. Clearly, the rate of trade-off between consumption in period 2 and real balances in period 2 is given by:[7]

$$\frac{1 + i_1}{1 + (\Delta P/P)^e_1} \div \frac{1}{1 + (\Delta P/P)^e_1} = (1 + i_1) \qquad \textbf{7.3.3}$$

Thus, the market rates of trade-off between current consumption and future consumption depend on inflation and rate of interest. The market rate of trade-off between current consumption and future real balances depends only on inflation and not on rate of interest. Finally, the market rate of trade-off between future consumption and future real balances depends only on rate of interest, not on inflation.

respect to the price axis. Their argument seems to be similar to saying that, if society is on a given bowed-out intertemporal transformation function between C at times 1 and 2, then increases in present consumption are associated with increases in the interest rate. True, but not what is asked here, or by Hicks or Leijonhufvud.

7 If the real balances are used for buying consumption goods, the cost of tranferring wealth from period 1 to 2 in the form of real balances rather than bonds (i.e., the cost of using real balances) is i_1 in terms of period 2 consumption—hence the preceding section's use of i_t as the opportunity cost of using a dollar in period $t + 1$.

Assume all goods are superior. Then an increase in wealth, with no change in any market transformation rates, implies consumption of more real goods and money services in every period. Thus, the marginal propensity to consume out of real wealth is greater than zero and less than unity. Then,

$$C_1 = C\left[\frac{W_n}{P_1}, i, \left(\frac{\Delta P}{P}\right)_1^e, \frac{M_1}{P_1}\right]$$

$$1 > C_{W_n/P} = C_y > 0$$

$$C_i \gtreqless 0$$

$$\frac{dC_1}{di} = C_{W_n/P}\frac{\partial W_n/P}{\partial i} + C_i \gtreqless 0 \qquad\qquad \textbf{7.3.4}$$

$$C_{\Delta P^e/P} \gtreqless 0$$

$$\frac{dC_1}{d\left(\dfrac{\Delta P}{P}\right)_1^e} = C_{W_n/P}\frac{\partial W_n/P}{\partial \Delta P^e/P} + C_{\Delta P^e/P} \gtreqless 0$$

$$C_{M/P} \gtreqless 0$$

$$dC/d(M/P) = C_{W_n/P} \cdot 1 + C_{M/P} > 0$$

An increase in i makes consumption in the future relatively cheaper; so if $(W_n - PV_{Cn})/P$ were constant, current consumption would tend to decline. The partial C_i picks up not only this substitution effect but also part of the wealth effect, for PV_{Cn} also changes with an increase in i.[8] When the only rate of interest that increases is i_1, the substitution is negative but the wealth effect is positive.[9] When all short rates are equal, an increase gives many substitution effects—for all intertemporal relative prices change—and some may be positive, while the wealth effect may be positive or negative.[10]

The substitution effect of an increase in $(\Delta P/P)^e$ favors current real consumption by making it less expensive relative to all future consumption and money services. But the wealth effect is negative, so the results for C_1 are ambiguous.[11] $C_{W_n/P}\partial(W_n/P)/\partial(\Delta P/P)^e$, which is almost certainly positive, does not measure the wealth effect, for it neglects the

8 Empirical equations estimating, say, consumption demand as a function of W_n/P and i are simply misspecified. If some parameter α varies with i to keep W_n/P constant, PV_{Cn}/P may vary any way at all, depending on the α chosen. The analyst can then make C_i take on any value desired by choice of α.

9 See equation 7.2.9.

10 See Hicks, *op. cit.*; Leijonhufvud, *op. cit.*; and inequality 7.2.12.

11 See inequality 7.2.11 and footnote 3, page 111.

effect on the present value of future expenditures. Thus, the partial $C_{\Delta P^e/P}$ picks up some of the true wealth effect as well as the substitution effect and is ambiguous rather than positive.

An increase in M/P with no change in real wealth can raise or lower real consumption, depending on whether real balances were below the optimal level or not. Last period, society provided itself with the money balances to begin the current period, choosing the quantity on the basis of last period's expectations. If these expectations are wrong, society provides itself with an inoptimal quantity of real balances— members of society would have accumulated a different quantity had they known last period what they do now. Given wealth, if society has too few real balances to transact all the business it would like, an increase in real balances lowers transactions costs and increases consumption; but if society has too many real balances, an increase means it plans to convert these extra real balances into other assets; and since the process of conversion is costly, planned consumption falls. However, an increase in wealth in the form of real balances makes society better off and leads to an increase in real consumption. It is very likely that the total effect $dC/d(M/P)$ is positive, and is here assumed.

Similar to equations 7.3.4,

$$\frac{\Delta M_1^d}{P_1} = \phi\left[\frac{W_n}{P_1}, \ i, \ \left(\frac{\Delta P}{P}\right)_1^e, \ \frac{M_1}{P_1}\right]$$

$$1 > \phi\frac{W_n}{P} = \phi_y > 0$$

$$\phi_i \gtreqless 0$$

$$\frac{d(\Delta M^d/P)}{di} = \phi_{W_n/P}\frac{\partial W_n/P}{di} + \phi_i < 0 \qquad\qquad \textbf{7.3.5}$$

$$\phi_{\Delta P^e/P} \gtreqless 0$$

$$\frac{d(\Delta M^d/P)}{d(\Delta P/P)_1^e} = \phi_{W_n/P}\frac{\partial W_n/P}{\partial \Delta P^e/P} + \phi_{\Delta P^e/P} \gtreqless 0$$

$$\phi_{M/P} < 0$$

$$\frac{d(\Delta M^d/P)}{dM/P} = \phi_{W_n/P} \cdot 1 + \phi_{M/P} < 0$$

The derivatives are easily understood. Since all goods are assumed superior, the marginal propensity to consume money services out of wealth is positive and less than unity. An increase in the interest rate makes real balances relatively more expensive compared to future consumption. ϕ_i does not measure these substitution effects alone, since it also picks up the influence of i on PV_{C_n}.[12] The true wealth effect is positive if only i_1 varies, or ambiguous if all i vary. Nevertheless, assume the total effect is to reduce the flow demand for money, giving the LM curve a positive slope.

An increase in $(\Delta P/P)_1^e$ makes future real balances more expensive relative to current consumption, since giving up a unit of consumption now and accumulating dollars brings a smaller increment than before to next period's real balances. Thus, an increase in $(\Delta P/P)_1^e$ leads to substitution of current consumption for future real balances. This is reinforced by the negative effect on wealth of an increase in $(\Delta P/P)_1^e$. But it is not clear that the demand for nominal dollars falls. The question deals with the price elasticity of demand for real balances next period in terms of this period's consumption good. If this demand has unitary elasticity, the demand for nominal dollars is constant when expected inflation rises. If the demand is elastic, the quantity of dollars demanded falls; and if the demand is inelastic, the number of dollars demanded will rise. Both the wealth and substitution effects on the demand for real balances of an increase in expected inflation are negative, but these two negative effects on the demand for real balances have ambiguous effects on the current demand for nominal balances.[13]

Since an increase in wealth leads to consumption of more of each good, the flow demand falls with an increase in real balances, for some of the increase in wealth is diverted to present and future consumption.[14]

7.4. The Comparative Statics Results with Excess Capacity

The system:

$$I^d + G + C^d - Y = 0$$

$$-\frac{\Delta M^s}{P} + \phi(W_n/P, \dots) = 0 \qquad \textbf{7.4.1}$$

$$-AQ + AQ(Y^d, i - \Delta P^e/P, \dots) = 0$$

12 See footnote 8, page 116, all the comments applying here, *mutatis mutandis*. Note that if all i vary, all intertemporal relative prices change, creating many substitution effects, the net effect of which is ambiguous.

13 As footnote 6, page 114, mentions, if all expected rates of inflation are equal and vary together, the wealth effect is ambiguous—and thus the effect on money demand is ambiguous. Further, an increase changes many intertemporal relative prices, and the net result of these many substitution effects is ambiguous.

14 $\phi_{M/P}$ is negative while $C_{M/P}$ is ambiguous. The higher is M_1, the lower is $\Delta M^d/P$ to reach a given M_2^d. If M/P is "excessive," an increase lowers $\Delta M^d/P$ by raising M_1 and also by lowering M_2^d by imposing costs of rearranging wealth. If M_1 is "too small," an increase of \$1 lowers transactions costs, but not, presumably, by so much that M_2^d increases by more than \$1.

describes the economy for the case of excess capacity. As before, assume that the IS curve is less steep than the LM, and I_y is less than unity. Assume:

$$I_i + C_y \frac{\partial W_n/P}{\partial i} + C_i < 0 \qquad \textbf{7.4.2}$$

$$I_y - 1 + C_y \gtreqless 0 \qquad \textbf{7.4.3}$$

$$\phi_i + \phi_y \frac{\partial W_n/P}{\partial i} < 0 \qquad \textbf{7.4.4}$$

$$\phi_{\Delta P^e/P} + \phi_y \frac{\partial W_n/P}{\partial \Delta P^e/P} \gtreqless 0 \qquad \textbf{7.4.5}$$

Inequality 7.4.2 gives the IS curve a negative slope when inequality 7.4.3 is negative, and implies that an increase in wealth raises the IS curve. Inequality 7.4.4 gives the LM curve a positive slope and inequality 7.4.5 has strong implications about the effects of inflationary expectations.

Differentiating system 7.4.1 yields:

$$
\begin{bmatrix}
(I_y - 1 + C_y) & \left(I_i + C_i + C_y \frac{\partial W_n/P}{\partial i} \right) & C_y \frac{1 + (\Delta P/P)^e}{1 + i_1} \\[2ex]
\phi_y & \left(\phi_i + \phi_y \frac{\partial W_n/P}{\partial i} \right) & \phi_y \frac{1 + (\Delta P/P)^e}{1 + i_1} \\[2ex]
AQ_y & AQ_i & -1
\end{bmatrix}
$$

$$
\begin{bmatrix}
\dfrac{dY}{d\alpha} \\[2ex]
\dfrac{di}{d\alpha} \\[2ex]
\dfrac{dAQ}{d\alpha}
\end{bmatrix}
= -
\begin{bmatrix}
\dfrac{d(I^d + g - Y + C^d)}{d\alpha} \\[2ex]
\dfrac{d[-\Delta M^s/P + \phi\,(\cdot)]}{d\alpha} \\[2ex]
\dfrac{d[-AQ + AQ\,(\cdot)]}{d\alpha}
\end{bmatrix}
\qquad \textbf{7.4.6}
$$

$$
[D^*]
\begin{bmatrix}
dY \\
di \\
dAQ
\end{bmatrix}
= -
\begin{bmatrix}
d\alpha_1 \\
d\alpha_2 \\
d\alpha_3
\end{bmatrix}
$$

The sign of the determinant of D^* is ambiguous, but section I's assumption that wealth effects themselves never reverse the change in future income from what it is if they are ignored implies $|D^*|$ is negative. For suppose the AQ curve is steeper than the LM. Then an increase in G raises AQ in the absence of wealth effects. Introducing wealth effects should leave AQ increased. But dAQ/dG is positive in this example if and only if $|D^*|$ is negative.[15]

Table 7-1 lists the comparative statics results. The circled effects are those different from the comparable Table 3-2, but the differences are easily understood. First, an increase in T lowers wealth, shifting both the IS and LM curves down, so i_1 falls, but Y_1 can rise or fall as the LM shifts down more or less relative to the IS curve.

Increases in ΔM^s or decreases in ΔM^d have unambiguous effects on i_1 in Chapter 3 but do not have here when the IS curve has a negative slope, as Figure 7-2 illustrates. The LM curve shifts from LM_1 to LM_2, the intersection of LM_2 and IS_1 at Y_1'' increasing AQ. This increase induces a rise in both IS_1 and LM_2, and the new $IS-LM$ intersection may be above or below i_1'.[16] Then i_1 may rise enough (say, i_1'') to reduce I^d at the new higher Y_1. Since the change in $\Delta P/P$ due to these monetary

TABLE 7-1

SUMMARY OF COMPARATIVE STATICS RESULTS WITH WEALTH EFFECTS: EXCESS CAPACITY

Parameters	Variables								
	Y	i_1	i_1	$\dfrac{\Delta P}{P}$	$\dfrac{\Delta P}{P}$	AQ	ΔN^d	$\dfrac{\Delta w}{w}$	I^d
		$\dfrac{di}{dY}(IS) < 0$	$\dfrac{di}{dY}(IS) > 0$	$\dfrac{di}{dY}(IS) < 0$	$\dfrac{di}{dY}(IS) > 0$				
G	$+$	$+$	$+$	$+$	$+$	?	?	?	?
T	Ⓐ	$-$	$-$	$-$	$-$	?	?	?	?
APS	$-$	$-$	$-$	$-$	$-$	?	?	?	?
ΔM^s	$+$	(?)	$+$	(?)	$+$	$+$	$+$	$+$	(?)
M	$+$	(?)	$+$	(?)	$+$	(?)	(?)	(?)	(?)
ΔM^d	$-$	(?)	$-$	(?)	$-$	$-$	$-$	$-$	(?)
Nu	(?)	$+$	$+$	(?)	?	$+$	$+$	?	(?)
$\dfrac{\Delta P}{P} e$	(?)	(?)	(?)	(?)	(?)	(?)	(?)	(?)	(?)
$\dfrac{w}{P}$	(?)	$-$	$-$	(?)	?	$-$	$-$	$-$	(?)
$\dfrac{\Delta w}{w} e$	(?)	$-$	$-$	(?)	?	$-$	$-$	?	(?)

15 In conjunction with inequalities 7.4.2 through 7.4.5, this sign of $|D^*|$ is sufficient to derive many of the unambiguous results in Table 7-1. The only other needed assumption is that interest effects on consumption are not "too" positive, as footnote 17, page 122, discusses.

16 This ambiguity follows directly from the ambiguity of the minor $|D_{22}^*|$, whose sign is determinate only when the IS curve has a positive slope.

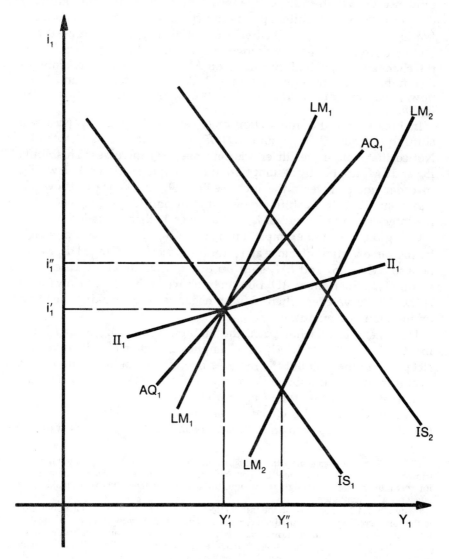

FIGURE 7-2

WEALTH EFFECTS, ΔM^s, AND EXCESS CAPACITY

changes depends only on the change in i_1, the effects on inflation are now ambiguous when $di/dy(IS)$ is negative.

An increase in M shifts the LM down by reducing the flow demand for money but shifts the IS curve up by increasing wealth. The initial impact on i_1 is ambiguous if the IS curve's slope is negative, and the influence of wealth-induced changes only adds to the ambiguity. If the IS curve initially shifts up very much relative to the LM, and if the LM is steeper than the AQ curve, the initial effect may, but need not, be to reduce AQ. Thus, the change in i_1 is ambiguous, and hence so is the change in $\Delta P/P$; and the effects on ΔN^d, $\Delta w/w$, and I^d are ambiguous in the same way as the effect on AQ. Changes in Nu, w/P, and $\Delta w/w$ now have ambiguous effects on Y_1 and $\Delta P/P$. Consider an increase in Nu.

In Figure 7–3, the intersection of IS_1 and LM_1 gives Y_1'. Nu rises, shifting II_1 and AQ_1 to II_2 and AQ_2. IS_1 rises to IS_2, as in Chapter 3.[17] Notice that before wealth effects impinge, AQ increases. This shifts IS_2 and LM_1 up; but by assumption, the new intersection is below AQ_2 in order not to reverse the increase in AQ, and hence is above IS_2 and below AQ_2. If IS_2 shifts up only slightly and LM_1 shifts "enough," the intersection of IS_3 and LM_2 is at a lower Y_1 than initially.

Going on with the example, an increase in Nu raises ΔP_1 and AQ_1 by the same vertical distance at Y_1'; for if AQ were unchanged, P_2 would be also. When IS_2 and LM_1 shift up through wealth effects, the intersection is to the right of AQ_2 but can be above (point H) or below (point J) the ΔP_2 curve even when IS has a negative slope, making the effect on inflation ambiguous.

This example also illustrates the ambiguity of changes in I^d. The intersection of IS_2 and LM_1 at Y_1'' implies a higher I^d if II curves are steeper than the LM. But the increase in AQ leads both IS_2 and LM_1 to rise. If they intersect above II_2, at say point H, I^d falls. In any case, the wealth effects obscure the results for I^d.

Finally, consider the effects of an increase in expected inflation, $(\Delta P/P)^e$. As long as such an increase has an indeterminate effect on the

---

17 The IS_1 curve rises exactly the same distance as the II_1 curve if and only if the consumption function is completely interest-inelastic. Since the effect on consumption of interest rate changes is ambiguous in sign, the text understates the case of making the effect on $\Delta P/P$ ambiguous.

Inequality 7.4.2 is negative, so the initial effect is to shift IS_1 up. The usual assumption is that an increase in i_1 when all short rates are equal and vary together has a negative effect on current consumption, making inequality 7.4.2 larger in absolute value than I_i and implying the IS shifts up a smaller distance than the II curve. See J. R. Hicks, *Value and Capital: An Inquiry into Some Fundamental Principles of Economic Theory* (2d ed.; London: Oxford University Press, 1946); Axel Leijonhufvud, *On Keynesian Economics and the Economics of Keynes: A Study in Monetary Theory* (London: Oxford University Press, 1968); Boris Pesek and Thomas Saving, *Money, Wealth, and Economic Theory* (New York: Macmillan Co., 1967). Footnote 6, page 114, provided plausible reasons why such an interest effect may be negative. But if the effect is positive, the IS curve may conceivably shift up more than the AQ curve; and if the LM is steeper than the AQ curve, the initial effect may be a decrease in AQ. However, section 1's assumption that taking account of discounted future incomes does not reverse the direction of change in these incomes from when they are ignored rules this out. Thus, the interest effect on consumption cannot be "too" positive. Note that the assumption that the interest effect on consumption is not "too" positive continues to ensure that the II is steeper than the IS curve, even when the latter has a positive slope.

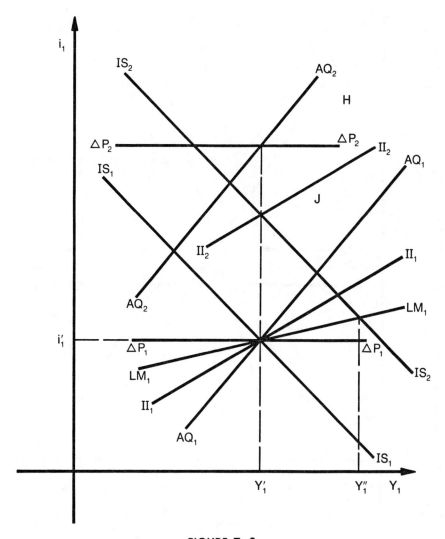

FIGURE 7-3

WEALTH EFFECTS, N_u, AND EXCESS CAPACITY

demand for money, as in inequality 7.4.5, the LM may initially shift up or down, and the effects on aggregate demand and aggregate supply are indeterminate. Figure 7-4 illustrates this by considering only the initial impact and by assuming that an increase in $(\Delta P/P)^e$ shifts the IS curve up.[18] The LM curve may rise far enough to lower Y_1 and AQ

---

18 An increase in $(\Delta P/P)^e$ has a positive effect on I^d but an ambiguous effect on C^d. As drawn, the effect on C^d may be negative or positive. If negative, the effect does not overwhelm the influence on I^d; and if positive, it does not overcome the larger influence of $(\Delta P/P)^e$ on AQ than on I^d (see Appendix 1, section 7) to shift the IS up more than the AQ curve.

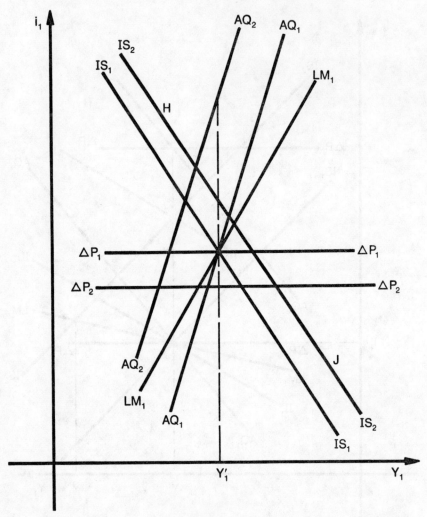

FIGURE 7-4

WEALTH EFFECTS, EXPECTED INFLATION, AND EXCESS CAPACITY

(point H). If the LM curve initially falls, Y_1^d and AQ rise. The effect on i_1 can go either way, as long as the IS curve has a negative slope. This also renders ambiguous the effect of expected on actual inflation. The initial ΔP_1 curve shifts down to ΔP_2; but since i_1 can fall, it may fall far enough to reduce $\Delta P/P$ (point J). The effects on ΔN^d, $\Delta w/w$, and I^d are ambiguous in the same way as AQ. The secondary shifts caused by changes in AQ just intensify the ambiguity.

Note that Chapter 3 found no such ambiguity, and in fact derived the commonly accepted proposition that expected inflation encourages actual inflation. Section 6 of this chapter shows that an increase in the expected rate of inflation increases business' demand for money, making the ambiguous effects on Y_1 and AQ more likely but making less likely the chance that an increase in expected inflation reduces actual inflation. In Chapter 3, an increase in $(\Delta P/P)^e$ raised $\Delta P/P$ but offered partial compensation by increasing I^d, AQ, and ΔN^d. Here, if an increase in $(\Delta P/P)^e$ raises the demand for money, due to business demand, perhaps, $\Delta P/P$ likely rises but may well be accompanied by even larger excess capacity and decreased I^d, AQ, and ΔN^d. Thus, though $(\Delta P/P)^e$ cannot be unambiguously shown to fuel inflation, such anticipations seem capable of encouraging "stagflation"—high inflation but low growth, weak labor demand, and excess capacity.

7.5. Comparative Statics Results with Positive Excess Aggregate Demand

It is more difficult to derive results for this model when there is positive excess demand for output. Assume the money and bond markets continue to clear in the sense defined in Chapter 4, and that all the disappointed excess demand in the product market is borne by business, thus allowing continued use of the LM curve.[19]

To illustrate the derivation of comparative statics results and the associated difficulties, Figure 7-5 uses the graphical apparatus of Chapter 4, sections 6 and 7, to consider an increase in G. The intersection of LM_1 and Y_1^c locates the market rate of interest, i_1'. The intersection of IS_1 and Y_1^c locates ρ', the rate of interest at which the product market would clear. IS_1' shows aggregate demand $Y_1^{d'}$ for the interest rate i_1'. Excess demand for output equals $Y_1^{d'} - Y_1^c$. When the business sector decides on, say, AQ, it does so on the basis of aggregate demand and actual investment, with i_1' irrelevant as long as business is rationed. However, there is some rate r' such that business demands at $(r', Y_1^{d'})$ exactly what actual investment is at $(i_1', Y_1^{d'})$. Business decides on AQ as though it were at $(r', Y_1^{d'})$. The II_1 curve through $(r', Y_1^{d'})$ runs through (ρ', Y_1^c) if actual investment is the same at (ρ', Y_1^c) and $(i_1', Y_1^{d'})$.[20]

An increase in G raises IS_1 and IS_1' to IS_2 and IS_2' in Figure 7-5. Neglect wealth effects for a moment. This, then, leads to a new equilibrium with the same market rate i_1', the higher level of aggregate demand, $Y_1^{d''}$, and new higher ρ and r. Specifically, r'' is at the intersection of $Y_1^{d''}$ and II_2. This intersection may be above or below the AQ_1 curve, causing negative or positive wealth effects. These effects, in turn, cause

19 See especially sections 2, 3, and 4 of Chapter 4.
20 This is so only if consumption is perfectly interest-inelastic. The results of the analysis do not require this assumption, but the graphical interpretation is much aided by it.

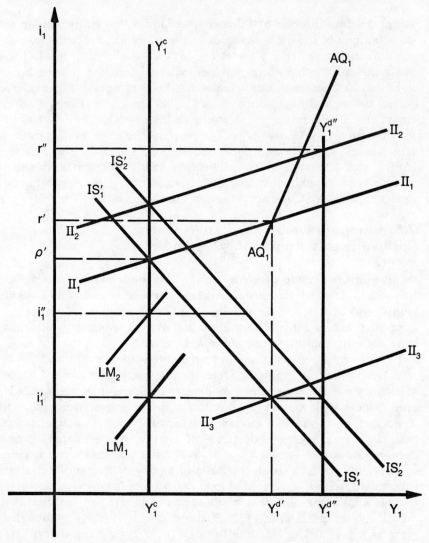

FIGURE 7-5

WEALTH EFFECTS, G, AND EXCESS DEMAND

changes in $Y_1^{d''}$. But by assumption they do not reverse the change in AQ.

This last assumption is crucial for comparative statics results, as continuing the example of an increase in G shows. The first question is whether the initial impact is to increase or decrease AQ. It is positive as drawn if the slope of the AQ curve, $\frac{di}{dY}(AQ)$, is greater than the ratio of the change in r over the change in Y_1^d. The change in Y_1^d is the upward shift in the IS' curve, $\frac{di}{dG}(IS')$, times the inverse of (minus) the slope

of the IS' curve, $-1/\frac{di}{dY}(IS')$, or is $-\frac{di}{dG}(IS')/\frac{di}{dY}(IS')$. The increase in

r equals the increase in ρ—the upward shift of the IS' curve, $\frac{di}{dG}(IS')$—

plus the slope of the II curve, $\frac{di}{dY}(II)$, times the change in Y, $-\frac{di}{dG}(IS')/$

$\frac{di}{dY}(IS')$. The ratio of the change in r to the change in Y_1^d is:[21]

$$\frac{dr}{dG}\bigg/\frac{dY}{dG} = \frac{dr}{dY} = \frac{\dfrac{di}{dG}(IS') - \dfrac{di}{dY}(II)\,\dfrac{di}{dG}(IS')\bigg/\dfrac{di}{dY}(IS')}{-\dfrac{di}{dG}(IS')\bigg/\dfrac{di}{dY}(IS')}$$ 7.5.1

$$= \frac{di}{dY}(II) - \frac{di}{dY}(IS') > 0$$

and the condition for the increase in G to have a positive initial effect on AQ is:

$$\frac{di}{dY}(AQ) > \frac{di}{dY}(II) - \frac{di}{dY}(IS')$$ 7.5.2

By assumption, if inequality 7.5.2 is positive, the ultimate effect on AQ of an increase in G must be positive.

The system:

$$-Y_1^d + I^d(Y_1^d, i_1, \ldots) + G + C^d(Y_1^c + \ldots, i_1, \ldots) = 0 = IS'(\cdot)$$

$$-\frac{\Delta M^s}{P} + \phi(Y_1^c + \ldots, i_1, \ldots) = 0 = LM(\cdot)$$ 7.5.3

$$-Y_1^c + I^d(Y_1^d, r, \ldots) + G + C^d(Y_1^c + \ldots, i_1) = 0 = r(\cdot)$$

$$-AQ + AQ(Y_1^d, r, \ldots) = 0 = \overline{AQ}(\cdot)$$

determines Y_1^d, i_1, r, and AQ.[22] Shocking system 7.5.3 by varying some parameter α yields:

21 Recall from footnote 20, page 125, this $di/dY(IS')$ neglects the effects of interest changes on consumption.

22 ρ is only an intermediate variable used in graphical analysis. Business makes its decisions on the basis of Y_1^d and the rate of interest r that would make business desire exactly the actual investment it can do (see Appendix 1, section 3), and households make their decisions on the basis of i_1 and AQ.

$$
\begin{bmatrix}
-1 + I_y & I_i + C_i + C_y\dfrac{\partial W_n/P}{\partial i} & 0 & C_y\dfrac{1 + (\Delta P/P)^e}{1 + i_1} \\[2ex]
0 & \phi_i + \phi_y\dfrac{\partial W_n/P}{\partial i} & 0 & \phi_y\dfrac{1 + (\Delta P/P)^e}{1 + i_1} \\[2ex]
I_y & C_i + C_y\dfrac{\partial W_n/P}{\partial i} & I_i & C_y\dfrac{1 + (\Delta P/P)^e}{1 + i_1} \\[2ex]
AQ_y & 0 & AQ_i & -1
\end{bmatrix}
\begin{bmatrix}
\dfrac{dY^d}{d\alpha} \\[2ex]
\dfrac{di_1}{d\alpha} \\[2ex]
\dfrac{dr}{d\alpha} \\[2ex]
\dfrac{dAQ}{d\alpha}
\end{bmatrix}
$$

7.5.4

$$
= - \begin{bmatrix}
\dfrac{dIS'(\cdot)}{d\alpha} \\[2ex]
\dfrac{dLM(\cdot)}{d\alpha} \\[2ex]
\dfrac{dr(\cdot)}{d\alpha} \\[2ex]
\dfrac{dAQ}{d\alpha}
\end{bmatrix}
\qquad [D^{**}] \qquad
\begin{bmatrix}
dY \\[2ex]
di \\[2ex]
dr \\[2ex]
dAQ
\end{bmatrix}
= - \begin{bmatrix}
d\alpha_1 \\[2ex]
d\alpha_2 \\[2ex]
d\alpha_3 \\[2ex]
d\alpha_4
\end{bmatrix}
$$

The sign of the determinant of D^{**} is ambiguous. But,

$$
\frac{dAQ}{dG} = \frac{-1}{|D^{**}|}\left(\phi_i + \phi_y\frac{\partial W_n/P}{\partial i}\right)I_i AQ_i
$$

7.5.5

$$
\cdot\left\{\frac{di}{dY}(AQ) - \left[\frac{di}{dY}(II) - \frac{di}{dY}(IS')\right]\right\}
$$

Whether or not inequality 7.5.2 holds, $|D^{**}|$ must be positive if wealth effects are not to reverse the initial change in AQ. Consequently, the assumption that wealth effects do not reverse the initial impact on AQ implies $|D^{**}|$ is positive.[23]

Table 7-2 presents the comparative statics results under the assumption that it makes no difference whether a derivative is evaluated at i_1 or r, at Y_1^d or Y_1^c. Those circled are different from the results in Table 4-1, and the differences are interesting and easily explained.

23 The sign of $|D^{**}|$ is sufficient to deduce most of the comparative statics results. Many of the ambiguous results—for example, dAQ/dG and dY/dNu—become determinate if inequality 7.5.2 is assumed and also $di/dAQ(IS) > di/dAQ(LM)$, though there is no very good reason for making either. Indeed, whether inequality 7.5.2 holds is one of several important empirical questions posed for the first time in this book.

TABLE 7-2

SUMMARY OF COMPARATIVE STATICS RESULTS
WITH WEALTH EFFECTS: EXCESS DEMAND

Parameters	Y^d	i	$\dfrac{\Delta P}{P}$	AQ	ΔN^d	$\dfrac{\Delta w}{w}$	I^d
			Variables				
G	$+$	Ⓩ	$+$	?	?	?	Ⓩ
T	Ⓩ	Ⓩ	?	?	?	?	Ⓩ
APS	$-$	Ⓩ	$-$	?	?	?	Ⓩ
ΔM^s	$+$	Ⓩ	$+$	$+$	$+$	$+$	Ⓩ
M	$+$	Ⓩ	$+$	Ⓩ	Ⓩ	Ⓩ	Ⓩ
ΔM^d	$-$	Ⓩ	$-$	$-$	$-$	$-$	Ⓩ
Nu	Ⓩ	⊕	?	$+$	$+$	?	Ⓩ
$\dfrac{\Delta P}{P}e$	Ⓩ	Ⓩ	Ⓩ	Ⓩ	Ⓩ	Ⓩ	Ⓩ
$\dfrac{w}{P}$	Ⓩ	⊖	?	$-$	$-$	$-$	Ⓩ
$\dfrac{\Delta w}{w}e$	Ⓩ	⊖	?	$-$	$-$	?	Ⓩ

A rise in G (or a fall in the average propensity to save, APS) may induce either a positive or negative wealth effect (AQ initially rises or falls), causing the LM curve to rise and increase i_1, as in Figure 7-5, or to fall and lower i_1; while in Chapter 4, the LM curve and i_1 were unchanged. The final (i_1, Y_1^d) point may be above or below II_3, making the effect on I^d ambiguous.

An increase in ΔM^s or a decrease in ΔM^d shifts the LM curve down initially to LM_2 in Figure 7-6, inducing a positive wealth effect that shifts both the IS and LM curves up. The change in i_1 depends on whether LM rises to LM_3 or LM_4. The final (i_1, Y_1^d) point may or may not be above II_2, making the effect on I^d ambiguous.

An increase in T initially lowers both the IS' curve, as with a decrease in G, and the LM curve, as with an increase in ΔM^s. Since the effects on Y_1^d and $\Delta P/P$ of a decrease in G and an increase in ΔM^s are in opposite directions (both effects on i_1 and I^d are ambiguous), the effects of an increase in T are ambiguous.[24] An increase in M shifts the IS' curve up, as does an increase in G, and the LM curve down, as does an increase in ΔM^s. Only the positive effects on aggregate demand and inflation are necessarily in the same direction for both influences.

24 If $Cy/\phi y$ is large (small) enough, the results are the same as a decrease in G (increase in ΔM^s); and since the ratio is unknown, the results are ambiguous.

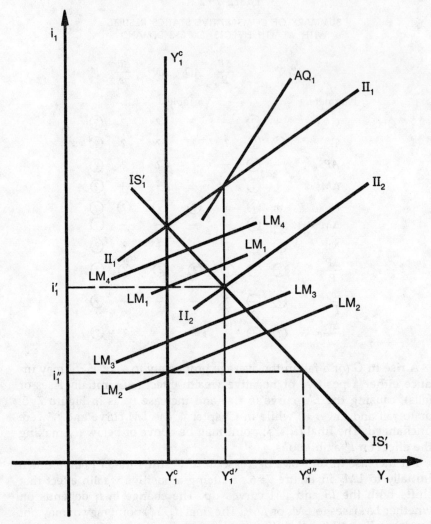

FIGURE 7–6

WEALTH EFFECTS, ΔM^s, AND EXCESS DEMAND

In Chapter 4, increases in Nu or decreases in w/P or $(\Delta w/w)^e$ caused an increase in Y_1^d and no change in i_1, since ΔM^s, ΔM^d, and M are unchanged. Initially, the IS_1', II_1, and AQ_1 curves rise, as in Figure 7–7. With an unchanged i_1, there is an increase in AQ—since the AQ shifts up more than the II curve, $(Y_1^{d''}, r'')$ is below AQ_2—and a positive wealth effect.[25] Both the IS and LM curves rise in response to the increase in

25 See Chapter 3, section 4, and Appendix 1, section 7.

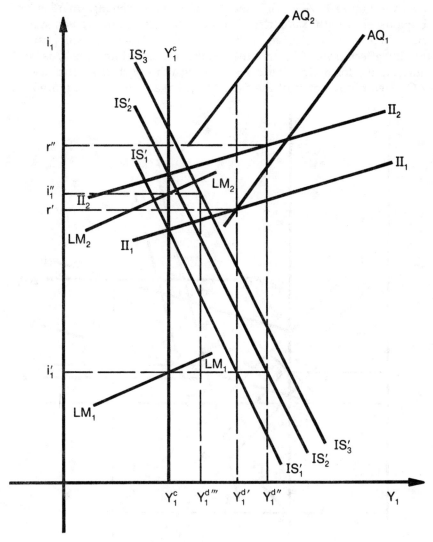

FIGURE 7-7

WEALTH EFFECTS, Nu, AND EXCESS DEMAND

wealth, the LM rise implying i rises. The new intersection of the IS' curve and the i_1 line must be below AQ_2 to keep the wealth effect positive and above IS_2' since a positive wealth effect shifts IS_2' up; but Y_1^d may fall to $Y_1^{d'''}$, as in Figure 7-7.

An increase in $(\Delta P/P)^e$ has ambiguous effects because both the IS and LM curves can initially shift. If there is no initial shift in the LM curve, $di/d(\Delta P/P)^e(LM) = 0$, the analysis is similar to an increase in

Nu as in Figure 7-7—i_1, *AQ*, and ΔN^d rise and the change in Y_1^d is ambiguous—but with $\Delta w/w$ rising because N_2^d rises along a given supply curve here. If the *LM* curve initially shifts down, there is a still positive wealth effect from *AQ*, and the results are as before save i_1 is now ambiguous; for as in Figure 7-6, the wealth effect of an increase in *AQ* may or may not shift the final *LM* curve above LM_1 in Figure 7-8.

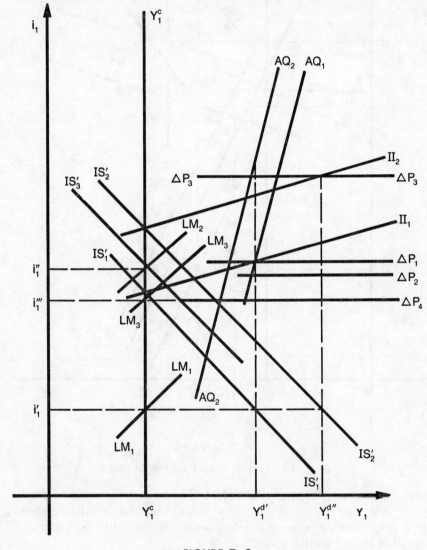

FIGURE 7-8

WEALTH EFFECTS, EXPECTED INFLATION, AND EXCESS DEMAND

However, LM_1 may initially shift up. As section 3 of this chapter showed, an increase in $(\Delta P/P)^e$ both reduces society's wealth and causes a substitution effect away from real balances; but the demand for nominal balances may rise, shifting LM_1 up. If the initial impact on AQ is still positive, the results are as before; but if it is negative, the results for ΔN^d and $\Delta w/w$ are ambiguous.

Chapter 4 derived the intuitively plausible result that inflationary expectations contribute to actual inflation, or an increase in $(\Delta P/P)^e$ increases $\Delta P/P$, with the partial compensation that AQ and ΔN^d increase. When the effect of $(\Delta P/P)^e$ on wealth is recognized, the result becomes ambiguous. The initial ΔP_1 shifts down to ΔP_2. With no wealth effects on LM or through AQ, the index on the higher curve ΔP_3 gives inflation. However, if LM initially shifts up, the intial impact on AQ may be negative (on IS_2' at, say, i_1'') and the final position may be $Y_1^{d'''}$, IS_3', i_1''', and ΔP_4 with reduced inflation. Intuitively, the only offset to business's inflationary expectations, disregarding negligible induced changes in actual investment, is a reduction in demand. The LM curve may shift up far enough to cause such an increase in i_1 that I^d falls enough to lower Y_1^d and more than offset inflationary expectations. Notice that this result depends upon increases in $(\Delta P/P)^e$ increasing ΔM^d, for the next section derives such a relationship for the business sector.

In both Chapter 3 (excess capacity) and Chapter 4 (excess demand), an increase in $(\Delta P/P)^e$ raised actual inflation and increased AQ and ΔN^d. This section and the preceding section find no such unambiguous relationship between $(\Delta P/P)^e$ and $\Delta P/P$. However, when $(\Delta P/P)^e$ positively affects ΔM^d, as it does business's demand for money in the next section, increases in $(\Delta P/P)^e$ may stimulate $\Delta P/P$ and at the same time are quite capable of adversely affecting AQ and ΔN^d, allowing the realistic possibility of inflationary expectations fueling inflation in a stagnating economy.

Finally, I^d is hopelessly ambiguous, for while wealth-induced changes in the IS and LM curves do not reverse the direction of change of AQ, this does not preserve the direction of change of I^d.

7.6. Business Demand for Money

Introducing a simple type of business demand for money does little to the results, but lends completeness. A new item, transactions costs, TC_t, is used here to help explain the demand for money. These costs are those associated with arranging transactions and depend on the value of transactions and the stock of money on hand to facilitate transactions. For example, if a firm buys a unit of capital in period t, it can pay cash on delivery—if it has the cash. If the firm does not have money on hand, it must go to the time and trouble of arranging some sort of trade credit. The cost of the trade credit and the cost of arranging it both enter TC_t.

The model adopts the simple hypothesis that the money balances which a business desires to hold during any period t depend only on the *scale* of its operations and the rate of interest. *Scale* of operations means precisely its revenue, P_tQ_t. This hypothesis eliminates the possibility that the demand for money might make the system of marginal conditions indecomposable. Chapter 3 pointed out that business's flow demand for money in period $t-1$ depended on the stock of money it desired to hold at time t. These desired holdings presumably depend on anticipated revenue in period t, P_tQ_t, and the uses of this revenue— investment, $P_{K,t}\Delta K_t$, the wage bill, w_tN_t, accumulation of money, ΔMB_t^d, the costs incurred in making transactions, TC_t, and a residual item, dividends, making the uses of revenue equal to revenue.

It is quite possible that the usefulness of cash balances depends on the distribution of revenue among the different uses in addition to this total value (equals total revenue). If the usefulness of cash balances depends on whether a dollar of revenue is spent on investment or otherwise used, then business's desired money holdings in period t, MB_t^d, depends on ΔK_t^d. This in turn means that decisions about MB_t^d depend on the stock of capital desired for period $t+1$, since:

$$\Delta K_t^d \equiv K_{t+1}^d - K_t \qquad \text{7.6.1}$$

With this dependence, the system of necessary conditions is no longer decomposable, and there is little hope of deriving comparative statics results.

To avoid this disaster, assume that there is no need to distinguish among the uses to which revenue is put, and only the total amount of uses matters. Total revenue must equal the total value of the uses of revenue, and thus MB_t^d depends on P_tQ_t which depends only on K_t and N_t. The system is again decomposable.

To make the argument more formal, let the costs of making transactions in period t, TC_t, be a function of revenue and the cash balances held in that period, the value of investment, the wage bill, transactions costs themselves, the accumulation of money, ΔMB_t, and dividend payments, DIV_t. Since dividends in period t are:

$$DIV_t = P_tQ_t - w_tN_t - P_{K,t}\Delta K_t - TC_t - \Delta MB_t \qquad \text{7.6.2}$$

TC_t can be written as:

$$TC_t = \overline{TC}_t(P_tQ_t, MB_t, P_{K,t}\Delta K_t, w_tN_t, TC_t, \Delta MB_t) \qquad \text{7.6.3}$$

Expressing TC_t as a function of the other variables,

$$TC_t = \overline{\overline{TC}}_t(P_t Q_t, MB_t, P_{K,t}\Delta K_t, w_t N_t, \Delta MB_t) \qquad \textbf{7.6.4}$$

The present value of the stream of dividends is:

$$P_1 Q_1 - w_1 N_1 - P_{K,1}(K_2 - K_1) - TC_1 - (MB_2 - MB_1)$$

$$+ \sum_{t=2}^{h} \frac{1}{\displaystyle\prod_{j=2}^{t}(1 + i_{j-1})} \cdot [P_t Q_t - w_t N_t - P_{K,t}(K_{t+1} - K_t) \qquad \textbf{7.6.5}$$

$$- TC_t - (MB_{t+1} - MB_t)]$$

where h is the firm's horizon. The firm desires to maximize this expression subject to the conditions that K_1, N_1, and MB_1 are given and that:

$$K_{h+1} = 0 \qquad \textbf{7.6.6}$$

since the firm goes out of business after period h. The necessary conditions for an interior maximum are:

$$MRP_{K,t}\left(1 - \frac{\partial TC_t}{\partial P_t Q_t}\right) + P_{K,t}\left(1 + \frac{\partial TC_t}{\partial P_{K,t}\Delta K_t}\right)$$

$$-(1 + i_{t-1})P_{K,t-1}\left(1 - \frac{\partial TC_{t-1}}{\partial P_{K,t-1}\Delta K_{t-1}}\right) = 0$$

$$(t = 2,h) \qquad \textbf{7.6.7}$$

$$\frac{\partial TC_t}{\partial \Delta MB_t}\left(1 - \frac{\partial TC_t}{\partial MB_t}\right) - (1 + i_{t-1})\left(1 - \frac{\partial TC_{t-1}}{\partial \Delta MB_{t-1}}\right) = 0$$

$$MRP_{N,t}\left(1 - \frac{\partial TC_t}{\partial P_t Q_t}\right) - MFC_{N,t}\left(1 + \frac{\partial TC_t}{\partial w_t N_t}\right) = 0$$

Now, if three equations are to depend only on K_t, N_t, and MB_t, in order to solve for these variables alone,

$$\frac{\partial TC_t}{\partial P_t Q_t}, \ \frac{\partial TC_t}{\partial P_{K,t}\Delta K_t}, \ \frac{\partial TC_{t-1}}{\partial P_{K,t-1}\Delta K_{t-1}}, \ \frac{\partial TC_t}{\partial w_t N_t},$$

$$\frac{\partial TC_t}{\partial \Delta MB_t}, \ \frac{\partial TC_t}{\partial MB_t}, \ \text{and} \ \frac{\partial TC_{t-1}}{\partial \Delta MB_{t-1}}$$

must not depend on:

$$P_{K,t}\Delta K_t, \ P_{K,t-1}\Delta K_{t-1}, \ \Delta MB_t, \ \text{or} \ \Delta MB_{t-1}$$

for,

$$\Delta K_t \equiv K_{t+1} - K_t, \ \Delta K_{t-1} \equiv K_t - K_{t-1}$$

$$\Delta MB_t \equiv MB_{t+1} - MB_t, \ \Delta MB_{t-1} \equiv MB_t - MB_{t-1}$$

7.6.8

One way of ensuring decomposibility is to assume that a dollar of income influences transactions costs the same way no matter how it is used.[26] Thus, assume:

$$TC_t = TC_t^*(P_tQ_t, MB_t, w_tN_t + P_{K,t}\Delta K_t + \Delta MB_t + TC_t + DIV_t)$$

$$(t = 1,h) \qquad \textbf{7.6.9}$$

$$= TC_t^*(P_tQ_t, MB_t, P_tQ_t)$$

Transactions costs in any period depend on the revenue in that period, the stock of money with which the firm begins the period, and the sum of the values of the different uses to which the revenue is put, the latter condition being equal to revenue itself.

Equation 7.6.9 can be rewritten as:

$$TC_t = TC_t(P_tQ_t, M_t) \qquad (t = 1,h) \qquad \textbf{7.6.10}$$

Let transactions costs increase with the scale of the operation, P_tQ_t, and increase at an ever increasing rate, so:

$$\frac{\partial TC_t}{\partial P_tQ_t}, \ \frac{\partial^2 TC_t}{\partial P_tQ_t^2} > 0 \qquad \textbf{7.6.11}$$

Assume an increase in the firm's initial money holdings diminishes transactions costs, but further increases in MB_t reduce TC_t at a diminishing rate, and a given increase in P_tQ_t produces a smaller increase in transactions costs the larger is MB_t, or:

$$\frac{\partial TC_t}{\partial MB_t} < 0$$

$$\frac{\partial^2 TC_t}{\partial MB_t^2} > 0$$

$$\textbf{7.6.12}$$

$$\frac{\partial^2 TC_t}{\partial P_tQ_t\partial MB_t} = \frac{\partial^2 TC_t}{\partial MB_t\partial P_tQ_t} < 0$$

26 Another way is to assume TC_t is linear in $(P_{K,t}\Delta K_t, \Delta MB_t)$ $(t = 1, h)$.

Inequalities 7.6.11 and 7.6.12 are intuitively plausible. Transactions costs are expected to increase with the scale of operations. The firm makes the cheaper transactions first, so increases in the scale of the operation confront it with ever more costly transactions. Holding another dollar at the start of the period saves the firm from some costly transactions, but the next dollar the firm has is used on less costly transactions and hence saves the firm less than the first dollar did. Increasing the scale of operations, and hence transactions, increases transactions costs less, the larger are money holdings.

Figure 7–9 illustrates these relationships. An increase in revenue and its uses from OA to OB increases costs from OH to OE. If MB is OG instead of OF, the same increase from OA to OB brings an increase in transactions costs of $OD - OJ$, where JD is less than HE. Finally, changes in MB reduce TC; but although FG equals RS, UV exceeds WZ.

The necessary conditions equations 7.6.7 now reduce to:

$$MRP_{K,t}\left(1 - \frac{\partial TC_t}{\partial P_t Q_t}\right) - P_{K,t-1}\left(i_{t-1} - \frac{\Delta P^e_{K,t-1}}{P_{K,t-1}}\right) = 0$$

$$MRP_{N,t}\left(1 - \frac{\partial TC_t}{\partial P_t Q_t}\right) - MFC_{N,t} = 0, \quad (t = 2,h) \quad \textbf{7.6.13}$$

$$\left(1 - \frac{\partial TC_t}{\partial MB_t}\right) - (1 + i_{t-1}) = 0$$

Appendix 1 shows that the functions describing wage and price changes, and desired investment, hiring, and future aggregate supply have exactly the same arguments and qualitative properties as those used earlier in this chapter. Thus, the apparatus of IS, IS', II, AQ, ΔP, and NN curves can be used as before. To help establish the LM curve, this section concentrates on the demand for money on the part of business. The new LM curve has exactly the properties of the one developed earlier in this chapter. Thus the system with business demand for money gives qualitative results identical to those derived with only wealth effects because all functions have the same qualitative reactions to parameters as before.

From equations 7.6.13,

$$\left(1 - \frac{\partial TC_t}{\partial MB_t}\right) - (1 + i_{t-1}) = 0 \qquad \textbf{7.6.14}$$

can be rewritten as:

$$\frac{\partial TC_t}{\partial MB_t} = -i_{t-1} \qquad \textbf{7.6.15}$$

Equation 7.6.15 says that if the firm is maximizing wealth, the decrease in transactions costs due to holding one more dollar must equal the

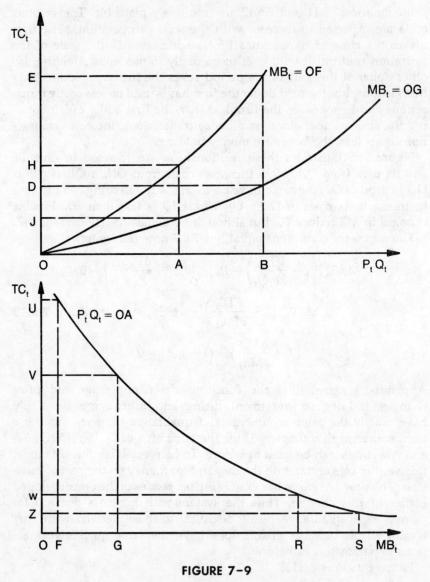

FIGURE 7-9

TRANSACTIONS COSTS OF THE FIRM

interest foregone. This relation determines MB_{t+1}^d as a function of $(P_{t+1}Q_{t+1})$ and i_t, and thus ΔMB_t^d as a function of $(P_{t+1}Q_{t+1})$, i_t, and MB_t. From equation 7.6.15,

$$\frac{dMB_t}{dP_tQ_t} = -\frac{\partial^2 TC_t/\partial MB_t\partial P_tQ_t}{\partial^2 TC_t/\partial MB_t^2} \qquad 7.6.16$$

and is positive from inequality 7.6.12. Again from equation 7.6.15 and inequality 7.6.12,

$$\frac{dMB_t}{di_{t-1}} = -\frac{1}{\partial^2 TC_t/\partial MB_t^2} < 0 \qquad \textbf{7.6.17}$$

Thus, the individual firm's money demand function is of the form:

$$MB_t = MB_t(P_t Q_t, i_{t-1}), \frac{\partial MB_t}{\partial P_t Q_t} > 0, \frac{\partial MB_t}{\partial i_{t-1}} < 0 \qquad \textbf{7.6.18}$$

These micro functions for period 1 can be aggregated by writing:

$$MB_2^d = B\phi^*(P_2 AQ_1, i_1) = B\phi^*[(1 + \Delta P_1/P_1) P_1 AQ_1, i_1]; \qquad \textbf{7.6.19}$$

$$B\phi^*_{P_2 AQ_1} > 0, B\phi^*_{i_1} < 0$$

where AQ_1 tells, from the point of view of period 1, the aggregate output business plans for period 2.[27] Similar to Chapter 2, inflation, $\Delta P/P$, depends on the position of expected demand curves. Thus, given AQ, $\Delta P/P$ varies positively with Y^d and $(\Delta P/P)^e$ and, given Y^d and $(\Delta P/P)^e$, depends only—and negatively—on AQ. As long as firms operate in the elastic regions of demand curves, as a wealth-maximizing monopolist always tries to do, an increase in AQ raises revenue. Thus,

$$\frac{\Delta P}{P} = f^*\left(Y^d, \frac{\Delta P}{P}e, AQ\right); f_y^*, f_{\Delta P^e/P}^* > 0; f_{AQ}^* < 0$$

$$\frac{\partial(1 + \Delta P_1/P_1) P_1 AQ_1}{\partial AQ_1} = f_{AQ}^* P_1 AQ_1 + \left(1 + \frac{\Delta P_1}{P_1}\right) P_1 > 0 \qquad \textbf{7.6.20}$$

Assuming $B\phi^*$ is homogeneous of degree one in price,[28]

$$\frac{MB_2^d - MB_1}{P_1} = \frac{P_1(1 + \Delta P_1/P)B\phi^*(AQ_1, i_1) - MB_1}{P_1} \qquad \textbf{7.6.21}$$

or

$$\frac{\Delta MB^d}{P} = B\phi\left(AQ, i_1, Y_1^d, \frac{\Delta P}{P}e, \frac{MB}{P}\right) \qquad \textbf{7.6.22}$$

$$B\phi_{AQ}, B\phi_{(\Delta P/P)^e}, B\phi_y > 0; B\phi_i, B\phi_{MB/P} < 0$$

---

27 Assume transactions costs are intra-business sector flows, so they are not counted in AQ which includes only final goods and services. An increase in the difficulty of making transactions shows up as a downward shift in the aggregate production function; for with given N and K, more resources are devoted to intrasector transactions, and Y is consequently smaller.

28 This assumption is not crucial. It merely makes the function more tractable.

Comparing the money demand function of the household and business sectors, the essay has derived:

$$sgn(B\phi_{AQ}) = sgn(\phi_{AQ}) > 0$$

$$B\phi_y > 0, \phi_y \geq 0 \text{ as } Y^d \gtrless Y \qquad \textbf{7.6.23}$$

$$sgn(B\phi_{MB/P}) = sgn(\phi_{MH/P}) < 0$$

where MH/P is the household sector's initial supply of real balances. $B\phi_y$ differs in sign from ϕ_y only when $Y^d > Y$ and does not significantly affect section 5's ambiguity:

$$sgn(B\phi_i) = sgn(\phi_i) < 0 \qquad \textbf{7.6.24}$$

where an increase in the interest rate reduces the household sector's flow demand for money by assumption, but the result is derived for the business sector. Thus, confidence that the LM curve has a positive slope—the assumption common everywhere—is strengthened.

Further,

$$B\phi_{(\Delta P/P)^e} > 0 \qquad \textbf{7.6.25}$$

while:

$$\phi_{\Delta(P/P)^e} \gtreqless 0 \qquad \textbf{7.6.26}$$

Sections 4 and 5 of this chapter point out that the effects of an increase in expected inflation on the system are totally ambiguous as long as such an increase has ambiguous effects on the demand for money. However, if $(\Delta P/P)^e$ affects money demand positively, it is likely that an increase that raises actual inflation will also reduce AQ and ΔN^d, producing "stagflation." While there are no a priori grounds for assuming that the effect on the household sector can or cannot be positive, by derivation, an increase in expected inflation increases business demand for money (see equation 7.6.22). Taking the demand for money for both sectors together, an increase in expected inflation will quite possibly lead to an increase in the demand for money, thus enhancing the possibility that expected inflation will produce stagflation.

Combining the two sectors' money demands barely alters the form of the aggregate demand function for money. Virtually all the partial derivatives of the household and business sectors' money demand functions agree in sign, but while some of the partials of the household money demand function are merely assumed to have the conventional signs, often these signs are derived for the business money demand function.

Positive excess aggregate demand for output implies some form of rationing to allocate the given or capacity level of output. Chapter 4 pointed out that the usual *LM* curve assumes there is no rationing. Chapters 4 and 6 continued to use the conventional *LM* curve by assuming that the household and government sectors were not subject to rationing and that only these sectors held and supplied money. These assumptions left the excess demand for money unaffected, and hence the same *LM* curve could be used.[29]

With a business demand for money, the excess demand for money is inextricably linked to the rationing process; for some sector is affected by rationing, and each sector either demands or supplies money. Nonetheless, continue to assume that the full burden of rationing falls on the business sector and that both the household and government sectors can buy all the output they demand. Thus, rationing does not influence households' money demand and government's money supply, and analysis can continue to use precisely the same household money demand function as before. This assumption is further simplifying by the fact that rationing affects business's demand for money only indirectly through AQ. For the purposes of business's money demand, it does not matter whether AQ is based on actual investment less than desired investment or actual equal to desired investment. Whether there is rationing or not, the business money demand function is equation 7.6.22. Thus, since rationing does not affect household money demand, total money demand is simply the sum of the usual household money demand function and equation 7.6.22. Row 2 in system 7.5.4 simply has $B\phi_y$ added to the first element (this is the only element whose sign changes), $B\phi_i$ added to the second element, and $B\phi_{AQ}$ added to the fourth element.

Changing the rationing scheme so it affects housholds and government would very likely alter the total excess demand for money equation. At many points, all analysis needs, though, is some excess demand function when there is rationing. The assumption that government and households are not rationed has simplicity, but removing this assumption is unlikely to introduce drastic changes in comparative statics.[30]

---

29 As pointed out, especially in Appendix 2, these are special assumptions; but the analysis and its results are not dreadfully dependent on them. That is, there is some *LM* curve for any given rationing scheme, and only the existence of an *LM* curve is needed for some results. Results which conceivably vary with the rationing scheme are, in fact, unlikely to do so.

30 See Appendix 2. The assumption sidesteps the question of how the *LM* curve changes with varying rationing schemes, but this issue is quite tangential.

7.7. Policy Implications of The Extended Model

The policy implications of this model are not too different from those of the model with no wealth effects or business demand for money. Consider the two "hard" cases of Chapter 6: the case of excess capacity, inflation, unemployment, and slow growth; and the case of positive excess aggregate demand, inflation, unemployment, and slow growth. In each case, the unorthodox policy prescriptions remain the same, recommending restrictive fiscal policy (or not too expansionary fiscal policy) and expansionary monetary policy. Expansionary monetary policy is to be interpreted here as low interest rates.

Introducing wealth variables and a business demand for money increases the ambiguity of the effects of some policy variables. Consider the case of excess capacity. Suppose the AQ is steeper than the LM curve. In such a case as that of Chapter 3, increases in G or decreases in T increase AQ, for only the IS curve shifts with these parameters, tracing out the LM curve. In the more sophisticated model with wealth effects and a business demand for money, an increase in G increases AQ if the AQ curve is steeper than the LM; but a decrease in T has ambiguous effects on AQ (see Table 7-1). These asymmetrical effects arise because the money demand function does not depend on G, but now does depend on T, since taxes subtract from wealth and the demand for money depends on wealth.[31]

Another case of ambiguity is the effect on the rate of interest of an increase in the flow supply of money. In the simpler model with excess capacity, such increases trace out the IS curve; so the rate of interest falls, assuming the IS curve has a negative slope. Now, increases in ΔM^s shift the LM curve to the right, and this rightward shift induces an increase in AQ and hence in wealth. This increase in wealth increases consumption demand and the demand for money; so both the IS and LM curves shift up, and their intersection may be at a new higher rate of interest.

Nevertheless, the policy results of Chapter 6 can be derived here again, for the most part. The easiest approach is to allow the monetary

---

31 Notice the asymmetry of treatment between G and T. Here changes in government spending per se do not affect household behavior, while changes in taxation to finance this expenditure do. It can be argued that increases in G should make society feel wealthier, since it now has the benefit of some government goods or services. See Martin J. Bailey, *National Income and the Price Level: A Study in Macroeconomic Theory* (2d ed.; New York: McGraw-Hill Book Co., 1971), Chapter 10, for wholehearted advocacy of this view. But this increase in government spending may have effects one way or another. If government now provides real goods that members of society would have bought, there should be substitution towards money services if T is unchanged. However, provision of more national defense may make each person feel better off, with no a priori bias in favor of more current goods or money services. With more defense, each person sees his budget constraint unchanged, and there is no way to predict how this changes his utility function and hence his purchasing pattern.

authority to control the rate of interest, circumventing the ambiguous effects of a change of ΔM^s.

Consider a policy designed to increase income, reduce excess capacity, lower inflation, and raise both the rate of growth and the demand for labor. The initial equilibrium in Figure 7–10 is $(i_1' Y_1')$. (The *LM* curve is not drawn.) The indices on the curves NN_1, AQ_1, and ΔP_1 give, respectively, business's desired change in employment, its aggregate planned output, and the rate at which prices rise. Lowering i_1 to,

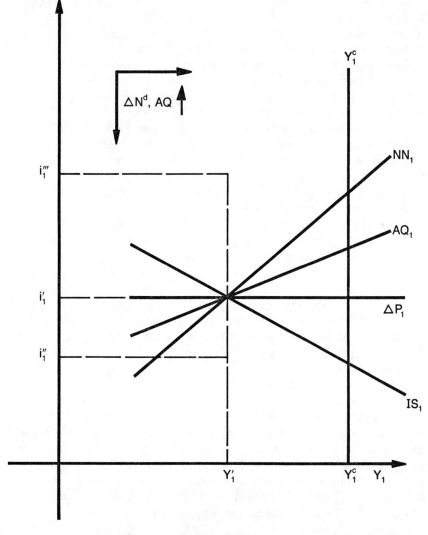

FIGURE 7–10

WEALTH EFFECTS, EXCESS CAPACITY, AND POLICY

say, i_1''', and holding Y_1 constant at Y_1' raises AQ and ΔN^d and lowers inflation. To hold Y_1 at Y_1' when lowering the interest rate, the government must increase taxation or cut its spending to lower the IS curve; for the induced increase in AQ shifts the IS curve to the right, so the decrease in the interest rate moves the system down an IS curve which is moving to the right. But government need not keep income at Y_1' to reduce inflation. It can allow income to rise up to Y_1^c and still have lower inflation because Y_1 does not affect inflation. The higher is Y_1, the more stimulated are AQ and labor demand.

High interest rates remain inimical to the policy goals of low inflation, high employment, and fast growth. Consider holding income at Y_1' and increasing the interest rate to i_1'''. This increases inflation and reduces growth and employment. If expansionary fiscal policy is not used to keep Y_1 at Y_1', income falls; and this reduces growth and employment even more, while increasing excess capacity.[32]

Given i_1, restrictive fiscal policy has no effect per se on inflation but harms growth and labor demand. Hold i_1 at i_1' and reduce G or increase T. The IS curve shifts leftward, reducing AQ and ΔN^d. The fall in AQ induces a further leftward shift in IS. Inflation is unchanged, since Y_1 affects it only when aggregate demand exceeds capacity. Thus, even with wealth effects and a business demand for money, high interest rates stimulate inflation; and the combination of restrictive monetary and fiscal policy increases excess capacity, lowers real income, hurts growth and the demand for labor, and stimulates inflation.

Wealth effects and a business demand for money do not seriously affect Chapter 6's policy conclusions for the case of positive excess aggregate demand for output. There, an increase in the rate of interest lowered aggregate demand, making business expect worse conditions than otherwise and thus decreasing AQ, ΔN^d, excess demand for output, and inflation. Restrictive fiscal policy decreased both inflation and excess demand for output. The effect on AQ and ΔN^d depended on the steepness of the initial AQ and NN curves. The same qualitative results hold with wealth effects.

In Figure 7–11, the IS' curve determines aggregate demand as a function of the rate of interest without household multiplier effects. Chapters 4 and 6 argued that increases in aggregate demand stimulate increases in investment demand, thus increasing aggregate demand even more in a typical multiplier process. Since real income and not aggregate demand influences household behavior, increases in aggregate demand unaccompanied by increases in real income do not stimulate household multiplier reactions. With i_1 equal to i_1', aggregate demand is $Y_1^{d'}$. Excess demand for output equals $Y_1^{d'} - Y_1^c$, where Y_1^c is

32 Wealth effects reinforce any restrictive fiscal policy when that policy induces a decrease in AQ.

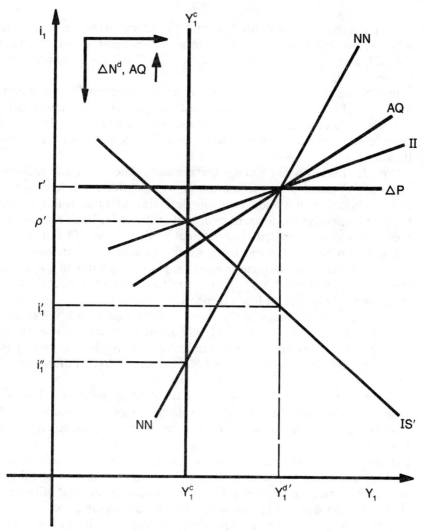

FIGURE 7-11

WEALTH EFFECTS, EXCESS DEMAND, AND POLICY

capacity output for period 1. Output is rationed and business does not get all the investment goods it would like. The curve II_1 in Figure 7-11 is chosen because its index indicates the amount business does get. II_1 shows combinations of aggregate demand and interest that make the business sector desire just the investment it can carry out, given the excess demand and the rationing. Thus if the interest rate is ρ', it desires to invest at $Y_1^{c'}$ the actual amount it is investing.[33]

---

[33] The II_1 curve may or may not intersect the Y_1^c curve just where the IS' curve does, depending on the interest elasticity of consumption demand. See section 5 of this chapter.

Decisions on AQ and ΔN^d depend on actual investment, not on whether rationing or the firm's choice determines the level.[34] Thus, the NN_1 and AQ_1 curves through II_1 at $(r', Y_1^{d'})$ tell the economy's decisions on AQ and ΔN^d.

In Chapter 6, increases in i_1 move along the given IS' curve and lower Y_1^d. This lower Y_1^d moves leftward along the II_1 curve, encountering NN, AQ, and ΔP curves with lower and lower indices. Thus, increases in i_1 reduce growth, labor demand, excess demand, and inflation.

Wealth effects do not change these results. The lower AQ reduces aggregate demand even more through wealth effects, reinforcing the initial effects. Households consume less due to this wealth effect, thereby increasing the amount of output left over for business investment. This increase in actual investment tends to raise AQ, but not by enough to return to the old level; for the decline in AQ induced the increase in actual investment in the first place. Consequently, even in this more sophisticated model, raising i_1 decreases inflation at the cost of damaging growth and labor demand.

Restrictive fiscal policy shifts the IS' curve downward. Given the rate of interest, aggregate demand falls, reducing inflation. The effects on AQ and ΔN^d are ambiguous as in the simpler model, depending as before on the slopes of the AQ and NN curves relative to the slopes of the IS' and II curves.[35]

In the extended model, if restrictive fiscal policy reduces AQ, it decreases wealth, thereby reducing consumption and increasing actual investment. This rise in actual investment increases AQ, so AQ does not fall as far as it would if consumption were unchanged. But if restrictive fiscal policy causes a rise in AQ, it then causes a wealth effect leading to more consumption. Higher consumption lowers actual investment, thereby dampening the increase in AQ, but not offsetting it; for the increase in AQ causes the increase in consumption.

In any case, policy recommendations are the same in this more sophisticated model as in the simpler. Restrictive monetary policy alone, reducing aggregate demand with high interest rates, reduces inflation and excess demand, but at a high cost in growth and employment demand. Restrictive fiscal policy alone reduces inflation and excess demand, but may harm growth and labor demand. A combination of restrictive monetary and fiscal policy reduces inflation and excess demand, but very likely causes adverse effects on growth and labor demand since the fiscal policy may harm these and the monetary policy certainly will.

---

34 Appendix 1 demonstrates this rigorously.

35 See Chapters 4 and 6 and section 5 of this chapter which develop these results and relationships in much detail.

A combination of restrictive fiscal policy and expansionary monetary policy, in the sense of low interest rates, decreases inflation and excess demand and raises growth and labor demand. In Figure 7–11, let fiscal policy lower the IS' curve until it intersects the Y_1^c curve below the NN_1 — Y_1^c intersection at i_1''. If the monetary authority chooses the rate of interest given by the IS' and Y_1^c curves' new intersection, then the system clearly enjoys larger labor demand and aggregate supply, zero excess demand, and lower inflation than initially. As in the simpler model, the cost of ensuring high growth and labor demand is making fiscal policy more restrictive than otherwise; for lowering the IS' curve means reducing G or increasing T, thus harming the household sector. The government could just raise i_1 to ρ', reducing inflation and setting excess demand equal to zero, but hurting growth and labor demand severely.

Thus, the model with wealth effects and a business demand for money gives the same policy recommendations as the simpler model.

8

A TWO-SECTOR VERSION OF THE SIMPLE MACRO MODEL

Macro models are useful because they reduce the complexity of more detailed descriptions of the world to a level where there are clear analytical results. However, because of this simplification, there always remains the question of whether the definite analytical results vanish in more complex models. In particular, definite policy implications are desiderata, but they must not depend "too" strongly on the model's simplifications.

8.1. Introduction

One kind of simplification is aggregation. While one-sector models dominate theoretical macroeconomics, the implications of two-sector models are becoming better known. In growth theory, in monetary theory, and in general disequilibrium theory, research on two-sector models has often yielded richer implications than has research on one-sector models.[1]

This chapter extends the basic one-sector model by sketching some of the policy implications of broadening the analysis to two sectors. This extension enriches the model and leads to more finely detailed policy recommendations, but does not change the basic indictments of current theoretical models and policy making.

Chapters 3 and 4 discussed the only two possible cases: (1) aggregate demand less than or equal to capacity, and (2) aggregate demand greater than capacity. With two sectors, there are four possible cases:

---

1 F. Hahn and R. C. O. Matthews, "The Theory of Economic Growth: A Survey," *Surveys of Economic Theory* (London: Macmillan & Co., 1966), II, are a source of early two-sector growth models. A major insight of this research is the capital-intensity condition for stability. William C. Brainard and James Tobin, "Pitfalls in Financial Model Building," *American Economic Review*, Vol LVIII (May, 1968), pp. 99–122, state clearly that financial policy has real effects by affecting the yield on capital goods. While not a new insight, it is often lost to sight. Axel Leijonhufvud, *On Keynesian Economics and the Economics of Keynes: A Study in Monetary Theory* (London: Oxford University Press, 1968), discusses general disequilibrium systems in terms of a two-sector model and shows that many results and insights cannot be understood in terms of a one-sector model.

(1) demand less than or equal to the capacity in both sectors; (2) consumer good demand greater than the capacity of that sector, and investment demand less than or equal to the capacity of that sector; (3) demand for consumer goods less than or equal to the capacity of that sector, and investment demand greater than capacity; and (4) demand greater than capacity in both sectors. Intuitively, the first and last are the most interesting cases, and this chapter considers only these.

8.2. Variations in Government Spending
—Excess Capacity in Both Sectors

In case (1), *IS* and *LM* curves formally similar to the others in this essay can be used, and this facilitates analysis. This cannot be done in many two-sector models, for these models allow the relative price of the outputs to vary. Here all prices are assumed constant during the period of analysis, so the relative price is also constant.[2]

Consider the *LM* curve of Chapter 3. If desired money holdings depend on real income and not its composition, extending the model to two sectors does not affect the *LM* curve.

The *IS* curve is the locus of (i_1, Y_1) points where:

$$-Y_1 + C_{pri}^d(Y_1 - T) + C_G^d + \frac{P_K}{P}I_{pri}^d + \frac{P_K}{P}I_G^d = 0 \qquad 8.2.1$$

holds, with C_{pri}^d and C_G^d being, respectively, private and government demand for consumer goods; I_{pri}^d and I_G^d being private and government demand for investment goods; and P_K/P being the relative price of capital goods in terms of consumer goods. Assume C_G^d and I_G^d are exogenous, and as before the private demand for consumer goods depends only on real disposable income in terms of consumer goods. This leaves the private demand for investment goods to be discussed.

Business demand for investment goods is made up of the capital goods sector's demand, I_{cap}^d, and the consumer goods sector's demand, I_{con}^d. The capital goods sector's demand, in sketch form, follows. Similar to Chapter 2, the capital goods sector's demand for investment depends on the demand it faces for its output (total investment demand, equal to $I_{pri}^d + I_G^d$), the expected real rate of interest in terms of capital goods, $i_1 - (\Delta P_K/P_K)^e$, the average rate at which producers expect their rivals to raise prices, $(\Delta P_K/P_K)^e$, the real wage rate in terms of capital goods, w/P_K, the rate at which rivals are expected to raise wages, $\Delta w^e/w$, and the aggregate percentage rate of unemployment, Nu. Then, I_{cap}^d is:

---

2 The period of analysis is the length of time over which the wealth-maximizing firms do not change prices. See Chapter 5, especially sections 1 and 3.

$$I_{cap}^d = \bar{I}_{cap}\left[I_{pri}^d + I_G^d, i - \frac{\Delta P_K}{P_K}e, \frac{\Delta P_K}{P_K}e, \frac{w}{P_K}\left(1 + \frac{\Delta w}{w}e\right), Nu\right] \quad \textbf{8.2.2}$$

But, since:

$$I_{pri}^d \equiv I_{cap}^d + I_{con}^d \qquad\qquad \textbf{8.2.3}$$

$$I_{cap}^d = \bar{I}_{cap}(I_{cap}^d + I_{con}^d + I_G^d, \dots) \qquad\qquad \textbf{8.2.4}$$

or rewriting,

$$I_{cap}^d = I_{cap}(I_{con}^d + I_G^d, \dots) \qquad\qquad \textbf{8.2.5}$$

The consumer goods sector's demand for investment depends on the demand it faces (total consumer good demand, equal to $C_{pri}^d + C_G^d$), the real implicit rental rate of capital services in terms of consumer goods,

$$\frac{P_K}{P}\left(i_1 - \frac{\Delta P_K}{P_K}e\right)$$

the rate at which the average producer expects his rivals to raise prices, $\Delta P^e/P$, the real wage rate in terms of consumer goods, w/P, the expected rate of rivals' wage increases, $\Delta w^e/w$, and the aggregate percentage rate of unemployment, Nu. Thus,

$$I_{con}^d = I_{con}\left[C_{pri}^d + C_{G'}^d \frac{P_K}{P}\left(i - \frac{\Delta P_K}{P_K}e\right), \frac{\Delta P}{P}e, \frac{w}{P}\left(1 + \frac{\Delta w}{w}e\right), Nu\right] \quad \textbf{8.2.6}$$

and considering the private demand for consumers goods,

$$I_{con}^d = I_{con}[C(Y - T) + C_{G'}^d \dots] \qquad\qquad \textbf{8.2.7}$$

Now, substituting equation 8.2.7 into equation 8.2.5,

$$I_{cap}^d = I_{cap}\{I_{con}[C(Y - T) + C_{G'}^d \dots] + I_{G'}^d \dots\} \qquad \textbf{8.2.8}$$

Finally, from equation 8.2.3, I_{pri}^d is the sum of equation 8.2.7 and equation 8.2.8, and the only endogenous variables affecting I_{pri}^d are Y_1 and i_1. Thus, the equation 8.2.1 of the *IS* curve has two endogenous variables, i_1 and Y_1, and many exogenous variables.[3]

Consider the case where there is excess capacity in both industries. As long as:

---

3 Notice that no distinction is made between the two sectors' expectations of the rate of wage increases, $(\Delta w/w)^e$. This could easily be done being merely a matter of notation, but the implications of such a distinction are not used here, and so it is omitted.

$$\frac{di}{dY}(IS) < \frac{di}{dY}(LM) \qquad\qquad \textbf{8.2.9}$$

any change in G ($= C_G^d + (P_K/P)I_G^d$), T, or ΔM^s has the same qualitative effects on Y_1 and i_1 as before. However, a given change in G has quantitatively different effects on $\Delta P/P$, the rate of change of the Consumer Price Index (CPI), depending on what this expenditure goes for. Now, the increase in i_1 may be greater when C_G^d rises than when I_G^d rises, and it is very likely that C^d will rise more if C_G^d rather than I_G^d increases.[4] Continuing to assume that per unit costs are constant and changes in aggregate demand induce isoelastic (to the price axis) shifts in the demand curves firms expect, the effect of G on CPI depends only on the increase in i_1.[5] Thus, a given fiscal jolt affects the CPI more if it is completely devoted to the consumer goods sector and if and only if this increases i_1 more than it devotes the spending to I_G^d. In any case, the CPI is almost certainly differentially affected by the two kinds of expenditures.

8.3. The Consumer Price Index and Monetary and Fiscal Policies

Continue to assume excess capacity in both industries. Another problem involving the CPI is the efficiency of various anti-inflation policies. Suppose the government wants to lower $\Delta P/P$ and to this end is willing to have Y_1 fall by, say, 1. Suppose there are two ways to accomplish this, by reducing the money supply or by reducing C_G^d (changes in I_G^d are not considered in this problem). The reduction in Y_1 has no effect per se on inflation. But reducing the money supply to reduce aggregate demand raises i_1 if the IS curve has a negative slope, and the effect of this is to raise the rate of increase of the CPI. However, whatever the slope of the IS curve, lowering C_G^d lowers i_1, hence reducing $\Delta P/P$. Given equation 8.2.9, a one unit decline in Y_1 is accompanied by a greater fall in i_1 with a decrease in C_G^d even if the IS curve's slope is positive.

The interpretation of this exercise is interesting. Many income-expenditure theories ignore the question of the optimal anti-inflationary mixture of monetary and fiscal policy in the closed economy. This view can be summarized by the conventional Keynesian fixed wage

---

4 A one dollar increase in G raises i_1 more, the same, or less when devoted to C_G^d rather than I_G^d as:

$$\frac{\partial I_{con}}{\partial C^d} \gtrless \frac{\partial I_{cap}/\partial I^d}{\left(1 + \frac{\partial I_{cap}}{\partial I^d}\right)\frac{P_K}{P}}$$

5 See Chapter 2, sections 3 and 4; and Appendix 1, section 5.

analysis.[6] The sequence of conclusions on anti-inflationary policy is as follows. Given w equals $\overline{w}$, the real wage rate determines current price and, given past prices, the rate of inflation between last period and this. The real wage rate is determined by the quantity of labor used, since the system is always on the labor demand curve. The number of workers used is always just sufficient to produce output exactly equal to aggregate demand. Going through the logical sequence in the opposite direction, there is a one-to-one relationship between aggregate demand and inflation—determining aggregate demand determines inflation, and this is so whether monetary or fiscal policy determines aggregate demand.

When this naive view is applied to policy making, the results may be disastrous. The politically sensitive price index is the CPI. Since fiscal policy can sometimes be politically impractical, decision makers may fall back on monetary policy. The rate of growth of the money supply is restrained, raising the cost of using capital, severely depressing the capital goods sector, and decreasing real income. Multiplier effects lower the demand for consumer goods (government's object all along); but since the typical firm sees isoelastic demand shifts, the only effect of the fall in demand is to hurt growth and labor demand, leaving $\Delta P/P$ unaffected. Further, the increase in i_1 may raise costs, thus *raising* $\Delta P/P$ and harming growth and planned hiring.[7]

While this example violently disputes the standard income-expenditure analysis, it is very similar in spirit to the one-sector model in Chapter 3. It would be necessary to analyze every conceivable problem with both a one- and two-sector model to find the degree of distortion involved in going to the one-sector model. But here is a case where the distortion is relatively unimportant.

8.4. Positive Excess Aggregate Demand in Both Sectors

The second analytical situation this chapter considers is demand greater than capacity in each sector. The vehicle is to consider the relative effects of monetary and fiscal policy on consumer goods price inflation and on changes in employment.

The analysis is not so different from that of the one-sector case. Since each industry is at capacity and both prices are given,

$$Y_1 = Y_{con}^c + \frac{P_K}{P} Y_{cap}^c \qquad \qquad 8.4.1$$

6 See, in particular, Warren Smith, "A Graphical Exposition of the Complete Keynesian System," *Southern Economic Journal*, Vol. XXIII (October, 1956), pp. 115–125.

7 Note that, as throughout, this is a short-run policy discussion. In the long run, the rate of growth of the money supply determines inflation. See footnote 18, Chapter 6, page 92.

where Y^c_{cap} and Y^c_{con} are, respectively, capacity output in the capital and consumer goods sectors. Thus, Y_1 is given; and from the *LM* equation, ΔM_s determines i_1, with i_1 varying inversely with ΔM^s.

Restrictive monetary policy raises the interest rate.[8] On the cost side, this has no effect on either sector.[9] When investment demand exceeds the capacity of that industry, rationing must begin. It does no good to say that using capital goods is now more expensive if they can be had—they cannot be had. All that happens is unfulfilled investment demand falls.

In the consumer sector, demand has not changed; for it depends only on the unchanging Y_1 (consumer demand depends on real income, not aggregate demand) and the unchanged C^d_G.[10] Thus neither cost nor demand for consumer goods varies, implying there is no effect on consumer goods prices, and hence none on the CPI, and no effect on the sector's demand for hiring, and hence none on its rate of increase of wages.

In the capital goods sector, the rise in i_1 has no effect on the cost side. On the demand side, the rise in i_1 reduces the partially unfulfilled investment demand of both sectors; and there are demand multiplier effects.[11] In the end, each capital good producer finds his costs unchanged but his expected demand lower. When producers cannot buy all the capital they want, per unit costs are rising, not constant.[12] Consequently, the rate of inflation of capital goods prices falls, as does this sector's demand for labor, and hence its rate of wage increases.[13] For both sectors together, a decrease in ΔM^s has no effect on the CPI's rate of increase and lowers aggregate desired hiring.

The analysis of the effect on actual employment and unemployment is somewhat complex. The rate of wage increase in the consumer goods sector is unaffected, but falls in the capital goods sector. Thus, the average rate of wage increases falls. But the rate of change in the CPI is unaffected, so next period's average real wage rate, in terms of the relevant consumer good, is lower. Thus, the quantity of labor supplied falls. Since both labor demand and supply fall, actual employment falls. The percentage rate of unemployment rises or falls depending on the fall in demand relative to supply.

8 This depends on the continuing assumption of positive excess aggregate demand.

9 See Chapter 4, section 6; and Appendix 1, section 3.

10 See Chapter 4, section 5; and Chapter 6, section 3.

11 See Chapter 4, section 5; and Chapter 6, section 3.

12 See Chapter 4, section 6; and Appendix 1, section 3. The assumption that neither sector's costs change implies that the decrease in investment demand by the investment relative to the consumer goods sector does not divert more investment to the latter—not implausible, but not necessarily true either. See Appendix 2.

13 Note that the system is in period 1, so the rate of change in capital goods prices between periods 1 and 2 falls. But consumer goods producers do not learn of this until period 2.

Chapter 6's policy discussion of the one-sector model concluded that a decrease in ΔM^s adversely affects hiring, but has some beneficial effect on inflation. But that chapter rejected reliance on monetary policy in favor of a mixture of policies on the basis that the mixture gives more benefits for the pain. Here, the two-sector model says the pain of monetary policy, lowered employment, brings no change in the CPI and hence no benefits.[14] Or, if some index of both consumer and capital goods prices is the target, the two-sector model just says that labor market pain will buy some arrest to the average price increases. Again, the one- and two-sector models are similar in spirit and recommendations. If anything, the two-sector model only strengthens the radical conclusions of the previous analysis; for here monetary policy has no effect on consumer prices, only on capital goods prices.

As an alternative to monetary restraint, the government can cut its expenditures either on consumer goods or capital goods. Suppose it lowers its demand for consumer goods. Each such firm finds no change in its cost situation but faces lower expected demand. Consequently, the rate of consumer goods price increase falls as does the desired rate of hiring and the actual rate of change of wages in this sector.

The declining demand for consumer goods makes this sector lower its investment demand, and hence the investment sector faces a lower demand. With unchanged costs but lower demand, the investment good sector lowers its rate of price increase, its desired hiring, and its rate of wage increases.

The effects, then, of a decrease in C_G^d are to lower price inflation in both industries, lower wage inflation, and lower aggregate desired hiring. This is basically what the one-sector model said, save that some of the goods the government foregoes in the one-sector model are investment goods which, when released to the private sector, lower costs; and these lower costs tend to stimulate desired hiring, an effect not felt here.

Alternatively, the government can reduce its expenditure on investment goods. This leads to adverse demand multiplier effects in the capital goods sector and hence tends to lower price and wage inflation and desired hiring there. However, the investment goods the government foregoes will go to previously unfulfilled private demand, thus lowering costs. Supposing these released goods go to both industries, the investment sector finds its marginal cost curves falling. This intensifies the decline in investment price inflation, but mitigates to some extent the fall in desired hiring and wage increases.

Some of the released investment goods presumably go to the consumer goods sector. Here, demand conditions are unchanged, but

14 But see footnote 12, page 153.

marginal cost falls with the increase in fulfilled investment. Thus, price inflation decreases, and hiring demand and wage increases are spurred.

Price inflation falls in each sector. Labor demand increases in the consumer goods sector as does the rate of wage change there. Things are much more complex in the capital goods sector. The parametric fall in government demand for investment goods and the induced multiplier effects on demand within the sector lower expected demand curves and thus reduce price inflation, the demand for labor, and wage increases there. But this reduced government demand frees some investment goods. This lowers marginal cost and price, and tends to increase labor demand and wages. Here, then, are two conflicting tendencies, the relative strengths of which there is no a priori means of judging. The final result on labor demand, and thus on wage increases, in this sector depends on: the sensitivity of estimates of future demand to changes in current demand; how far the multiplier effects on demand work themselves out during the period; the sensitivity of the capital goods sector's demand for capital to the demand it faces for its output; the proportion of the investment goods which the government releases that goes to this sector; and the sensitivity of the marginal revenue product of labor here to the stock of capital. Clearly, then, the effect on labor demand in this sector is ambiguous, and thus the changes in aggregate labor demand and in the average rate of wage increases are also ambiguous. But this ambiguity is just the kind of thing encountered in Chapters 4 and 6 where reductions in G increased actual private investment.

As in those chapters, several policy recommendations suggest themselves. Suppose the government acts to reduce the demand for investment goods to that sector's capacity. Now, if the government further lowers its demand for investment goods but also lowers the interest rate to keep total investment demand equal to capacity, both private sectors invest more, and thus both raise their demand for labor. In reducing investment demand to capacity, government reduces the capital goods sector's demand for labor. But once investment demand is held at capacity, the lower is government demand, the more the private sector invests and the higher is labor demand. At some point, the influence of this increased private investment on labor demand just offsets any decline in demand due to reducing investment demand to capacity. Further reductions in government demand for investment goods, accompanied by reductions in the interest rate to hold total investment demand at capacity, lead to net increases in labor demand. Thus, if the government desires to decrease inflation in either the consumer- or capital-goods index or both and not hurt or actually stimulate labor demand, the prescription is to lower its spending on investment goods to free these goods for industry and thus lower industrial costs and prices, and to lower the interest rate to stimulate demand for the released investment goods. If enough investment goods are released in this fashion, the positive effects of having more capital goods to work with overwhelm the negative effects on labor demand of reducing investment demand to capacity.

The analysis here is more detailed (and interesting) than the analysis of the one-sector model. But the basic spirit of policy and the basic condemnation of current short-run policy making are remarkably similar in both the one- and two-sector models. The analysis of this chapter illustrates and helps sustain the conjecture that no major violence is done to policy implications by choosing to work with the simpler one-sector model rather than the richer two-sector model.

A final word is needed, though, on the role of the relative price of capital and consumer goods. Many theories accord this relative price a central role, and many make variations in this price a prime equilibrating device.[15] But this relative price is fixed in the single period discussed, whether in the one-sector or two-sector version, and hence plays no equilibrating role in the single period. The price is fixed because of the fundamental perceptions on which the model is based—the period of the model is the length of time it takes the entrepreneur to discover he has possibly set the wrong price and to decide to change the price. Thus, it makes no sense to complain that variations in the relative price play no role in the single period—they logically cannot.

Nevertheless, the relative price varies over time in the two-sector model. The two-sector model will have a different time path from the one-sector model by virtue of this variability. This, however, says nothing more than that two models which differ in an essential way will have different non-steady-state time paths. Variations in the relative price are a necessary condition for the two-sector model to reach long-run, steady-state equilibrium unless the price is accidentally frozen at the long-run equilibrium level. But it is highly doubtful that there is a meaningful sense in which the variability of the relative price in a two-sector model gives such a model equilibrating tendencies more powerful than in a one-sector model which necessarily lacks such variability.

15 See, for example, Axel Leijonhufvud, *On Keynesian Economics and the Economics of Keynes: A Study in Monetary Theory* (London: Oxford University Press, 1968).

1 MATHEMATICAL NOTES

This appendix discusses the necessary and sufficient conditions for the firm to maximize the present value of its operations.[1] These conditions help derive the micro comparative statics results of Chapters 2 and 4. This appendix considers the effects of a rather general scheme of depreciation, discusses isoelastic shifts in demand, and shows the effects of a business demand for money. Finally, the parametric shifts in the IS, II, AQ, NN, Δw, and ΔP curves relative to each other (used in Chapters 3, 4, 6, and 7) are derived.

A.1. Profit Maximization

Assume that each firm knows the maximum stock of capital that rationing allows it to have on hand in any period t. Call this maximum stock K_t^*. The firm wishes to maximize the present value of its operations from the present, time $t = 1$, to the end of its horizon in period h, subject to the constraint that it sell K_h by the end of that period, or:

$$K_{h+1} = 0 \qquad \text{A.1.1}$$

and subject to the $h - 1$ constraints:

$$(K_t^* - K_t) \geq 0 \qquad (t = 2, h) \qquad \text{A.1.2}$$

The present value of the firm's operations is:

$$PV = P_1 Q_1 - w_1 N_1 - P_{K,1}(K_2 - K_1)$$

$$+ \sum_{t=2}^{h-1} \frac{1}{\prod_{j=2}^{t}(1 + i_{j-1})} \cdot [P_t Q_t - w_t N_t - P_{K,t}(K_{t+1} - K_t)] \qquad \text{A.1.3}$$

$$+ \frac{1}{\prod_{j=2}^{h}(1 + i_{j-1})}(P_h Q_h - w_h N_h + P_{K,h} K_h)$$

---

[1] These notes are intended neither as an exercise in formal elegance nor as a complete, coherent mathematical restatement of the text, but rather as an aid in understanding the text. The mathematical techniques are elementary.

The firm wishes to maximize PV subject to the inequalities A.1.2 and:

$$K_t \geq 0, N_t \geq 0 \quad (t = 2, h) \tag{A.1.4}$$

According to the Kuhn-Tucker theorem, if PV is a concave function of K_t, N_t $(t = 2, h)$ and if the constraints in inequalities A.1.2 are convex when they hold as equalities—that is, are convex when $(K_t^* - K_t) = 0$—then maximizing PV subject to the constraints is equivalent to maximizing:[2]

$$PV^* = P_1 Q_1 - w_1 N_1 - P_{K,1}(K_2 - K_1)$$

$$+ \sum_{t=2}^{h-1} \frac{1}{\prod_{j=2}^{t}(1 + i_{j-1})} \cdot [P_t Q_t - w_t N_t - P_{K,t}(K_{t+1} - K_t) + \tag{A.1.5}$$

$$\lambda_t(K_t^* - K_t)] + \frac{P_h Q_h - w_h N_K + P_{K,h} K_h + \lambda_h(K_h^* - K_h)}{\prod_{j=2}^{h}(1 + i_{j-1})}$$

where λ_t are multipliers,

$$\lambda_t \geq 0, \quad (t = 2, h) \tag{A.1.6}$$

The constraints in inequalities A.1.2 are linear equations when they hold as equalities, and can then be taken to be convex; for linear equations can be treated as either convex or concave as desired. Assume that the function PV is concave. Then the necessary and sufficient conditions for a set of values K_t, N_t $(t = 2, h)$ to maximize PV subject to inequalities A.1.2 and A.1.4 are:

$$MRP_{K,t} - P_{K,t-1}\left(i_{t-1} - \frac{\Delta P_{K,t-1}^e}{P_{K,t-1}^e}\right) - \lambda_t \leq 0, K_t \geq 0$$

$$MRP_{N,t} - MFC_{N,t} \leq 0, N_t \geq 0$$

$$(K_t^* - K_t) \geq 0, \lambda_t \geq 0$$

$$(t = 2, h) \tag{A.1.7}$$

$$[MRP_{K,t} - P_{K,t-1}\left(i_{t-1} - \frac{\Delta P_{K,t-1}^e}{P_{K,t-1}^e}\right) - \lambda_t]K_t = 0$$

$$(MRP_{N,t} - MFC_{N,t})N_t = 0$$

$$(K_t^* - K_t)\lambda_t = 0$$

2 H. W. Kuhn and A. W. Tucker, "Non-Linear Programming," *Proceedings of the Second Berkeley Symposium on Mathematical Statistics and Probability*, edited by J. Neyman (Berkeley: University of California Press, 1951), pp. 481–92.

A.2. The Comparative Statics of Chapter 2

Chapter 2 discusses the case in which K_t and N_t are positive, and the maximum capital constraint K_t^* does not apply. Then system A.1.7 becomes:

$$MRP_{K,t} - P_{K,t-1}\left(i_{t-1} - \frac{\Delta P_{K,t-1}^e}{P_{K,t-1}^e}\right) = 0$$

$$MRP_{N,t} - MFC_{N,t} = 0 \qquad (t = 2, h) \quad \text{A.1.8}$$

Concavity of PV implies that, for all t, the matrix:

$$[D]_t = \begin{bmatrix} \dfrac{\partial MRP_{K,t}}{\partial K_t} & \dfrac{\partial MRP_{K,t}}{\partial N_t} \\[3mm] \dfrac{\partial MRP_{N,t}}{\partial K_t} & \dfrac{\partial MRP_{N,t}}{\partial N_t} - \dfrac{dMFC_{N,t}}{dN_t} \end{bmatrix} \qquad \text{A.1.9}$$

is negative definite; that is, the nested principal minors alternate in sign, the first one being negative:

$$|D_{11}|_t = \frac{\partial MRP_{N,t}}{\partial N_t} - \frac{dMFC_{N,t}}{dN_t} < 0$$

$$|D_{22}|_t = \frac{\partial MRP_{K,t}}{\partial K_t} < 0 \qquad \text{A.1.10}$$

$$|D|_t > 0$$

Chapter 2 explicitly assumed that an increase in one factor raises the marginal revenue product of the other, or:

$$\frac{\partial MRP_{K,t}}{\partial N_t} = \frac{\partial MRP_{N,t}}{\partial K_t} = |D_{21}|_t = |D_{12}|_t > 0 \qquad \text{A.1.11}$$

Shocking system A.1.8 for $t = 2$ by varying the parameter α yields the system:

$$\begin{bmatrix} \dfrac{\partial MRP_{K,2}}{\partial K_2} & \dfrac{\partial MRP_{K,2}}{\partial N_2} \\[3mm] \dfrac{\partial MRP_{N,2}}{\partial K_2} & \dfrac{\partial MRP_{N,2}}{\partial N_2} - \dfrac{dMFC_{N,2}}{dN_2} \end{bmatrix} \begin{bmatrix} \dfrac{dK_2}{d\alpha} \\[3mm] \dfrac{dN_2}{d\alpha} \end{bmatrix} =$$

$$- \begin{bmatrix} \dfrac{\partial\left[MRP_{K,2} - P_{K_1}\left(i_1 - \dfrac{\Delta P_{K,1}^e}{P_{K,1}}\right)\right]}{\partial\alpha} \\[5mm] \dfrac{\partial(MRP_{N,2} - MFC_{N,2})}{\partial\alpha} \end{bmatrix} \qquad \text{A.1.12}$$

(continued)

$$[D]_2 \begin{bmatrix} dK \\ dN \end{bmatrix} = - \begin{bmatrix} d\alpha_1 \\ d\alpha_2 \end{bmatrix}$$

where, throughout, the vectors $[d\alpha]$ are the initial impacts of α on each equation. Table A-1 lists the vectors $-[d\alpha_1, d\alpha_2]$ for the various parametric changes discussed in Chapter 2. Table 2-1 lists the comparative statics results for K_2 and N_2, found by solving system A.1.2 for the vectors in Table A-1 and using equations A.1.10 and A.1.11. Since K_2 and N_2 vary in the same direction, there are no ambiguous changes in Q_2. Table 2-1 lists these also. The text aggregated these results to find the social investment function, the aggregate planned output function, and the function which describes the changes in employment the business sector desires.

When the parametric change does not affect the demand curve or does not affect the labor supply curve, the effect on P_2 is opposite in sign to the effect on Q_2; and the sign of the effect on w_2 is the same as on N_2, as Table 2-1 shows. When the parameter shifts the demand or supply curve, the analysis is more complicated; and the remainder of this section takes up, in order, the effects of P_2^e, $(\Delta P/P)^e$, Nu, and $(\Delta w/w)^e$.

TABLE A-1

VECTORS FOR THE COMPARATIVE STATICS EXPERIMENTS OF CHAPTER 2

Parameter	Vector
Y_1	$-\left[\dfrac{\partial MRP_{K,2}^+}{\partial Y}, \dfrac{\partial MRP_{N,2}^+}{\partial Y} \right]$
i_1	$-\left[-P_{K,1}, 0 \right]$
Nu	$-\left[0, -\dfrac{\partial MFC_{N,2}^-}{\partial Nu} \right]$
$\widetilde{P}_1$	$-\left[\dfrac{\partial MRP_{K,2}^+}{\partial \widetilde{P}_1}, \dfrac{\partial MRP_{N,2}^+}{\partial \widetilde{P}_1} \right]$
$\Delta P^e/P$	$-\left[\dfrac{\partial MRP_{K,2}^+}{\partial \Delta P^e/P}, \dfrac{\partial MRP_{N,2}^+}{\partial \Delta P^e/P} \right]$
$\widetilde{w}_1$	$-\left[0, -\dfrac{\partial MFC_{N,2}^+}{\partial \widetilde{w}_1} \right]$
$\Delta w^e/w$	$-\left[0, -\dfrac{\partial MFC_{N,2}^+}{\partial (\Delta w/w)^e} \right]$
$P_{K,1}$	$-\left[-\left(i_1 - \dfrac{\Delta P_{K,1}^e}{P_{K,1}} \right), 0 \right]$
$\dfrac{\Delta P_{K,1}^e}{P_{K,1}}$	$-\left[\overline{P}_{K,1}, \overline{0} \right]$

Chapter 2 assumes that an increase in Y_1 raises the typical firm's current demand, increasing proportionately the expectational parameter $u_{P,2}$; and $u_{P,2}$ shifts period 2's expected demand curve proportionately and isoelastically relative to the price axis. Further, a change in P_2^e shifts the expected demand curve proportionately and isoelastically relative to the quantity axis. Section 5 of this appendix shows that these two assumptions imply that the expected demand function is:

$$P_2 = P_2^e \overline{P}(Q_2/u_{P,2}) \qquad \text{A.1.13}$$

Assuming marginal cost is constant (c equals average and marginal cost), profits are:

$$P_2^e \overline{P}(Q_2/u_{P,2})Q_2 - cQ_2 \qquad \text{A.1.14}$$

and the necessary and sufficient conditions for Q_2 to yield an interior maximum are:

$$P_2^e \left(\overline{P} + \overline{P}_Q \cdot \frac{Q}{u_P} \right) - c = 0 \qquad \text{A.1.15}$$

$$P_2^e \left(2\overline{P}_Q \cdot \frac{1}{u_P} + \overline{P}_{QQ} \cdot \frac{Q}{u_P^2} \right) < 0 \qquad \text{A.1.16}$$

From equation A.1.15, varying $u_{P,2}$ gives:

$$\frac{dQ_2}{du_{P,2}} = -\frac{P_2^e(-2\overline{P}_Q \cdot Q/u_P^2 - \overline{P}_{QQ} \cdot Q/u_P \cdot Q/u_P^2)}{P_2^e(2\overline{P}_Q \cdot 1/u_P + \overline{P}_{QQ} \cdot Q/u_P^2)} = \frac{Q_2}{u_{P,2}} > 0 \quad \text{A.1.17}$$

and from the demand function in equation A.1.13,

$$\frac{dP_2}{du_{P,2}} = P_2^e \left(\overline{P}_Q \frac{dQ}{du_P} \cdot \frac{1}{u_P} - \overline{P}_Q \frac{Q}{u_P^2} \right) = P_2^e \left(\overline{P}_Q \frac{Q}{u_P} \cdot \frac{1}{u_P} - \overline{P}_Q \frac{Q}{u_P^2} \right) = 0 \quad \text{A.1.18}$$

Thus, dP_2/dY_1 equals zero in Table 2–1.

From equation A.1.15, varying P_2^e yields:

$$\frac{dQ_2}{dP_2^e} = -\frac{\overline{P} + \overline{P}_Q \cdot Q/u_P}{P_2^e(2\overline{P}_Q \cdot 1/u_P + \overline{P}_{QQ} \cdot Q/u_P^2)} \qquad \text{A.1.19}$$

which is known to be negative from inequality A.1.16 and from the fact that, when equation A.1.15 is divided by P_2^e, $-c/P_2^e$ is negative. From equation A.1.13,

$$\frac{dP_2}{dP_2^e} = \overline{P} + P_2^e \overline{P}_Q \cdot \frac{1}{u_P} \cdot \frac{dQ}{dP_2^e}$$

$$= \overline{P} - \frac{P_2^e \overline{P}_Q \cdot 1/u_P \cdot \overline{P} + P_2^e \overline{P}_Q \cdot (1/u_P)\overline{P}_Q(Q/u_P)}{P_2^e(2\overline{P}_Q \cdot 1/u_P + \overline{P}_{QQ} Q/u_P^2)} \qquad \text{A.1.20}$$

which is positive if and only if:

$$\overline{P}\overline{P}_Q + \overline{P}\overline{P}_{QQ}\frac{Q}{u_P} - \overline{P}_Q^2\frac{Q}{u_P} < 0 \qquad \text{A.1.21}$$

Only $\overline{P}_{QQ}$ can make inequality A.1.21 positive, and thus inequality A.1.21 holds if the demand curve does not fall at "too" decreasing a rate. Intuitively, the faster the demand falls, the less likely is an upward shift to increase output so much that price actually declines. If the demand curve is always linear in Q, for example, $\overline{P}_{QQ}$ is zero and inequality A.1.21 holds. Make the very mild assumption that inequality A.1.21 holds. Then, since $\widetilde{P}_1$ and $(\Delta P/P)^e$ positively influence P_2^e, for:

$$P_2^e = P_1\left(1 + \frac{\Delta P}{P}e\right) \qquad \text{A.1.22}$$

Table 2–1 lists $dP_2/d\widetilde{P}_1$ and $dP_2/(d\Delta P/P)^e$ as positive.

An increase in $(\Delta P/P)^e$ really has two roles. The higher the rate of inflation the firm expects, the higher it believes demand will be next period (as just seen); but the higher the rate of price increase of capital goods, the lower the marginal factor costs of capital services, $P_{K,1}(i_1 - \Delta P_{K,1}^e/P_{K,1})$. Thus, an increase in the expected rate of change of all prices raises the firm's demand curve and lowers its marginal cost curve. These two effects reinforce each other on I^d, $\Delta w/w$, ΔN^d, and AQ; and thus as far as the II, NN, Δw, and AQ curves go, the previous analysis is sufficient, though it deals only with the first role of $(\Delta P/P)^e$. The effects are offsetting on $(\Delta P/P)$.

From equation A.1.22,

$$\frac{dP_2^e}{d(\Delta P/P)^e} = \widetilde{P}_1 \qquad \text{A.1.23}$$

Then, from equation A.1.15,

$$\frac{dQ_2}{d(\Delta P/P)^e} = -\frac{\widetilde{P}_1[\overline{P} + \overline{P}_Q(Q/u_p)] - \dfrac{\partial c}{\partial(\Delta P/P)^e}}{P_2^e(2\overline{P}_Q \cdot 1/u_p + \overline{P}_{QQ}Q/u_p^2)} > 0 \qquad \text{A.1.24}$$

Intuitively, an increase in $(\Delta P/P)^e$ raises output demand and lowers the cost of capital services. An increase in demand increases the use of both factors when they are complements, as assumed right along; and a fall in the price of one factor increases the use of both if they are complements—and output rises.

From equation A.1.13,

$$\frac{dP_2}{d(\Delta P/P)^e} = \widetilde{P}_1\bar{P} + P_2^e\bar{P}_Q \cdot \frac{1}{u_P} \cdot \frac{dQ}{d(\Delta P/P)^e}$$

$$= \widetilde{P}_1\bar{P} - P_2^e\bar{P}_Q \cdot \frac{1}{u_P} \cdot \frac{\widetilde{P}_1(\bar{P} + \bar{P}_Q Q/u_P) - \partial c/\partial(\Delta P/P)^e}{P_2^e(2\bar{P}_Q \cdot 1/u_P + \bar{P}_{QQ} Q/u_P^2)}$$

A.1.25

The assumptions made so far do not determine the sign of equation A.1.25; but similar to equation A.1.20, the smaller is $\bar{P}_{QQ}$, the more likely is Equation A.1.25 to be positive.

However, temporarily assume $\bar{P}_{QQ}$ equals zero. Then for equation A.1.25 to be positive,

$$\widetilde{P}_1\bar{P} - P_2^e \cdot \bar{P}_Q \cdot \frac{1}{u_P} \cdot \frac{\widetilde{P}_1(\bar{P} + \bar{P}_Q \cdot Q/u_P) - \partial c/\partial(\Delta P/P)^e}{2P_2^e \cdot \bar{P}_Q \cdot 1/u_P} > 0 \quad \text{A.1.26}$$

$$\widetilde{P}_1\bar{P} - \frac{\widetilde{P}_1(\bar{P} + \bar{P}_Q \cdot Q/u_P) - \partial c/\partial(\Delta P/P)^e}{2} > 0 \qquad \text{A.1.27}$$

$$\widetilde{P}_1\bar{P} > \frac{\widetilde{P}_1(\bar{P} + \bar{P}_Q Q/u_P) - \partial c/\partial(\Delta P/P)^e}{2} \qquad \text{A.1.28}$$

Let the change in demand price, $\widetilde{P}_1\bar{P}$, be dP_2; and let the changes in marginal revenue, $\widetilde{P}_1(\bar{P} + \bar{P}_Q Q/u_P)$, and marginal cost, $\partial c/\partial(\Delta P/P)^e$, be dMR_2 and dMC_2. Then inequality A.1.28 says an increase in $(\Delta P/P)^e$ raises P_2 if the induced rise in demand price at the initial output is larger than the fall in price caused by the induced increase in Q, this fall equalling 1/2 of the increase in marginal revenue minus the decrease in marginal costs, or if:

$$dP_2 > \tfrac{1}{2}(dMR_2 - dMC_2) \qquad \text{A.1.29}$$

Dividing inequality A.1.29 by P_2,

$$\frac{dP_2}{P_2} > \frac{1}{2}\left(\frac{dMR_2}{MR_2}\frac{MR_2}{P_2} - \frac{dMC_2}{MC_2}\frac{MC_2}{P_2}\right) \qquad \text{A.1.30}$$

or, since MR_2 equals MC_2,

$$\frac{dP_2}{P_2} > \frac{1}{2}\left(\frac{dMR_2}{MR_2} - \frac{dMC_2}{MC_2}\right)\frac{MC_2}{P_2} \qquad \text{A.1.31}$$

The percentage change in demand price equals the percentage change in rivals' prices, or:

$$\frac{dP_2}{P_2} = \frac{dP_2^e}{P_2^e}\frac{\widetilde{P}_1}{P_2^e} \qquad \text{A.1.32}$$

Using equation A.1.32 and noting that:

$$\frac{dMR}{MR} = \frac{\widetilde{P}_1(\overline{P} + \overline{P}_Q Q/u_P)}{P_2^e(\overline{P} + \overline{P}_Q Q/u_P)} = \frac{\widetilde{P}_1}{P_2^e}$$

inequality A.1.31 becomes:

$$\frac{\widetilde{P}_1}{P_2^e} > \frac{1}{2}\left(\frac{\widetilde{P}_1}{P_2^e} - \frac{dMC_2}{MC_2}\right)\frac{MC_2}{P_2} \qquad \text{A.1.34}$$

$$\frac{\widetilde{P}_1}{P_2^e} - \frac{1}{2}\frac{\widetilde{P}_1}{P_2^e}\frac{MC_2}{P_2} = \frac{\widetilde{P}_1}{P_2^e}\left(1 - \frac{1}{2}\frac{MC_2}{P_2}\right) > -\frac{1}{2}\frac{dMC_2}{MC_2}\frac{MC_2}{P_2} \qquad \text{A.1.35}$$

or

$$\frac{P_2}{P_2^e}\frac{\widetilde{P}_1}{MC_2}\left(1 - \frac{1}{2}\frac{MC_2}{P_2}\right)2 > -\frac{dMC_2}{MC_2} \qquad \text{A.1.36}$$

The assumption that an increase in one factor raises the marginal revenue product of the other implies that the factors are technical complements; that is, an increase in one raises the marginal physical product of the other. A change in the marginal factor cost of one of two complements changes marginal cost, but the percentage change in marginal cost is less than the percentage change in the marginal factor cost.[3] Thus, since the decrease in the cost of capital services is less than 100 percent, $-dMC_2/MC_2$ is positive but less than unity. Comparing this to the right-hand side of inequality A.1.36, $1 - \frac{1}{2}MC_2/P_2 \cdot 2$ is greater than unity since MC_2 is less than P_2; and thus inequality A.1.36 is likely to hold under many different and plausible circumstances. For example, if most firms charge about the same price (P_2 and P_2^e are about equal), and if costs are not rising "too" fast ($\widetilde{P}_1$ exceeds MC_2), inequality A.1.36 holds.

The two relatively weak assumptions that $\dfrac{P_2}{P_2^e} \cdot \dfrac{\widetilde{P}_1}{MC_2}$ is not "too" much

less than unity and P_{QQ} is not "too" positive ensure that $dP_2/d(\Delta P/P)^e$ is positive when both influences of $(\Delta P/P)^e$ are included. This implies that, from equations 2.5.3,

$$\frac{\Delta P}{P} = f(Y, i - \frac{\Delta P}{P}e, \frac{\Delta P}{P}e, \dots) \qquad \text{A.1.37}$$

and

$$\frac{\partial(\Delta P/P)}{\partial(\Delta P/P)^e} = -f_2 + f_3 > 0 \qquad \text{A.1.38}$$

3 For a demonstration, see Richard J. Sweeney, "Firm Decision-Making and Macroeconomic Disequilibria" (Doctoral dissertation, Princeton University, 1972), appendix to Chapter 3.

As section 7 of this appendix shows, inequality A.1.38 implies that an increase in $(\Delta P/P)^e$ shifts the initial ΔP curve down, an important step in the determination of the effect of expected $(\Delta P/P)^e$ on actual $\Delta P/P$ inflation in Chapters 3, 4, and 7.

Consider the effect on next period's wage offer of a decrease in current aggregate unemployment, Nu, or an increase in the wage the firm thinks its rivals are offering currently, $\tilde{w}_1$, or in the percentage rate at which the firm thinks its rivals are changing their wage offers, $(\Delta w/w)^e$. All such changes reduce the labor supply, but the ultimate effect on w_2 is doubtful. However, if the net marginal revenue product of labor curve —capital having been adjusted to its optimal level given the quantity of labor—has a sufficiently negative slope, and if the labor supply function does not flatten at "too" fast a rate, then, as in Table 2−1,

$$dw_2/dNu < 0 \qquad dw_2/d\tilde{w}_1 > 0 \qquad dw_2/d\Delta w^e/w > 0 \qquad \textbf{A.1.39}$$

Assume the firm believes that next period's labor supply price varies positively with rivals' offers. Let the number of workers who currently apply to the firm for a job vary positively with the current aggregate unemployment rate, Nu, and let an increase in applications raise $u_{w,2}$, an expectational parameter that affects proportionately the number of workers the firm believes will accept a job next period for any given wage offer. Then the labor supply function is: **A.1.40**

$$w_2 = \overline{w}\left(\frac{N}{u_{w,2}}\right) + \beta\left(w_2^e\right) = \overline{w}\left(\frac{N}{u_{w,2}}\right) + \beta\left[\tilde{w}_1\left(1 + \frac{\Delta w}{w}e\right)\right]; \ \overline{w}', \beta' > 0$$

The wage bill is:

$$wN = \overline{w} \cdot N + \beta \cdot N \qquad\qquad \textbf{A.1.41}$$

and marginal factor cost is positive:

$$MFC_{N,2} = w + \overline{w}'\frac{N}{u_w} > 0 \qquad\qquad \textbf{A.1.42}$$

and, by assumption, rising:

$$\frac{dMFC_{N,2}}{dN_2} = \frac{2}{u_w}\overline{w}' + \frac{N}{u_w^2}\overline{w}'' > 0 \qquad\qquad \textbf{A.1.43}$$

The net revenue due to labor, R, is the total revenue minus the total rent on capital when capital is adjusted to its optimal value given the quantity of labor. (R thus implies a prior optimization problem.)[4] The firm chooses N to maximize $R(N) - \overline{w}N - \beta N$, and the necessary and sufficient conditions for a positive N to yield a maximum are:

4 *Ibid.*

$$R' - \overline{w} - \frac{N}{u_w}\overline{w}' - \beta = 0 \qquad \text{A.1.44}$$

$$R'' - \frac{2}{u_w}\overline{w}' - \frac{N}{u_w^2}\overline{w}'' < 0 \qquad \text{A.1.45}$$

From equation A.1.44,

$$\frac{dN_2}{du_{w,2}} = -\frac{(N/u_w)[(2/u_w)\overline{w}' + (N/u_w^2)\overline{w}'']}{R'' - (2/u_w)\overline{w}' - (N/u_w^2)w''} \qquad \text{A.1.46}$$

which is positive from increasing MFC_N (see inequality A.1.43) and the second-order inequality A.1.45. From equation A.1.40,

$$\frac{dw_2}{du_{w,2}} = -\overline{w}'\frac{N}{u_w^2} + \frac{1}{u_w}\overline{w}'\frac{dN}{du_{w,2}}$$

$$= -\frac{1}{u_w}\left[-\overline{w}'\frac{N}{u_w} - \overline{w}'\frac{N}{u_w}\frac{(2/u_w)\overline{w}' + (N/u_w^2)\overline{w}''}{R'' - (2/u_w)\overline{w}' - (N/u_w^2)\overline{w}''}\right] \qquad \text{A.1.47}$$

$$= \frac{-1/u_w \cdot N/u_w \cdot \overline{w}'\,R''}{R'' - (2/u_w)\overline{w}' - (N/u_w)\overline{w}''}$$

which is negative if and only if R'' is negative.

R'' is the slope of the net marginal revenue product of labor curve. It is consistent with an interior profit maximum that this curve have a positive slope, but only if the MFC_N curve is rising and at a fast enough rate; for otherwise equation A.1.44 yields a profit minimum (inequality A.1.45 is reversed).[5] Assume that R'' is negative, avoiding this unpleasant possibility and ensuring that equation A.1.47 is negative. Regarding w_2^e, increase $(\Delta w/w)^e$, lowering N_2^d for differentiating equation A.1.44,

$$\frac{dN_2}{d(\Delta w/w)^e} = -\frac{-\beta'\widetilde{w}_1}{R'' - (2/u_w)\overline{w}' - (N/u_w^2)w''} \qquad \text{A.1.48}$$

which is known to be negative from inequality A.1.45. Differentiate the labor supply function in equation A.1.40 to find:

$$\frac{dw_2}{d(\Delta w/w)^e} = \frac{1}{u_w}\overline{w}' \cdot \frac{dN}{d(\Delta w/w)^e} + \beta'\widetilde{w}_1$$

$$= \frac{(1/u_w)\overline{w}'\beta'\widetilde{w}_1}{R'' - (2/u_w)\overline{w}' - (N/u_w^2)\overline{w}''} + \beta'\widetilde{w}_1 \qquad \text{A.1.49}$$

$$= \left[\frac{(1/u_w)\overline{w}'}{R'' - (2/u_w)\overline{w}' - (N/u_w^2)w''} + 1\right]\beta'\widetilde{w}_1 < \beta'\widetilde{w}_1$$

5 The net marginal revenue product of labor curve may have a positive slope even when the marginal revenue product of labor curve, evaluated at a given capital stock, has a negative slope. For when N rises, the increase this induces in $K(K$ and N are complements) may actually cause MRP_N to rise.

Thus, equation A.1.49 is positive just when:

$$\frac{(1/u_w)\,\overline{w}'}{R'' - (2/u_w)\overline{w}' - (N/u_w^2)\overline{w}''} > -1 \qquad \text{A.1.50}$$

or

$$R'' - \frac{1}{u_w}\overline{w}' - \frac{N}{u_w^2}\overline{w}'' < 0 \qquad \text{A.1.51}$$

The rate at which the supply curve flattens is $\overline{w}''$, given the slope $\overline{w}'$. The more negative is $\overline{w}''$, the faster the curve flattens and the less likely it is that inequality A.1.51 holds. Intuitively, the faster the supply curve flattens, the larger the reduction in N^d with an upward shift in the curve; and the larger is the fall in N^d, the larger the fall in w_2, given $\overline{w}'$, and the more likely is the upward shift to be offset. If R'' is assumed negative as before, then inequality A.1.51 holds and equation A.1.49 is positive under the very weak assumption that the supply curve does not flatten "too" fast.

If the representative firm's wage rate, w_1, equals the average wage rate, and if beliefs about rivals wages are correct, then from equation A.1.49:

$$\frac{\dfrac{dw_2}{d(\Delta w/w)^e}}{w_1} < \beta'\frac{\widetilde{w}_1}{w_1} = \beta' \qquad \text{A.1.52}$$

But recall from Chapter 2, equation 2.5.7, that the sign of the partial derivative of the aggregate wage change function with respect to the real wage rate, $g_{w/P}$, depends on G_4^* which equals $[dw_2/d(\Delta w/w)^e]/w_1$. Thus, G_4^* is something less than β'.

It may well be that β' approximates unity. On the average, matching wage increases should keep workers who were earning no rent from leaving. Most of those who leave one firm do so to go to another, so the effects of the increases, which are really wealth effects on workers' behavior, may approximately cancel in the aggregate. There may be some net movement in or out of the labor force or an industry's labor pool, but the direction of such movement is ambiguous—ignore it. Then G_4^* is less than unity, and from equations 2.5.7, $g_{w/P}$ is negative when actual and expected wage inflation are approximately equal.

A.3. The Comparative Statics of Chapter 4

Chapter 4 analyzed the case in which the representative firm has a positive stock of capital but cannot invest as much as it wants, or:

$$K_t^* = K_t \qquad K_t > 0,\ (t = 2, h) \qquad \text{A.1.53}$$

Assume also that:

$$N_t > 0, (t = 2, h) \qquad \text{A.1.54}$$

which is entirely reasonably when discussing a representative firm. Then for $t = 2$, system A.1.7 becomes:

$$MRP_{K,2} - P_{K,1}\left(i_1 - \frac{\Delta P_{K,1}^e}{P_{K,1}}\right) - \lambda_2 = 0$$

$$MRP_{N,2} - MFC_{N,2} = 0 \qquad \text{A.1.55}$$

$$\lambda_2(K_2^* - K_2) = 0$$

Shock system A.1.55 by varying some parameter α to get the system:

$$
\begin{bmatrix}
\dfrac{\partial MRP_{K,2}}{\partial K_2} & \dfrac{\partial MRP_{K,2}}{\partial N_2} & -1 \\[2ex]
\dfrac{\partial MRP_{N,2}}{\partial K_2} & \dfrac{\partial MRP_{N,2}}{\partial N_2} - \dfrac{dMFC_{N,2}}{dN_2} & 0 \\[2ex]
-\lambda_2 & 0 & 0
\end{bmatrix}
\begin{bmatrix}
\dfrac{dK_2}{d\alpha} \\[2ex]
\dfrac{dN_2}{d\alpha} \\[2ex]
\dfrac{d\lambda_2}{d\alpha}
\end{bmatrix}
= -
\begin{bmatrix}
d\alpha_1 \\[2ex]
d\alpha_2 \\[2ex]
d\alpha_3
\end{bmatrix}
\qquad \text{A.1.56}
$$

The only case in which $d\alpha_3$ is nonzero is when K_2^* changes. Leave this case until last. Then from system A.1.56,

$$\frac{dN_2}{d\alpha} = -d\alpha_2\left(\frac{\partial MRP_{N,2}}{\partial N_2} - \frac{dMFC_{N,2}}{dN_2}\right) \qquad \text{A.1.57}$$

An implication of the assumption that the *PV* function is concave, at least in the region considered, is that:

$$\left(\frac{\partial MRP_{N,2}}{\partial N_2} - \frac{dMFC_{N,2}}{dN_2}\right) < 0 \qquad \text{A.1.58}$$

so

$$sgn\left(\frac{dN_2}{d\alpha}\right) = sgn(d\alpha_2) \qquad \text{A.1.59}$$

Chapter 4 asserted that, comparing the case in which the K_2^* constraint is binding for the firm to the one in which it is nonbinding, the only differences in comparative statics results are: (1) an increase in Y_1^d raises P_2, (2) changes in i_1 and $\Delta P_{K,1}^e/P_{K,1}$ no longer affect firms' decisions, and (3) a change in K_2^* through I^a now affects the variables.

Aside from the variables in (1)–(3), equation A.1.59 and the appropriate entries for $d\alpha_2$ in Table A–1 verify that the effect on N_2^d of parametric variations is the same as in Table 2–1. In Chapter 2, N_2, K_2, and Q_2 always vary in the same direction. Here,

$$\frac{dQ}{d\alpha} = Q_N \frac{dN}{d\alpha} \qquad \textbf{A.1.60}$$

and since N_2 varies in the same way as before, so does Q_2. Aside from changes in P_2^e or Y_1, P_2 varies inversely with Q_2, just as before. If w_2^e or Nu does not change, w_2 varies positively with N_2, as before. As in section 2, an increase in Nu lowers w_2 if and only if R'' is negative; and an increase in w_2^e raises w_2 if and only if $R'' - (1/u_w)\overline{w}' - (N/u_w^2)\overline{w}''$ is negative.[6] But both are more likely to be negative now, since here R'' is evaluated at K_2^* and not at the optimal value of K_2. At the higher optimal value of K_2, R'' is larger in algebraic value since the factors are complements.[7]

As for changes in the demand curve, consider first (1). Increases in Y_1^d increase $u_{P,2}$, and $u_{P,2}$ shifts the firm's expected demand curve proportionately and isoelastically relative to the price axis. As long as K_2^* exceeds K_2^d, the marginal cost curve is horizontal. When K_2^d exceeds K_2^*, marginal cost is rising in the same way that fixing one factor in the short run makes increasing short-run marginal cost consistent with constant long-run marginal costs.[8] With increasing per unit costs, marginal cost, c, in the necessary condition, equation A.1.15, now varies positively with Q_2 ($c_Q > 0$), and inequality A.1.16 becomes:

$$P_2^e \left[2P_Q \frac{Q}{u_P^2} - P_{QQ} \frac{Q}{u_P} \frac{Q}{u_P^2} \right] - c_Q = P_2^e \{\cdot\} - c_Q < 0 \qquad \textbf{A.1.61}$$

An increase in $u_{P,2}$ caused by an increase in Y_1^d yields:

$$\frac{dQ_2}{du_{P,2}} = - \frac{P_2^e \left[-2\overline{P}_Q \frac{Q}{u_P^2} - \overline{P}_{QQ} \frac{Q}{u_P} \frac{Q}{u_P^2} \right]}{P_2^e \{\cdot\} - c_Q} = \frac{Q_2}{u_P} \cdot \frac{P_2^e \{\cdot\}}{P_2^e \{\cdot\} - c_Q} > 0 \qquad \textbf{A.1.62}$$

and thus,

$$\frac{dP_2}{du_{P,2}} = - P_2^e \overline{P}_Q \frac{Q_2}{u_P^2} + P_2^e \overline{P}_Q \frac{1}{u_P} \frac{dQ_2}{du_{P,2}}$$

$$= \frac{Q_2}{u_P^2} P_2^e \overline{P}_Q \left(\frac{P_2^e \{\cdot\}}{P_2^e \{\cdot\} - c_Q} - 1 \right) > 0 \qquad \textbf{A.1.63}$$

6 R'' is the slope of the curve showing the net marginal revenue product of labor. See section 2 of this appendix.

7 See footnote 5, page 166.

8 For an example under perfect competition, see Robert Kuenne, *The Microeconomic Theory of The Market Mechanism: A General Equilibrium Approach* (New York: Macmillan Co., 1968), Chapter 4.

When P_2^e varies and shifts the demand curve, the necessary and sufficient condition for dP_2/dP_2^e to be positive is no longer inequality A.1.21 but is:

$$\overline{P}\,\overline{P}_Q + \overline{P}\,\overline{P}_{QQ} - \overline{P}_Q^2 \frac{Q}{u_P} - \overline{P}c_Q < 0 \qquad \text{A.1.64}$$

which is clearly more likely to hold the larger is c_Q. Thus, the result here is, if anything, stronger than claimed in Chapter 2.

Consider (2). From system A.1.56, an increase in i_1 yields:

$$\frac{dK_2}{di_1} = \frac{dN_2}{di_1} = 0, \frac{d\lambda_2}{di_1} = -P_{K,1} \qquad \text{A.1.65}$$

Chapter 4 considered small increases in i_1 that left K_2^d greater than K_2^*. Thus when i_1 rises, the K_2 in:

$$MRP_{N,2} - MFC_{N,2} = 0 \qquad \text{A.1.66}$$

does not change. The firm still takes K_2^*, all the capital it can. Hence N_2 is unchanged. With K_2 and N_2 unchanged in:

$$MRP_{K,2} - P_{K,1}\left(i_1 - \frac{\Delta P_K}{P_K}\right) - \lambda_2 = 0 \qquad \text{A.1.67}$$

variations in λ_2 must offset changes in i_1. The same argument applies, *mutatis mutandis*, for changes in $\Delta P_{K,1}^e/P_{K,1}$. Interpret $P_{K,1}(i_1 - \Delta P_{K,1}^e /P_{K,1}) + \lambda_2$ as the marginal factor cost of capital services such that, if this value holds, the firm just desires that equation A.1.53 hold for $t = 2$. K_2^*, however, is the maximum amount of capital the firm can have. The variable λ_2 is a shadow price telling the firm just how far short is the actual ruling marginal factor cost of capital services, $P_{K,1}(i_1 - \Delta P_{K,1} /P_{K,1})$, from inducing the firm to demand just the amount it can in fact have. The amount by which actual marginal factor cost falls short, λ_2, goes down by $P_{K,1}$ for every one unit increase in i_1, as equation A.1.65 says. As for the effect of i_1 on w_2, Q_2, and P_2, with no change in N_2, w_2 is unaffected; and with no change in N_2 or K_2, Q_2 does not vary and hence P_2 is unchanged. Since the effect of $\Delta P_{K,1}^e /P_{K,1}$ is just the opposite of i_1, this means that when $(\Delta P/P)^e$ increases equally both the rivals' prices and capital goods prices, only the former has an effect. $dP_2/d(\Delta P/P)^e$ is then positive as long as inequality A.1.64 holds, whereas the previous section required stronger assumptions (see inequality A.1.36).

When K_2^* increases, assume that the increase is small enough that the firm continues to take K_2^*. Then, from equation A.1.57,

$$\frac{dN_2}{dK_2^*} = \frac{\partial MRP_{N,2}/\partial K_2}{\partial MRP_{N,2}/\partial N_2 - dMFC_{N,2}/dN_2} > 0 \qquad \textbf{A.1.68}$$

since by assumption of inequality A.1.11:

$$\frac{\partial MRP_{N,2}}{\partial K_2} > 0 \qquad \textbf{A.1.69}$$

To induce an increase in labor supplied, the firm raises w_2. Since both K_2 and N_2 rise, so does Q_2, inducing a fall in P_2—all as Chapter 4 showed graphically.

It is possible to write micro functions showing the firm's reactions, as in Chapter 2. And again as in Chapter 2, these functions may be aggregated to derive macro functions. The functions have the same form as the macro functions in equations 2.5.3 but with the differences in partial derivatives shown in (1)–(3) in this section and discussed in Chapter 4, section 6.

A.4. Depreciation

Under a fairly general scheme of depreciation, the results for the model are virtually identical to those without depreciation. Thus, simplicity dictates ignoring depreciation, since very little is lost in so doing.

Assume that no matter how much the stock of capital depreciates, what is left can be represented by a scalar entirely comparable to new capital. During the period, capital depreciates; but what is left is economically identical to some amount of new capital. Given this assumption, treat depreciation as a factor of production. The production function may be written as:

$$Q_t = Q(K_t, N_t, B_t) \qquad \textbf{A.1.70}$$

where B_t is current physical depreciation. Net investment is now:

$$\Delta K_t = K_{t+1} - K_t = I_t - B_t \qquad \textbf{A.1.71}$$

There are other possible ways of introducing such depreciation; for example, the common formulation:[9]

$$B_t = \delta K_t, \ 1 \geq \delta \geq 0 \qquad \textbf{A.1.72}$$

9 See, for example, Kenneth Arrow, "Optimal Capital Policy with Irreversible Investment," *Value, Capital and Growth*, edited by J. Wolfe (Chicago: Aldine Publishing Co., 1968).

The firm ends the period with the same number of units of "old" capital as it started with, but the productive powers have diminished such that this left-over capital stock can be represented by $(1 - \delta)K_t$ units of new capital. Usually δ is taken as a constant, and hence the firm cannot control B_t separately from K_t. The present, more sophisticated approach in equation A.1.70 allows the firm to control the number of units of capital that die—subject to the production function.

The assumption that depreciation is economically identical with a certain number of units of capital dying while the other units are good as new avoids the problem of having to treat used units of capital as separate factors of production. If units of old capital of various ages and conditions cannot be treated as some fraction of one unit of new capital, there must be markets for various "used" types of capital; and each type enters the production function as different inputs and outputs. Thus, the firm starts the period with, say, 10 units of new capital, and it must decide how much output to produce and how much capital, and how used up is the capital, with which it wants to end the period.[10]

Let the production function display nonnegative and diminishing marginal physical productivity,

$$Q_K, Q_N, Q_B \geq 0; Q_{KK}, Q_{NN}, Q_{BB} < 0 \qquad \textbf{A.1.73}$$

and let the factors be technical complements. Let the present value function be concave and let an increase in the quantity of one factor increase the marginal revenue product of every other (the assumption throughout the book), or:

$$\frac{\partial MRP_K}{\partial B}, \frac{\partial MRP_K}{\partial N}, \frac{\partial MRP_N}{\partial B} > 0 \qquad \textbf{A.1.74}$$

Then all comparative statics results are qualitatively the same for the firm whether the capital constraint K_2^* is binding or not, except for anticipated inflation.[11] The firm plans to depreciate its capital stock in period 2 to the point at which the marginal revenue product of one unit of depreciation equals the $P_{K,2}$ the firm could get by selling the unit. The expected price $P_{K,2}^e$ is:

$$P_{K,2}^e = P_{K,1}\left(1 + \frac{\Delta P_{K,1}^e}{P_{K,1}}\right) \qquad \textbf{A.1.75}$$

10 T. Haavelmo, *A Study in the Theory of Investment* (Chicago: University of Chicago Press, 1960), devotes a good deal of space to depreciation and the markets for used capital goods.

11 For a detailed discussion of this depreciation model when the capital constraint K_2^* is nonbinding, see Richard J. Sweeney, "Firm Decision-Making and Macroeconomic Disequilibria" (Doctoral dissertation, Princeton University, 1972), Appendix 2 to Chapter 2.

Hence an increase in $\Delta P^e_{K,1}/P_{K,1}$ raises the cost of allowing depreciation, but lowers $P_{K,1}$ $(i_1 - \Delta P^e_{K,1}/P_{K,1})$, the marginal factor cost of capital services. When K^d_2 is less than K^*_2, such an increase tends to change K_2 and B_2 in opposite directions, giving totally ambiguous results. Allowing $(\Delta P/P)^e$ simultaneously to shift the demand function further obscures matters.

When K^d_2 exceeds K^*_2, $\Delta P^e_{K,1}/P_{K,1}$ has no effect on actual K_2; but through its adverse effect on B_2, it reduces B_2, Q_2, N_2, and w_2, and raises P_2. Combining this with an equal rise in $(\Delta P/P)^e$ in the demand function means P_2 definitely rises, for both demand and costs rise. In much the same way that section 2 of this appendix showed that P_2 likely rises when demand and capital services costs rise through an increase in $(\Delta P/P)^e$, it can be shown that Q_2 will likely rise on balance, implying N_2 and w_2 rise.

There is little purpose, then, in sacrificing the economy of the simple model to include even this tractable but general scheme of depreciation.

A.5. Isoelastic Demand Changes

The text assumed that variations in P^e_2 $(u_{P,2})$ shifted the expected demand curve proportionately and isoelastically relative to the quantity (price) axis and asserted this was a desirable property, since only such shifts were consistent with an inflationary stationary state (noninflationary steady-state growth).

A demand curve shifts isoelastically relative to the quantity (price) axis if an only if, at a given quantity (price), the elasticity is the same on both the old and new demand curves.[12] If P^e_2 and $u_{P,2}$ cause shifts isoelastic to the quantity and price axes respectively, and if such shifts are always proportionate, then:

$$P_2 = \overline{P}(Q; P^e_2, u_{P,2}), \quad \overline{P}_Q < 0 \qquad \text{A. 1.76}$$

can be rewritten:

$$P_2 = P^e_2 \overline{P}\left(\frac{Q_2}{u_{P,2}}\right)$$

$$P^e_2 \overline{P}_Q \frac{1}{u_{P,2}} < 0$$

A.1.77

The elasticity of demand, E, taken as a positive number, is:

---

12 Joan Robinson discusses briefly both types of isoelastic shifts, but uses only shifts isoelastic relative to the price axis, in Joan Robinson, *The Economics of Imperfect Competition* (London: Macmillan Co., 1964).

$$E = -\frac{dQ}{dP_2}\frac{P_2}{Q} = \frac{-1}{P_2^e \overline{P_Q}\frac{1}{u_{P,2}}}\frac{P_2}{Q_2} = -\frac{P_2}{P_2^e}\frac{u_{P,2}}{Q_2}\frac{1}{P_Q} \qquad \textbf{A.1.78}$$

Proportionate changes in P_2 and P_2^e at an unchanged Q_2 satisfy equation A.1.77 and leave E unchanged, and proportionate changes in $u_{P,2}$ and Q_2 at the given P_2 and P_2^e satisfy equation A.1.77 and leave E unchanged. Thus, equation A.1.77 provides the proportionate and isoelastic responses required.[13]

With constant marginal costs equal to c, the necessary condition for an interior wealth maximum in the product market is:

$$P\left(1 - \frac{1}{E}\right) - c = 0 \qquad \textbf{A.1.79}$$

If the firm's price and all other prices including factor prices rise by $\alpha\%$, then the necessary condition continues to hold at Q_2; and Q_2 remain the equilibrium output only if E is unchanged, for:

$$P(1 + \alpha)\left(1 - \frac{1}{E}\right) - (1 + \alpha)c = \left[P\left(1 - \frac{1}{E}\right) - c\right]\alpha \qquad \textbf{A.1.80}$$

Thus, all firms are in an inflationary steady state if and only if variations in P_2^e induce proportional demand shifts isoelastic to the quantity axis.

Suppose that growth in Y_1^d stimulates proportional growth in $u_{P,2}$, and growth in $u_{P,2}$ stimulates proportional changes in Q with no price changes. Then E must not change with proportional changes in $u_{P,2}$ and Q_2, and hence does not change with proportional changes in Y_1^d and Q_2. This would be the case if and only if variations in $u_{P,2}$ bring proportional and isoelastic, relative to the price axis, changes in demand.

If relative shifts in output composition are tolerated in noninflationary steady-state growth, variations in $u_{P,2}$ must cause isoelastic, relative to the price axis, changes in demand, though these changes need not be proportional to $u_{P,2}$, and variations in $u_{P,2}$ need not be proportional to those of Y_1^d. Any kind of nonproportional relationship between Y_1^d and isoelastic demand shifts can always be written as equation A.1.77, provided $u_{P,2}$ and Y_1^d need not vary proportionally.

Note that appropriate continuing percentage changes in Y^d and P^e can generate any desired kind of inflationary steady-state growth.

A.6. Business Demand for Money

The firm has the same qualitative reactions to parametric changes when it has a demand for money as when it holds no money. Thus,

---

13 It is simple to show that only equation A.1.77 provides the required responses.

introducing Chapter 7's simple business demand for money introduces no new complications or insights into the functioning of the economy as a whole different from those of the analysis when household wealth effects are included. Parallel to Chapter 2, the argument assumes business can buy all the capital it wants. Extending the argument to the case of rationing of capital goods, as in Chapter 4, is trivial.

The system 7.6.13 gives the necessary conditions for an interior maximum with the simplified transactions costs assumption. Shocking system 7.6.13 for $t = 2$ by changing some parameter α yields system A.1.81 on page 176.

It is known from the second-order conditions that D' must be negative definite if the firm is, in fact, at an interior maximum. Thus, the earlier assumption:

$$\partial^2 TC_2 / \partial MB_2^2 > 0 \qquad \textbf{A.1.82}$$

is implied by the second-order conditions. The text also assumed:

$$\partial^2 TC_2 / \partial MB_2 \partial P_2 Q_2 < 0 \qquad \textbf{A.1.83}$$

and while this need not be true for the second-order conditions to be satisfied, continue to assume that it holds. Assume also:

$$\frac{MRP_{K,2}\left(1 - \dfrac{\partial TC_2}{\partial P_2 Q_2}\right)}{\partial N_2} = \frac{\partial MRP_{N,2}\left(1 - \dfrac{\partial TC_2}{\partial P_2 Q_2}\right)}{\partial K_2} > 0 \qquad \textbf{A.1.84}$$

or an increase in the use of one factor increases the net marginal revenue product of the other, the usual assumption, but applied to this system where transactions costs must be netted out of marginal revenue product.

Assuming D' is negative definite implies:

$$|D'_{11}|, |D'_{22}|, |D'_{33}| > 0; |D'| < 0 \qquad \textbf{A.1.85}$$

From inequalities A.1.82 through A.1.85,

$$|D'_{11}|, |D'_{13}|, |D'_{22}|, |D'_{31}|, |D'_{33}| > 0$$

$$\textbf{A.1.86}$$

$$|D'_{12}|, |D'_{21}|, |D'_{23}|, |D'_{32}| < 0$$

Chapter 7 asserted that this addition of a simplified business demand for money does not alter the signs of the partial derivatives of the business sector behavior functions, and hence exactly the same graphical apparatus of II, AQ, NN, Δw, and ΔP curves as before can be used. This is demonstrated by solving system A.1.81 for the vectors $-[d\alpha_1, d\alpha_2,$

$$
\begin{bmatrix}
\dfrac{\partial MRP_{K,2}\left(1-\frac{\partial TC_2}{\partial P_2 Q_2}\right)}{\partial K_2} & \dfrac{\partial MRP_{K,2}\left(1-\frac{\partial TC_2}{\partial P_2 Q_2}\right)}{\partial N_2} & -MRP_{K,2}\dfrac{\partial^2 TC_2}{\partial P_2 Q_2 \partial MB_2} \\[3ex]
\dfrac{\partial MRP_{N,2}\left(1-\frac{\partial TC_2}{\partial P_2 Q_2}\right)}{\partial K_2} & \dfrac{\partial MRP_{N,2}\left(1-\frac{\partial TC_2}{\partial P_2 Q_2}\right)}{\partial N_2}-\dfrac{dMFC_{N,2}}{dN_2} & -MRP_{N,2}\dfrac{\partial^2 TC_2}{\partial P_2 Q_2 \partial MB_2} \\[3ex]
-MRP_{K,2}\dfrac{\partial^2 TC_2}{\partial P_2 Q_2 \partial MB_2} & -MRP_{N,2}\dfrac{\partial^2 TC_2}{\partial P_2 Q_2 \partial MB_2} & -\dfrac{\partial^2 TC_2}{\partial MB_2^2}
\end{bmatrix}
$$

$$
\begin{bmatrix}
\dfrac{dK_2}{d\alpha} \\[2ex]
\dfrac{dN_2}{d\alpha} \\[2ex]
\dfrac{dMB_2}{d\alpha}
\end{bmatrix}
= -
\begin{bmatrix}
d\alpha_1 \\[1ex]
d\alpha_2 \\[1ex]
d\alpha_3
\end{bmatrix},
\quad [D']
\begin{bmatrix}
dK \\[1ex]
dN \\[1ex]
dMB
\end{bmatrix}
= -
\begin{bmatrix}
d\alpha_1 \\[1ex]
d\alpha_2 \\[1ex]
d\alpha_2
\end{bmatrix}
$$

A.1.81

$d\alpha_3$] listed in Table A–2. The effects of the parametric changes on K_2 and N_2 are identical to those for the model in which business held no money, and hence so are the effects on Q_2 and P_2 when the demand function does not shift and on w_2 when the labor supply function does not shift. The effects of increases in Y_1^d and P_2^e on the price the firm charges in period 2, and the effects of decreases in Nu and increases in w_2^e on the wage rate the firm offers in period 2 again depend on comparisons of the marginal revenue product of labor function and the labor supply functions and the derivatives of these functions. The introduction of money alters nothing in these problems.

The micro functions for $\Delta P/P$, $\Delta w/w$, ΔN^d, AQ, and I^d have exactly the same forms, arguments (since the partials with respect to MB_1 are zero), and signs of derivatives as before; and aggregating these functions yields the same macro functions as before. Thus, the II, AQ, NN, Δw, and ΔP curves are the same whether or not there is a business

TABLE A–2

VECTORS FOR THE COMPARATIVE STATICS EXPERIMENTS WHEN THE FIRM HOLDS MONEY

Parameter	Vector
Y_1	$-\left[\dfrac{\partial MRP_K^+\left(1-\dfrac{\partial TC}{\partial PQ}\right)}{\partial Y},\ \dfrac{\partial MRP_N^+\left(1-\dfrac{\partial TC}{\partial PQ}\right)}{\partial Y},\ -\dfrac{\partial\dfrac{^+\partial TC}{\partial MB}}{\partial Y}\right]$
i_1	$-\left[-P_{K,1},\ 0,\ -1\right]$
Nu	$-\left[0-\dfrac{\partial\overline{MFC}_N}{\partial Nu},\ 0\right]$
$\tilde{P}_1$	$-\left[\dfrac{\partial MRP_K^+\left(1-\dfrac{\partial TC}{\partial PQ}\right)}{\partial\tilde{P}_1},\ \dfrac{\partial MRP_N^+\left(1-\dfrac{\partial TC}{\partial PQ}\right)}{\partial\tilde{P}_1},\ -\dfrac{\partial\dfrac{^+\partial TC}{\partial MB}}{\partial\tilde{P}_1}\right]$
$\dfrac{\Delta P}{P}e$	$-\left[\dfrac{\partial MRP_K^+\left(1-\dfrac{\partial TC}{\partial PQ}\right)}{\partial(\Delta P/P)^e},\ \dfrac{\partial MRP_N^+\left(1-\dfrac{\partial TC}{\partial PQ}\right)}{\partial(\Delta P/P)^e},\ -\dfrac{\partial\dfrac{^+\partial TC}{\partial MB}}{\partial(\Delta P/P)^e}\right]$
$\tilde{w}_1$	$-\left[0,\ -\dfrac{\partial MFC_N^+}{\partial\tilde{w}_1},\ 0\right]$
$\dfrac{\Delta w}{w}e$	$-\left[0,\ -\dfrac{\partial MFC_N^+}{\partial(\Delta w/w)^e},\ 0\right]$
$P_{K,1}$	$-\left[i-\dfrac{\Delta P_{K,1}^e}{P_{K,1}},\ 0,\ 0\right]$
$\dfrac{\Delta P_{K,1}^e}{P_{K,1}}$	$-\left[P_{K,1},\ 0,\ 0\right]$
MB_1	$-\left[0,\ 0,\ 0\right]$

demand for money. The form of the equation for the IS curve is unchanged, for business's money holdings affect neither the consumption function nor the investment demand function. Finally, Chapter 7 derived the business money demand function:

$$\frac{\Delta MB^d}{P} = B\phi(AQ, i, Y^d, (\Delta P/P)^e, MB/P) \qquad \text{A.1.87}$$

There is no argument in this function that is not in the household money demand function; and as Chapter 7 showed, almost all derivatives agree for the two sectors.[14] Thus, the $IS, LM, \Delta P, \Delta w, NN, AQ$, and II curves are the same as when business holds no money. It was precisely on this assumption that Chapter 7 carried out the policy analysis. Thus, the results of that chapter are upheld. Business demand for money adds no new insights or results regarding the macrosystem.

A.7. Relative Slopes of the II, AQ, and NN Curves, and Parametric Shifts in the II, AQ, NN, Δw, and ΔP Curves

Many of the comparative statics results of Chapters 3, 4, and 7 depended on the NN being steeper than the AQ curve which is steeper than the II curve. Other comparative statics depended on the shifts parameters induce in these curves and the Δw and ΔP curves relative to each other.

Return to the model of the firm to investigate these questions. Allow some parameter α to change and then adjust the interest rate to keep desired capital and hence desired investment constant.[15] Naturally, desired hiring changes along with i_1. The interpretation of the derivative $dN_2/d\alpha$ gives the slope of the NN relative to the II curve and the relative shifts of the two curves.

Shock the system A.1.8 for $t = 2$ to get:

$$\begin{bmatrix} \dfrac{\partial MRP_{K,2}}{\partial N_2} & -P_{K,1} \\[3ex] \dfrac{\partial MRP_{N,2}}{\partial N_2} - \dfrac{dMFC_{N,2}}{dN_2} & 0 \end{bmatrix} \begin{bmatrix} \dfrac{dN}{d\alpha} \\[3ex] \dfrac{di}{d\alpha} \end{bmatrix} = - \begin{bmatrix} d\alpha_1 \\[3ex] d\alpha_2 \end{bmatrix} \qquad \text{A.1.88}$$

(continued)

---

14 Indeed, some signs of partial derivatives for the business sector were derived which were merely assumed for the household sector. See Chapter 7, section 6. Note that when $Y^d \geq Y$, $B\phi_Y > 0$ while $\phi_Y = 0$; but this has virtually no effect on results. It only reinforces the ambiguity in the case of positive excess aggregate demand.

15 Recall that net equals gross investment here because of the assumption of no depreciation. Desired net investment, I_1^d, equals the stock of capital desired for period 2, K_2^d, less the current stock, K_1, or $I_1^d = K_2^d - K_1$. Thus, any parametric change, other than in K_1, affects K_2^d and I_1^d exactly equally.

$$[D''] \qquad \begin{bmatrix} dN \\ \\ di \end{bmatrix} = - \begin{bmatrix} d\alpha_1 \\ \\ d\alpha_2 \end{bmatrix}$$

where:

$$|D''| = \left(\frac{\partial MRP_{N,2}}{\partial N_2} - \frac{dMFC_{N,2}}{dN_2} \right) P_{K,1} < 0$$

$$|D''_{11}| = 0, \; |D''_{12}| = \frac{\partial MRP_{N,2}}{\partial N_2} - \frac{dMFC_{N,2}}{dN_2} < 0 \qquad \text{A.1.89}$$

$$|D''_{21}| = -P_{K,1} < 0, \; |D''_{22}| = \frac{\partial MRP_{K,2}}{\partial N_2} > 0$$

As usual, $|D''_{22}|$ is positive by assumption; the second-order conditions give $|D''_{12}|$ and hence $|D''|$. Table A–3 lists $-[d\alpha_1, d\alpha_2]$ for four of the relevant parameters—current aggregate demand, Y_1^d (which affects $u_{P,2}$), the expected rate of rivals' price inflation, $(\Delta P/P)^e$, the percentage rate at which other businesses are expected to raise their wage offers, $(\Delta w/w)^e$, and the aggregate unemployment rate, Nu (which affects $u_{w,2}$). (The effect of the real wage rate, w/P, is discussed shortly.)

The results are:

$$dN/dY, \; di/dY > 0$$

$$dN/d\Delta P^e/P, \; di/d\Delta P^e/P > 0$$
$$\text{A.1.90}$$
$$dN/d\Delta w^e/w, \; di/d\Delta w^e/w < 0$$

$$dN/d\,Nu, \; di/d\,Nu > 0$$

The interpretation of the results is straightforward. By assumption, $di/d\alpha$ is the change in i_1 that keeps K_2^d and hence I^d constant. Thus, di/dY is the slope of the II curve (positive, of course). dN/dY is positive because the change in i_1 that holds I^d constant is too small to hold N^d constant. It would require a larger rise in i_1 to hold N^d constant since, from equations 2.5.3, increases in i_1 reduce N_2^d. Hence the NN is steeper than the II curve.

The rise in i_1 that holds I^d constant allows N^d and hence AQ to rise, for:

$$\frac{dQ}{d\alpha} = Q_N \frac{dN^d}{d\alpha} \qquad \text{A.1.91}$$

A larger increase in i_1 keeps AQ constant but causes I^d to fall. However, the rise in i_1 that holds N^d constant causes I^d and hence AQ to fall.

TABLE A-3

VECTORS TO DETERMINE RELATIONSHIPS OF II AND NN CURVES

Parameter	Vector
Y_1	$-\left[\dfrac{\partial MRP^+_{K,2}}{\partial Y_1},\ \dfrac{\partial MRP^+_{N,2}}{\partial Y_1}\right]$
$\dfrac{\Delta P}{P}e$	$-\left[\dfrac{\partial MRP^+_{K,2}}{\partial \dfrac{\Delta P}{P}e}+P_{K,1},\ \dfrac{\partial MRP^+_{N,2}}{\partial \dfrac{\Delta P}{P}e}\right]$
$\dfrac{\Delta w}{w}e$	$-\left[0,\ -\dfrac{\partial MFC^+_{N,2}}{\partial \dfrac{\Delta w}{w}e}\right]$
Nu	$-\left[0,\ -\dfrac{\partial M\overline{FC}_{N,2}}{\partial Nu}\right]$

Thus, the AQ curve is steeper than the II but less steep than the NN curve—as Chapter 3 asserted.

The other results are easily interpreted. By hypothesis, $di/d\alpha$ is the change in i_1 that keeps K^d_2 and hence I^d constant. Thus, $di/d\alpha$ now represents the vertical shift in the II curve. Increases in the rate at which all prices are expected to rise and increases in the aggregate rate of unemployment shift the II curve up, while increases in the rate at which rivals are expected to raise their wages shift the II curve down.[16]

If $dN/d\alpha$ is greater than zero, the change in i_1 that keeps I^d constant is too small to hold N^d_2 constant. To do this, i_1 would have to rise even more since, from equations 2.5.3, increases in i_1 reduce N^d. Thus, for increases in $(\Delta P/P)^e$ and Nu, the NN rises even more than the II curve; while for increases in $(\Delta w/w)^e$, the NN shifts down even more than the II curve.

When i_1 rises to hold K^d_2 and hence I^d constant, but N^d_2 also rises, so does AQ, from equation A.1.91. If i_1 were to rise enough to hold Q and hence AQ constant, then I^d would actually fall; and N^d_2 would still have to be larger than before in order to balance this fall in I^d. Thus, the AQ curve shifts farther than the II, but not as far as the NN curve; and all three shift in the same direction.

The result that the NN curve shifts down more than the II curve for an increase in $(\Delta w/w)^e$ implies:

$$\frac{di}{d\dfrac{\Delta w}{w}e}(II)=-\frac{I_{(\Delta w/w)^e}}{I_i}>\frac{di}{d\dfrac{\Delta w}{w}e}(NN)=-\frac{H_{(\Delta w/w)^e}}{H_i} \qquad \text{A.1.92}$$

---

16 The rate at which all prices are expected to rise includes the rate at which capital goods prices appreciate.

where $I_{(\Delta w/w)^e}$, $H_{(\Delta w/w)^e}$ and I_i, H_i are the partial derivatives of the investment and hiring functions with respect to expected wage changes and the interest rate. Since from equations 2.5.3,   **A.1.93**

$$I_{(\Delta w/w)^e} = I_{w/P} \cdot \frac{w/P}{[1+(\Delta w/w)^e]}, \quad H_{(\Delta w/w)^e} = H_{w/p} \cdot \frac{w/P}{[1+(\Delta w/w)^e]}$$

inequality A.1.92 implies that increases in w/P shift both curves down and the NN more than the II, or:

$$0 > \frac{di}{dw/P}(II) = -\frac{I_{w/P}}{I_i} > \frac{di}{dw/P}(NN) = -\frac{H_{w/P}}{H_i} \qquad \textbf{A.1.94}$$

With an increase in $(\Delta P/P)^e$, the NN and Δw curves vary exactly together, the same wage rate inducing the same labor supply as before. The shift in the Δw with an increase in Nu, $(\Delta w/w)^e$, or w/P depends on the partial derivatives of the aggregate wage change function, $g(\cdot)$. For example, from equations 2.5.3, the vertical shift of Δw with a change in $(\Delta w/w)^e$ is:

$$\frac{di}{d\frac{\Delta w}{w}e}(\Delta w) = -\frac{G_{(\Delta w/w)^e}}{G_i} \qquad \textbf{A.1.95}$$

Section 2 of this appendix established that $G_{(\Delta w/w)^e}$ is positive under very mild conditions; and since G_i is negative, an increase in $(\Delta w/w)^e$ shifts the Δw curve upward. In the same way, since G_{Nu} and $G_{w/P}$ are negative under mild conditions, an increase in either shifts the Δw curve down.

Changes in w/P, $(\Delta w/w)^e$, or Nu cause a change in $\Delta P/P$ only if Q changes, for:

$$\frac{dP_2}{d\alpha} = P_2^e \overline{P_Q} \frac{1}{u_p} \frac{dQ}{d\alpha}, \overline{P_Q} < 0 \qquad \textbf{A.1.96}$$

and thus for these parameters, the intersection of the ΔP and AQ curves shifts exactly vertically. If $(\Delta P/P)^e$ is taken to represent changes in rivals' prices and capital goods prices, the analysis is complex but the result determinate, as shown in section 2 of this appendix. From equations 2.5.3, the direction of shift of the ΔP curve is:

$$\frac{di}{d\frac{\Delta P}{P}e} = -\frac{-f_2 + f_3}{f_2} \qquad \textbf{A.1.97}$$

and since $f_2(=f_i)$ is positive, and from inequality A.1.38, $-f_2 + f_3$ is also positive, the ΔP curve shifts down.

The preceding section showed that introducing a business demand for money does not alter the business behavior functions, so this section's results also apply in Chapter 7.

2 THE RATIONING ASSUMPTION

This appendix shows that when only households demand money, the rationing assumption of Chapter 4 is relatively weak and deserves no particular objection. Chapter 4 assumes that when aggregate demand exceeds capacity output, all government and consumer demand is fulfilled. This puts all the burden of rationing on the business sector and implies that the conventional *LM* curve can be used for analysis.[1]

There are two primary effects of this assumption. First, changes in the rate of interest depend only on changes in money supply and changes in the money demand function. Second, changes in actual investment depend only on changes in desired consumption and in government demand.

The first effect of the rationing assumption is easy to understand. With capacity output given, then from the equation of the *LM* curve,

$$-\frac{\Delta M^s}{P} = \phi(Y_1^c, i_1, M/P) = 0 \qquad \text{A.2.1}$$

The only kind of comparative statics changes affecting i_1 are changes in ΔM^s, M, or the money demand function. Conversely, the effects of changes in other parameters can be traced without worrying about induced variations in i_1. Now making i_1 insensitive to all save money market parameters has no direct effect on $\Delta P/P$, $\Delta w/w$, ΔN^d, and AQ; when the business sector is subjected to rationing, whether or not any other sector is also, actual investment and not i_1 affects its decisions. But i_1 is important for aggregate demand, and Y_1^d is an overwhelmingly important variable throughout the system since it represents the state of demand each firm faces.

Nevertheless, under a rather general rationing scheme, Y_1^d varies in the same direction whether i_1 changes or not—variations in i_1 reduce the amplitude of variations in Y_1^d but do not change signs. Plot the usual downward sloping *IS'* curve in Figure A-1 (note *IS'*, not *IS*), showing aggregate demand as a function of i_1. Now consider the determination of i_1. Let the demand for money depend on given real income Y_1^c, the rate of interest, and the amount actual consumption falls short of desired consumption. If for some reason the household sector is more severely rationed, this frustrated expenditure necessarily shifts from

---

1 See Chapter 4, sections 2 through 4.

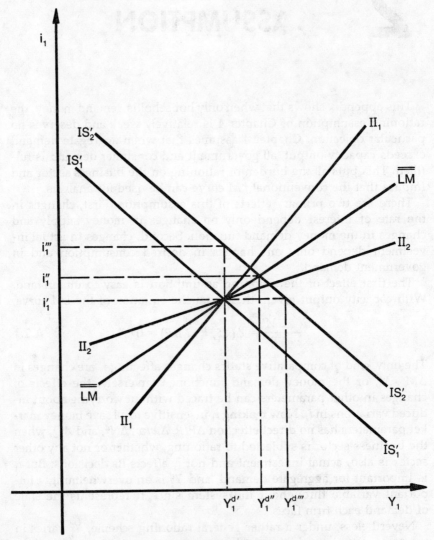

FIGURE A-1

RATIONING AFFECTS THE HOUSEHOLD SECTOR

consumption to saving; and if money services are a normal good, the household sector increases its demand for money. Now, let the rationing process be described by some rule that compares the household sector's demand to aggregate demand.[2] The amount of goods the household sector can buy depends positively on its demand, C^d (where C^d

2 This is a specialization of the assumption that the rationing process compares the demand of each sector to that of the others, and it is not a strong assumption. Since C^a varies negatively with Y^d, the slope of IS' is $- (-1 + I_y + C_y^d)/I_i < - (-1 + I_y)/I_i$ and is necessarily negative when I_y is less than unity, as assumed throughout.

depends only on real disposable income), and negatively on Y_1^d. This implies that now:

$$\frac{\Delta M^d}{P} = \phi^*(Y_1, i_1, Y_1^d), \phi_i^* < 0, \phi_{Yd}^* > 0 \qquad \text{A.2.2}$$

and the equation of the new LM curve, $\overline{\overline{LM}}$, is:

$$-\frac{\Delta M^s}{P} + \phi^*(Y_1, i_1, Y_1^d) = 0, \frac{di}{dY^d}(\overline{\overline{LM}}) = -\frac{\phi_{Yd}^*}{\phi_i^*} > 0 \qquad \text{A.2.3}$$

Plot the LM curve on the same axes as the IS' curve, and the intersection determines $(i_1', Y_1^{d'})$. Now let G rise. IS_1' shifts up to IS_2' and increases Y_1^d to $Y_1^{d''}$. This increase is not as large as it would have been had i_1 remained at i_1' instead of rising to i_1''. Thus, the rise in i_1 decreases the amplitude of the variation in Y_1^d but does not change the sign of the variation.

In this apparatus, variations in I^d are now ambiguous, whereas they are determinate in Chapter 4. The II curve through the point $(Y_1^{d'}, i_1')$ shows other values of (Y_1^d, i_1) that hold I^d at its initial value. This II curve may be steeper than the $\overline{\overline{LM}}$ curve, II_1, or less steep, II_2. With II_1, the increase in G increases I^d; with II_2, I^d decreases.

The first effect, then, of Chapter 4's rationing assumption is to limit severely the conditions under which i_1 varies. This, however, is virtually innocuous: the only variable qualitatively affected by making a much more general rationing assumption is I^d, and by itself I^d is not a particularly crucial variable. Indeed, the comparative statics effects for I^d become totally ambiguous in Chapter 7 with no great damage.

The second effect of Chapter 4's rationing assumption is to limit changes in actual investment to those induced by changes in government spending or taxation or in the propensity to save. A more general rationing assumption allows actual investment to vary with all parametric changes. This new variability of I^a is of vital importance only to the rate of inflation, $\Delta P/P$. But since $\Delta P/P$ is a crucial policy target, the matter deserves detailed discussion.

Assume that I^a depends positively on investment demand, I^d, and on total output to be rationed, Y_1^c, and negatively on consumer demand, C^d, and government demand, G^d, or:

$$I^a = \Gamma(Y_1^c, C^d, G^d, I^d), \Gamma_C < 0, \Gamma_G < 0, \Gamma_I > 0 \qquad \text{A.2.4}$$

Since I^d varies with every parametric change, much simplicity is lost.

The assumption of equation A.2.4 leads to increased ambiguity. In Chapter 4, increases in G^d reduce I^a. Here, an increase in G^d raises Y_1^d and i_1 and, as Figure A–1 shows, may raise or lower I^d. If I^d rises enough, I^a may rise.[3] In Chapter 4, a rise in G stimulates Y_1^d; and at an unchanged i_1, I^d rises. The higher Y_1^d stimulates AQ, $\Delta w/w$, and ΔN^d, but the increased G reduces I^a, dampening AQ, $\Delta w/w$, and ΔN^d, so the net effects are ambiguous. Equation A.2.4 intensifies this ambiguity for the three variables, because now it is not even clear that I^a falls.

Equation A.2.4 has a drastic effect on the sign of changes in $\Delta P/P$. Before, a rise in G^d stimulated Y_1^d and hence increased inflationary pressure, while the concomitant fall in I^a shifted cost curves up and also added to inflationary pressure. Now, G^d rises and induces an increase in Y_1^d, but I^a may actually rise. Thus, the inflationary effects of increased aggregate demand can conceivably be offset by the deflationary effects of a possible increase in I^a. This net result hardly seems likely, but damaging ambiguity with regard to inflation persists throughout the comparative statics.

Aside from changes in G, T, and APS, the comparative statics results are perfectly clear for I^d and I^a as long as the $\overline{LM}$ curve has a positive slope.[4] Further, the changes in I^a do not reverse any of the conclusions for AQ, $\Delta w/w$, and ΔN^d. Take, for example, an increase in the expected rate of inflation. In Figure A–2, the IS' curve shifts up, increasing Y_1^d and i_1. The initial II curve shifts up to II_2, and I^d rises. C^d and G^d are unchanged with the rise in Y_1^d; but I^d rises, so I^a rises. Now, the increase in Y_1^d reinforces the expansionary impact of the increase in $(\Delta P/P)^e$ and stimulates AQ, $\Delta w/w$, and ΔN^d, as in Chapter 4 where I^a does not change. Here I^a rises, but this also stimulates the three variables. The increases in Y_1^d and $(\Delta P/P)^e$ spur inflation, but the increase in I^a dampens $\Delta P/P$, so the net result for inflation is ambiguous.

Compare Table A–4 and Table 4–1. The circled changes are different. The several differences in the interest columns are due to the assumption that rationing of the household sector changes with Y_1^d, and thus these particular differences are independent of the assumption that I^a varies with I^d (they were found in Figure A–1 before equation A.2.4 was assumed). The effects of Y_1^d are precisely the same in both cases,

3 The increase in G^d reduces output going to the private sector, but it may so stimulate investment demand that the slice the business sector gets of the smaller private sector pie is actually larger than before. This ambiguity of changes in I^a occurs only with changes in G, T, or APS (as shown later) and is, in part, a reflection of the new ambiguity of changes in I^d.

4 Since the $\overline{LM}$ curve depends on how the government and household sectors are rationed, it also depends on I^d; for from equation A.2.4, I^d influences rationing. Thus, the $\overline{LM}$ curve actually shifts when I^d shifts, and to draw it unchanged is to have taken account implicitly of such shifts for each experiment. That the resulting $\overline{LM}$ curve has a positive slope is not a very strong assumption, requiring only that the true $\overline{LM}$ curve not shift up more than the IS'. It is possible that the $\overline{LM}$ curve in Figure A–2 have a negative slope, if, for example, an increase in I^d so diverts goods from the household sector that money demand greatly rises. But this seems unlikely.

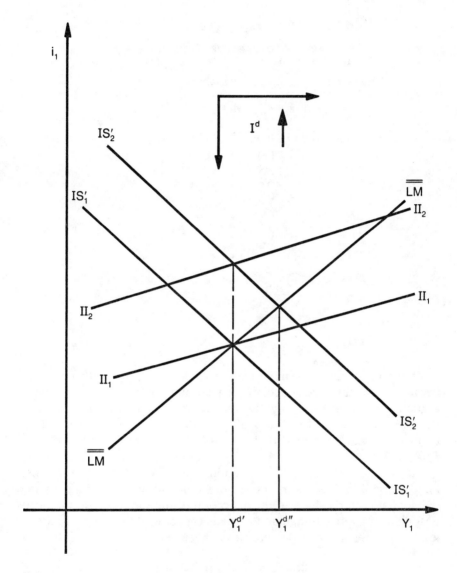

FIGURE A-2

DESIRED INVESTMENT AND ACTUAL INVESTMENT

as are the effects on ΔN^d, $\Delta w/w$, and AQ. The effects on I^d are now ambiguous for changes in G, T, or APS, where before they were known;
but this ambiguity again depends on changing the assumption about
household rationing, since the ambiguous results were derived earlier
in Figure A-1 before this appendix mentioned equation A.2.4.

TABLE A-4

SUMMARY OF COMPARATIVE STATICS RESULTS UNDER AN ALTERNATE RATIONING SCHEME

Parameters				Variables				
	Y^d	i	$\frac{\Delta P}{P}$	AQ	ΔN^d	$\frac{\Delta w}{w}$	I^d	I^a
G	+	(+)	(?)	?	?	?	(?)	(?)
T	−	(−)	(?)	?	?	?	(?)	(?)
APS	−	(−)	(?)	?	?	?	(?)	(?)
ΔM^d	−	+	(?)	−	−	−	−	(−)
ΔM^s	+	−	(?)	+	+	+	+	(+)
M	+	−	(?)	+	+	+	+	(+)
Nu	+	(+)	?	+	+	?	+	(+)
$\frac{\Delta P}{P}e$	+	(+)	(?)	+	+	+	+	(+)
$\frac{w}{P}$	−	(−)	?	−	−	−	−	(−)
$\frac{\Delta w}{w}e$	−	(−)	?	−	−	?	−	(−)

Inflation is the one case in which the results are significantly changed. Because I^a varies, the effects of all parametric changes are now ambiguous, where before only the results of changes in Nu, w/P, and $(\Delta w/w)^e$ were doubtful. But while this formal ambiguity cannot be removed, it can be argued that the effects are quite likely to be as in Table 4–1.[5]

The ambiguous effects on inflation result from two assumptions. First, marginal increases in one sector's demand must significantly increase that sector's share in the allocation of the rationed output. Suppose that, if aggregate demand exceeds capacity, all sectors feel rationing. But, in response to parametric changes, let:

$$\frac{dG^a}{dG^d} \cong 0, \frac{dC^a}{dC^d} \cong 0, \frac{dI^a}{dI^d} \cong 0 \qquad \text{A.2.5}$$

or marginal changes in a sector's demand bring no significant change in the allocation of output. This assumption surely has some plausibility. Often a clear ranking of customers determines who gets how much, and this happens without reference to relative intensity of demands. A firm's biggest and best customer is going to be well treated no matter how eager are smaller customers.

5 This formal ambiguity can only be removed by rationing assumptions virtually as strong as those of Chapter 4's text, one of which is discussed in the next paragraph.

Now, if I^a does not vary with $I^d(\Gamma_I = 0)$ or does not vary significantly with $I^d(\Gamma_I \cong 0)$, then a great deal of ambiguity is removed. Endogenous variations in inflation become perfectly determinate and have the same signs as in Chapter 4. Further, if variations in G^d and C^d do not affect I^a or C^a, even more ambiguity disappears. Previously, increases in G^d increased Y_1^d and G^a at the expense of I^a. The increase in Y_1^d stimulated AQ, but the decline in I^a dampened AQ, so the net result was ambiguous. Under the assumption that marginal changes in demand have virtually no effect on allocation of output, the increase in Y_1^d stimulates AQ, there is no change in I^a, and AQ rises.

Eliminating this ambiguity surrounding changes in AQ only reinforces the policy conclusions in Chapter 6. There, reductions in G^d reduce Y_1^d and hence tend to reduce $\Delta P/P$, AQ, and ΔN^d. But the decrease in G^d also raises I^a, reducing $\Delta P/P$ but tending to raise AQ and N^d. Thus, the effects on $\Delta P/P$ are clear and favorable, while the effects on AQ and ΔN^d are ambiguous. Chapter 6 argues that optimum anti-inflationary policy combines a reduction in interest rates with this restrictive fiscal policy. If restrictive fiscal policy alone hurts AQ and ΔN^d (a possibility), lowering i_1 can ensure high growth and labor demand while inflation in reduced. The force of the argument is weakened, though, by the possibility that reductions in G^d, and thus increases in I^a, actually stimulate AQ and ΔN^d, perhaps enough so there is no need to worry about these variables.

Equation A.2.5 assumes that marginal decreases in G^d have no effect on I^a, and hence AQ and ΔN^d unambiguously suffer. Large enough decreases in G^d (not marginal) that induce a fall in G^a will bring some small rise in I^a. Reduced interest rates are necessary to make up for all those units of reduced G^d that bring no mitigating increases in I^a. Chapter 6 argues for a mixture of monetary and fiscal policy on the grounds that the effects of fiscal policy by itself may not be totally satisfactory for hiring and growth. The new rationing assumption makes these unsatisfactory effects certain and thus makes the argument in favor of the mixture more compelling.

Comparing the assumption that rationing affects only business to equation A.2.5, the second assumption produces even more clear-cut results than the first, and seems no stronger. Wherever both assumptions have unambiguous results, they are the same; so the results of the first assumption are not particularly sensitive as long as a strong assumption is made. Though the second assumption is too strong, in a milder version it does have plausibility. The tendency for marginal shifts in demand not to change "too" drastically the allocation of output must work to make changes in I^a relatively unimportant and hence to make the results of Chapter 4's model more likely, even when I^a and I^d are free to vary.

The second cause of ambiguity in the effects of inflation is the assumption of only one produced good. Chapter 8 discusses some of the implications of generalizing Chapters 3 and 4 to two outputs. Consider such a model when all sectors endure rationing.

The ambiguous effects on inflation of the three policy variables G^d, T, and ΔM^s cause most concern. With two sectors, G^d is composed of demand for consumer goods, C_G^d, and demand for investment goods, I_G^d. Chapter 4 predicts that an increase in G increases $\Delta P/P$. With two sectors, suppose government contemplates an increase in G and considers three possible effects on the rate of increase of the Consumer Price Index (CPI).

First, if I_G^d rises, the consumer goods sector feels no increase in demand and hence initially has no tendency to raise CPI. Households have no new rivals for consumer goods output, so they presumably feel no different effects of rationing, and thus i_1 is unchanged.[6] Actual private investment falls if the business bears all or part of marginal rationing, or it remains unchanged if I_G^a is unchanged when I_G^d rises. In any case, total investment demand is higher, so capital goods prices tend to increase. This tendency is mitigated by any additional investment goods the capital goods sector can draw away from the consumer goods sector due to this shift in relative output demand. Thus, there is a tendency for the CPI to rise as the quantity of investment goods allocated to the consumer goods sector falls; and it is conceivable that the rate of increase in capital goods prices falls if the investment sector can draw enough investment away from the other sector.

Second, let government raise both C_G^d and I_G^d in such a way that there is zero net effect on the consumer goods sector's actual investment. That is, output demand rises and both sectors want to invest more; and for the consumer goods sector, it is a standoff. Then, demand in the consumer goods sector rises but its investment is unchanged, so the CPI rises.

Third, suppose the government raises C_G^d and changes (raises or lowers, but probably lowers) I_G^d so that the consumer goods sector's actual investment rises. Let this be accomplished by such a "small" enough rise in C_G^d (this makes it virtually certain that I_G^d is falling) that the increased demand for consumer goods is more than offset by the increased actual investment of the sector, and the rate of increase of the CPI falls. The point of these examples is that it takes a fairly specialized increase in total G^d to cause the CPI to dip, if such a thing is actually possible. I_G^d may have to fall so far to let the consumer goods sector's investment rise that G^d falls.

6 With two sectors, the graphical apparatus used in much of this essay is inapplicable. Some graphical analysis is possible, but it is not developed here since it adds little but is complex.

Changes in T parallel those in G, but changes in ΔM^s are rather interesting. An increase in ΔM^s causes a decrease in i_1 to induce the household sector to accept more dollars. This decrease in i_1 increases both business sectors' demands for investment, but only the capital goods sector sees it as an increase in demand for its output. There is a tendency, then, for this sector to deprive the other of investment goods. To this extent, the CPI will rise. It is conceivable, but only barely, that the rate of increase of capital goods prices will slow. But Section 7 of Chapter 4 predicts that an increase in ΔM^s by itself raises inflation.[7]

To summarize: Assumptions alternative to those of Chapter 4 lead to different variability in I^a than found there. The assumption that I^a varies directly with I^d and inversely with C^d and G^d leads to increased variability of I^a. This in turn has the one important effect of making changes in $\Delta P/P$ ambiguous. But another rationing assumption, that marginal changes in sectors' demands do not change output allocation, leads to no variability in I^a, thus making determinate all changes in $\Delta P/P$ and the changes in AQ, $\Delta w/w$, and ΔN^d due to changes in G, T, or APS. Thus, the effects on I^a of alternate rationing assumptions may strengthen or weaken Chapter 4's results. But examination of the more detailed two-sector model shows that allowing variability in I^a, which appears to weaken the results on inflation, is not very likely in fact to produce this weakening.

Considering the results of this appendix, the rationing assumption of Chapter 4 seems relatively unobjectionable.

---

7 See Chapter 8 for a discussion of the effects of changes in ΔM^s on AQ and ΔN^d. Note that Chapter 3, with excess capacity, not rationing, predicts that an increase in ΔM^s lowers inflation if the IS curve has a negative slope.

BIBLIOGRAPHY

Abramovitz, Moses, *et al. The Allocation of Economic Resources*. Stanford: Stanford University Press, 1959.

Ackley, Gardner. *Macroeconomic Theory*. New York: Macmillan Co., 1961.

Alchian, Armen A. "Information Costs, Pricing, and Resource Unemployment," in Edmund Phelps, *et al. Microeconomic Foundations of Employment and Inflation Theory*. New York: W. W. Norton & Co., 1970.

————, and William R. Allen. *University Economics: Elements of Inquiry*, 3d ed. Belmont, Calif.: Wadsworth Publishing Co., 1971.

Arrow, Kenneth, "Toward a Theory of Price Adjustment," in Moses Abramovitz, *et al. The Allocation of Economic Resources*. Stanford: Stanford University Press, 1959.

————. "Optimal Capital Policy with Irreversible Investment." *Value, Capital and Growth*, edited by J. Wolfe. Chicago: Aldine Publishing Co., 1968.

Bailey, Martin J. *National Income and the Price Level: A Study in Macroeconomic Theory*, 1st and 2d eds. New York: McGraw-Hill Book Co., 1962 and 1971.

Brainard, William C., and James Tobin. "Pitfalls in Financial Model Building." *American Economic Review*, Vol. LVIII (May, 1968), pp. 99–122.

Branson, William. *Macroeconomic Theory and Policy*. New York: Harper & Row, Publishers, 1971.

Clower, Robert. "The Keynesian Counterrevolution: A Theoretical Appraisal." *The Theory of Interest Rates*, edited by F. Hahn and F.P.R. Brechling. London: Macmillan & Co., 1965.

Cogerty, D., and G. Winston. "Patinkin, Perfect Competition and Unemployment Disequilibria." *Review of Economic Studies*, Vol. XXXI (April, 1964), pp. 121–126.

Dernberg, Thomas, and Duncan McDougall. *Macroeconomics*, 4th ed. New York: McGraw-Hill Book Co., 1972.

Duesenberry, James. *Business Cycles and Economic Growth*. New York: McGraw-Hill Book Co., 1958.

Enthoven, Alain C. "A Neo-Classical Model of Money, Debt and Economic Growth," mathematical appendix to John G. Gurley and Edward S. Shaw. *Money in a Theory of Finance*. Washington, D. C.: Brookings Institution, 1960.

Ferber, Robert (ed.). *Determinants of Investment Behavior*. New York: Columbia University Press, 1967.

Friedman, Milton. *The Optimum Quantity of Money and Other Essays.* Chicago: Aldine Publishing Co., 1969.

——. "A Theoretical Framework for Monetary Analysis." *Journal of Political Economy,* Vol. LXXVIII (March, 1970), pp. 193–238.

Gurley, John G., and Edward S. Shaw. *Money in a Theory of Finance.* Washington, D.C.: Brookings Institution, 1960.

Haavelmo, T. *A Study in the Theory of Investment.* Chicago: University of Chicago Press, 1960.

Hahn, F., and F.P.R. Brechling (eds.). *The Theory of Interest Rates.* London: Macmillan & Co., 1965.

Hahn, F., and R.C.O. Matthews. "The Theory of Economic Growth: A Survey." *Surveys of Economic Theory,* 3 Vols. London: Macmillan & Co., 1966.

Hicks, J.R. "Mr. Keynes and the 'Classics': A Suggested Interpretation." *Econometrica,* Vol. V (April, 1937), pp. 147–159.

——. *Value and Capital: An Inquiry into Some Fundamental Principles of Economic Theory,* 2d ed. London: Oxford University Press, 1946.

Horwich, George. "Tight Money, Monetary Restraint, and the Price Level." *Journal of Finance,* Vol. XXI (March, 1966), pp. 15–33.

Johnson, Harry G. "The Neo-Classical One-Sector Growth Model: A Geometrical Exposition and Extension to a Monetary Economy." *Economica,* Vol. XXXIII (August, 1966), pp. 265–287.

Jorgenson, Dale. "The Theory of Investment Behavior." *Determinants of Investment Behavior,* edited by Robert Ferber. New York: Columbia University Press, 1967.

Kalecki, M. *Theory of Economic Dynamics,* rev. 2d ed. New York: Monthly Review Press, 1968.

Koopmans, T. *Three Essays on the State of Economic Science.* New York: McGraw-Hill Book Co., 1957.

Kuenne, Robert. *The Microeconomic Theory of The Market Mechanism: A General Equilibrium Approach.* New York: Macmillan Co., 1968.

Kuhn, H.W. and A.W. Tucker. "Non-Linear Programming." *Proceedings of the Second Berkeley Symposium on Mathematical Statistics and Probability,* edited by J. Neyman. Berkeley: University of California Press, 1951.

Leijonhufvud, Axel. *On Keynesian Economics and the Economics of Keynes: A Study in Monetary Theory.* London: Oxford University Press, 1968.

McKenna, Joseph. *Aggregate Economic Analysis,* 3d ed. New York: Holt, Rinehart & Winston, 1970.

Modigliani, Franco. "Liquidity Preference and the Theory of Interest and Money." *Econometrica,* Vol. XXII (January, 1944), pp. 45–88.

——, and Merton Miller. "The Cost of Capital, Corporation Finance, and the Theory of Investment." *American Economic Review,* Vol. XLVIII (June, 1958), pp. 261–297.

————. "Dividend Policy, Growth, and the Valuation of Shares." *Journal of Business*, Vol. XXXIV (October, 1961), pp. 411–433.

Mortenson, Dale. "A Theory of Wage and Employment Dynamics," in Edmund Phelps, *et al. Microeconomic Foundations of Employment and Inflation Theory*. New York: W. W. Norton & Co., 1970.

Mundell, Robert. "An Exposition of Some Subtleties in the Keynesian System." *Weltwirtschaftliches Archiv*, Vol. XCIII (December, 1964), pp. 301–312.

Neyman, J. (ed.). *Proceedings of the Second Berkeley Symposium on Mathematical Statistics and Probability*. Berkeley: University of California Press, 1951.

Patinkin, Don. *Money, Interest, and Prices*, 2d ed. New York: Harper & Row, Publishers, 1965.

Pesek, Boris, and Thomas Saving. *Money, Wealth, and Economic Theory*. New York: Macmillan Co., 1967.

Phelps, Edmund. "Money Wage Dynamics and Labor Market Equilibrium," in Edmund Phelps, *et al. Microeconomic Foundations of Employment and Inflation Theory*. New York: W. W. Norton & Co., 1970.

Phelps, Edmund, and Sidney Winters. "Optimal Price Policy under Atomistic Competition," in Edmund Phelps, *et al. Microeconomic Foundations of Employment and Inflation Theory*. New York: W. W. Norton & Co., 1970.

Phelps, Edmund, *et al. Microeconomic Foundations of Employment and Inflation Theory*. New York: W. W. Norton & Co., 1970.

Robinson, Joan. *The Economics of Imperfect Competition*. London: Macmillan & Co., 1964.

Smith, Warren. "A Graphical Exposition of the Complete Keynesian System." *Southern Economic Journal*, Vol. XXIII (October, 1956), pp. 115–125.

————. *Macroeconomics*. Homewood, Ill.: Richard D. Irwin, 1970.

Solomon, Ezra. *The Theory of Financial Management*. New York: Columbia University Press, 1963.

Stein, Jerome. "Money and Capacity Growth." *Journal of Political Economy*, Vol. LXXIV (October, 1966), pp. 451–465.

————. "Monetary Growth Theory in Perspective." *American Economic Review*, Vol. LX (January, 1970), pp. 85–106.

Stiglitz, Joseph. "A Re-Examination of the Modigliani-Miller Theorem." *American Economic Review*, Vol. LIX (December, 1969), pp. 78–93.

Sweeney, Richard J. "Firm Decision-Making and Macroeconomic Disequilibria." Doctoral dissertation, Princeton University, 1972.

Witte, James. "The Microfoundations of the Social Investment Function." *Journal of Political Economy*, Vol. LXXI (October, 1963), pp. 441–456.

Wolfe, J. (ed.). *Value, Capital and Growth*. Chicago: Aldine Publishing Co., 1968.

INDEX